D1409211

Letters to Daniel

Amy Leigh McCorkle

Cover Art © 2015 by Delilah K. Stephans

Print ISBN: 978-1522864172

Published by: Amy McCorkle

Editors: Tanja Cilia and Ellen Eldridge

Dedicated to Daniel Craig, My Silent Witness

Mary)
Thank you
so much —
Amy Leigh
McCorkle

Acknowledgements

Too many to count but I thank Missy Goodman and Pamela Turner and of course Tim Druck and family. To Lea Schizas for the conversation which planted the seed that started all of this. Stephen Zimmer my project's film incarnations of this story. To mom and dad. (Faye and John). To Tanja Cilia and Ellen Eldridge for their editorial eyes. To my Aunt Debbie and Uncle Frank. And finally to Delilah K. Stephans. I thank all of these people and so many more for supporting me through the hard times and now celebrate with them through the good times.

Contents

Introduction

When Amy told me she was going to do this blog and write as if she were talking to Daniel Craig, I was not crazy about the idea. Amy is such an honest and sensitive person that I was wary of her getting hurt.And she did. Some of the comments by people she considered friends were selfish and hurtful. I am ashamed to admit that after one not so glowing post about yours truly, I got upset. It took me several days to realize that this blog is not about me. Sure, I play a supporting part in the best friend role, but this is about my friend. Who she was, who she is and who she hopefully one day will be.

Amy was also the first person I ever met to say she was a writer. Not I want to be a writer. Not, I'm working a day job, but I also write (insert your genre here). She has never strayed from stating saying she's a writer. Not even in the darkest moments of her life was her faith shaken.

It seems like I've known my best friend my entire life, but, in actuality, we met back in 1996. We were coworkers at a bookstore in the Jefferson Mall. It was a great job that introduced me to people who would change the course of my life. These people were different from my family in that they were interested in things like movies, art and, of course, books.

Amy was by far the weirdest person that I had ever met during my sheltered existence. Within days of meeting her, I knew her life story. I admired how open she was about everything from parents to customers to sexual abuse. It also scared me, if I'm being completely honest. Who talks that way with people they barely know? Amy does.

It's this openness that she projects that draws people from all walks of life to her. They understand that she won't discriminate or judge them. She will welcome them into the fold. Amy doesn't take the word "friendship" lightly. With social media like Facebook the word friend is thrown around loosely. Not so with Amy. If you are her friend, she will go the distance for you. Whatever you need, she will do it. Need someone to go to the ER at midnight, she's your girl. Need a shoulder to cry on or ears to listen? She's got those as well. I can only hope that I'm half the friend to her that she has been to me.

I had a front row seat to Amy's two nervous breakdowns. The first was in 2000. I admit I was stupid about mental illness even though I had been surrounded by it my whole life. It is only in the last decade or so that people have really opened up the conversation. Before that people just didn't talk about it as much.

When Amy realized that something was wrong, she actively sought help. The road wasn't an easy one. She went from doctor to doctor only to be turned away or told it was all in her head. We laugh at that now. Did I mention that during this breakdown Amy and I were sharing an apartment in San Antonio, Texas, trying to make a movie? It amazes me the courage and/or the stupidity of those girls that we were. Moving away from everything we had ever known. There was no family, friends or safety net to catch us.

I think it was that time in Texas that cemented the fact that we were going to be family for the rest of our lives. To me, it's like soldiers in battle: once you have been through things together, you are forever bonded. We did not dodge gunfire and cannons, but we did survive on very little. Meals consisted of eggs, bologna, Kool-Aid, pasta and Ramen. Our feet served as our mode of transportation. The car blew up (and then was crashed into), the next-door neighbor was a soft hearted cocaine addict, we didn't speak the language (neither Spanish nor Texan) and we had a run in with the man in one purple sock. We had no money, no furniture and no fear. While we eventually failed at this endeavour, it was epic. I wouldn't trade my experience there for anything in the world. It was truly an adventure.

Amy spent the next few years submerged in her healing process. There were times when it looked as if the illness would consume her in its vast ocean. Wave after wave would push her farther and farther out to sea. In the middle of this madness Amy made me promise to make sure that she was never committed to a psych ward. I believe that it was and is still to this day one of her greatest fears. I kept that promise because I had faith in my friend. I knew that she would eventually make her way to shore. And my faith was validated when she recently graduated from her group therapy and was asked to speak in front of the board at Seven Counties about her triumphs.

As Amy's friend I have gone on the journey with her as much as I could. I've listened when needed and I helped as much as possible. Mostly, I watched as she became the phoenix rising up out of the ashes. She is truly an amazing writer and an even better friend. Now it is her time to soar.

Dear Amy,

I struggled with this assignment. I'm not a writer because I generally don't do well writing when assigned subjects.One thousand words on a random subject that catches my fancy is an average Facebook post for me, but ask me to write a piece on a specific subject, person or place and I will procrastinate until I sweat blood on my keyboard. As a result, I rarely accept this sort of challenge. This is different.

You are, above all, my friend. That's been true for more than twenty years now, more or less. In that time, both of us have changed dramatically, while our common ground has remained. First as classmates, then casual friends, then during a long interlude as we pursued our own paths, and friends again through the miracle of modern technology, we've grown to appreciate each other. I value your opinion and creativity, and I certainly hope you value mine. We've worked together, cross-promoting your writing career and my musical aspirations, and I certainly hope my words on this page are worthy of your talent, and rise to the level of introduction that you deserve. I'm immensely thankful for our friendship on many levels. You bear the type of light that, even at first glance, appears impossible to extinguish.

Despite our long-term friendship, I did not know many of the things you wrote about in these letters. I was not aware of the trials you faced as an adolescent and young adult, and you never made many people aware of your internal struggles. These letters as written have been a revelation to me about my friend, about the person behind the cool, confident exterior—the girl who was a class ahead of me in school, who played field hockey and held her own with the future college professors, teachers, engineers and attorneys in a gifted group of high school students. You were the girl I always thought was far cooler than I. Some of the things you've related in these letters are simply remarkable.Your stream-of-conscious retelling of the things you've learned through education and experience as a student, a writer, a woman, a traveler and a fan is riveting to read, and, at times, rises to the level of must-read for young people in similar situations. There is wisdom in these pages: the kind of knowledge that only experience can grant, and the kind of things learned with the heart more than the head. Taken by themselves, the stories of events, situations and people in general, and specific persons, the things you learned simply by living, this book is worth reading and taking to heart—a sort of coming-to-adulthood story that Forrest Carter may have expressed had Little Tree been a young person in the late

1990s in an urban high school, progressing through college and the first half of an eventful life. But, if much of this book is a narrative of a life's learning, most of the rest is a catharsis—I nearly wrote 'confession,' but that wouldn't have been quite correct.

Amy, we didn't know. None of us. And I'm fairly sure you never knew how much we cared. By we, I mean people who will be shocked to find out just what you've endured, both during that time and after.

Your ability to tell a story is at times humorous and heartbreaking, uplifting and uncomfortable, but above all else it is the one thing about you that I admire the most—it is absolutely, completely authentic. In a world of cheap substitutes, you are the real thing, and your words paint pictures, sometimes of hope and joy, other times dark and desperate, but always real. And it is this reality, this stark honesty that draws me to your story, again and again.

I'm uncomfortable with the word 'heartbreaking' as painful as some of your experiences can read, but it is the reader's heart alone that breaks. Your own heart remains strong throughout, a testimony to a girl who knows what she wants, isn't always sure exactly how to get there, but won't let anyone or anything deflect her path, wherever it should happen to lead. I admire you for that.

The common thread is so unique, and so very you—these letters addressed to none other than Mr. Bond himself, Daniel Craig. The conversational tone with which you relate the good, the bad and the ugly to this artist you admire so much lends a delicacy to the proceedings, and a tenderness that doesn't seem possible with such weighty issues. These are real letters to a friend, and the answer to the rhetorical question, "What's On Your Mind?" Daniel Craig's penny for your thoughts, whatever they may be on that given day. I also happen to believe that Mr. Craig is a good, decent man, and I can only imagine his response to reading these letters. Daniel, if you're reading this, I assure you that Amy is no obsessed, weirdo of a fan. And I personally appreciate the anchor you've provided for her to organize her thoughts and emotions and to provide a focus for the things she needed to get off her chest. As someone who aspires to a certain level of fame, I have learned through this experience just how special and important one's work can be to someone watching or listening from afar, and I trust that you will treat Amy's work with the respect that her deepest confessions deserve. Amy, there will be a day when your work is as important to someone as Daniel's has been to you. I have the utmost confidence that you will not forget, that you will treat that person with tenderness and care.

I should wrap this up before I begin my habit of rambling pontification. Amy, I wish for you the success that you deserve. If I were the person who would chose who is entrusted with the things that come with fame and fortune, I would choose someone like you, a woman who will always remember what it was like to be that scared girl just starting her life, who's lived and loved and learned and survived to tell the story. I wish for you to meet your hero Daniel Craig on an equal footing, so that when you tell him what his work has meant to you, he can tell you what your work means to others. And I wish that this work, this remarkable collection of letters, saves even one person from abuse and mistreatment and shows them the value of hope and perseverance. You know why the caged bird sings, and someone, someday just might leave the door open.

I'm proud and thankful to be your friend. We are the music makers, and we are the dreamers of dreams.

Yours most faithfully,
Tim

Letters to Daniel

Dear Daniel,

Let's get the elephant out of the way. I don't know you. You don't know me. But I know your work. And it's impressive. And what it's done for me is really beyond anything I could've hoped for. Or even expected.

I'm a successful small press and soon to be indie writer. I write everything under the sun. Short stories, novellas, novels. I even write screenplays. None of which I'm sure you're ever going to read or see. But I'm big believer in paying it forward. So, I'll do what I do with anything I write and begin at the beginning.

This blog is really a platform to thank you for all that I've been blessed with over the last two and a half years. But the seeds were planted in September of 2009 when I rented "Casino Royale." I went out and bought it. And that's saying a lot because I wasn't much of a Bond girl myself. It's not that the movies were bad; I just found they weren't for me. But I'll admit, the scene where you came up out of the water at the beginning of the film did make an impression on me. However, there are plenty of films where I think men are nice to look at, but if the story isn't there I won't go see it. I'm a bit of a film snob in that regard.

That being said, I loved the movieand thought Vesper Lynd was the best Bond girl ever. I know people say Bond Woman now, but the reality is this: I'm from Kentucky and I am 37 years old, so I say girl. It's just the vernacular. I liked Vesper Lynd so much I chose Lynd for my last name on my sci-fi and dystopian books that I write. I digress. The May 2010 Coyote Con, an online writing conference, included a writing contest called MayNoWriMo. I wrote a 50,000-word book in 30 days. It was called "Another Way to Die." And, for the first time, I used you as the hero template. In February2011, at another online writing conference, called Digicon, I pitched the book and eventually landed a contract with a Canadian e-publisher called MuseItUp Publishing. I was 35. I'd been writing for 30 years. Seventeen of those years I'd been seeking publication. Finally, validation. I cried.

I had been through so much. And, really,I've been through so much in my life that I couldn't possibly cover it in just one post. Hence, the blog.

I've been emotionally and sexually abused. I live with a bipolar diagnosis. And right now I seem to be going through some sort of renaissance. I'm more confident than I've ever been. I have signed 23 publication contracts since February 2011. Seven of them are out under my given name, Amy McCorkle, or my pen name, Kate (for Kate Winslet) Lynd (Vesper Lynd). I've won awards, the high point so far being a 2012 Moondance International Film Festival award for Best Short Story.

There have been extreme highs and lows. At one point I was going to bed hungry and waking up hungry. Struggling with symptoms of bipolar disorder can be very hard. All in the name of trying to make a movie. It's just been recently that I've turned back to a love of mine, screenwriting. I'm better now. Sane now. And this summer and fall I'll be going out to promote two books, "Gemini's War" and "City of the Damned," which includes a huge double launch that is going to be a sanctioned event at Fandom Fest/Fright Night Film Festival. Kind of like SDCC only not as big. Although, for me it will be.

Your work has inspired me, even during some low and scary times, to hang onto my dreams and pursue my passion at all costs. As a thank you, I'd like to invite you, your wife and your daughter to the launch. Now, I don't know anyone who knows you. And this is a relatively new blog, so I won't hold my breath or even dare to think you would for a split second think about coming. I'm not that self-absorbed or self-involved. But all the same, I really think you should know that you're a big part of why this summer is going to be so huge for me. Again, thank you. I am forever indebted to you.

Sincerely,
Amy McCorkle

Dear Daniel Craig,

I need to tell you something. If I've learned anything over the years it's that people let you down. Depressing, right? I was taught early on that I was more likely to find my heroes in books, films and the theater than I was in real life. But as hard as my life was, I don't want to paint a lopsided picture. As bad as it was when it came to my biological father, his family (with the exception of his sister and her family), and his network of cop and marine buddies, my mother and stepdad, who I call dad, were at the other end of the spectrum. Most of the time.

The worst thing I can say about my mom is that she probably suffers from the same disease that I do, and without treatment bipolar disorder can make you one unstable human being. As warm and loving as she was while growing up, I never quite knew which mother I was going to get. But for all her flaws I never doubted once that she or my dad (stepdad) loved me.

I don't have this thing about my alcoholic father's behavior being my mother's fault. Mom is an early childhood education public school teacher. My dad (stepdad) went back to school later in life and went to law school to become a public defender. Neither of these jobs pay like, say, wealthy person's salary, and when I told them I wanted to become an author, my dad said you can be like John Grisham, a lawyer *and* a writer.

What I wanted was to be an author and to be involved with the movies. I had no idea how to do either so I just wrote, everyday. I even wrote a screenplay when I was 17 years old. It was bad. So bad that I think I burned it. My mother was a teacher and she believed in getting your education. So I went to college900 miles away from home. And I promptly experienced a continuation of mania. Homesickness. And the inability to sleep. The only noteworthy thingswerestarting my first serious relationship, and writing my first attempt at a novel. I also got addicted to soap operas, and because I was in two different zonesI watched them *all*.

I took a creative writing course, too, for poetry. And it was dark. All of it so dark. But Dr. Oldknow was so awesome. And he taught me a lot about how to write. So I guess it wasn't a total wash.

I saw a lot of bad movies too. A forgettable Charlie Sheen movie, a female centered western called "Bad Girls," which is really unintentionally funny. But anyway, I digress.

Daniel, I can count on one hand how many men have shown me love and kindness. And even they, my stepdadand an uncle, could break my heart. My stepdad would take my sisters and me to the library every weekend. My uncle and my aunt would pop popcorn and fill a large paper grocery bag with it and take me to the drive-in (yes drive-in) and we would sit in lawn chairs in the summer time and watch the latest blockbuster.

I didn't get to this point in my life alone. But, I see a lot of them in you in some ways. In the few interviews I've seen with you, you seem intensely private and protective of your friends and loved ones. And since I feel about as unprotected as a babe in the woods, I find that to be a highly admirable quality. And it gives me hope that someone out there will one day be protective of me.

There is so much to be grateful for in my life right now. And I have to say the success I've received over the last few years has given me the kind of confidence to believe other parts of my life will eventually iron themselves out. And whenever I doubt that, I just pop in a movie of yours and I watch it. I think you hit a homerun every time out, even if the film isn't perfect. And my personal favorite is "Cowboys & Aliens." (It's the geek in me). Again Fandom Fest is in July, so just in case hell does freeze over, you and your family are invited to attend.

Sincerely,
Amy McCorkle

Dear Daniel,

Ever been scared? Me, I'm scared of everything. Heights, bugs, closed-in places. But I'm not talking about that kind of scared. What I'm asking is, have you ever been afraid for your life because of what someone else was doing? Some say murder is the only capital crime there is. But I disagree. I think rape belongs up there. If you go by that, I've been scared for my life so many times by so many different men that maybe I should be used to it by now. One time stands out more than the others.

When I was 5, a cop stuck his service weapon in my mouth. Ever tasted gun metal? It gags you. And the worst part isn't the pain your predator is putting you through. No, it's the sheer terror of the gun going off in your mouth if you so much as cry, flinch, or scream—as my predator put it—for help. He will not just kill you, but kill your 3-year-old sister, who is sleeping just feet away on the bed.

You feel so alone at that point. Like no one loves you. Like no one will believe you. Like no one will ever find you worthy to be loved or find you beautiful again.

In some cases, the violators' faces blurred together, and their voices became just an amalgamation of every bad thing you ever heard.

In my biological father's case, it was hearing these words while he was molesting me.

Stupid. Ugly. Worthless. Whore. Slut. No one will ever believe you over me. And when I tested the waters by telling my mother as an adult she confronted him about it. So, do you think he said,"Yes, I did it. I irreparably harmed our daughter and I'll never be able to atone for what I've done to her"?

I honestly don't know what she expected him to say. Mom just assumes because she wills it that makes it so. So, when he feigned ignorance and denied it,Mom tried to put it off on another member of his family. And, while one of his brothers is guilty, too, he never shoved a gun into my mouth while he was raping me.

For the longest time I had this compelling need for people to believe me when I told them what had happened to me. Now, I realize the worst reaction is indifference. I've faced that within my own family. I had my mother tell me that she "would never ask me to be in the same room with him" about an uncle on her side who had preyed upon me. That wasn't really the reaction I needed from her. What I needed her to say was,"String the sonofabitch up by his toes." Since that wasn't what I got, I learned pretty fast family wasn't exactly the place to look for comfort and healing in this particular matter. What I realized was that only a therapist and my closest friends would ever stand by me in this matter. So, when the night terrors and nightmares plagued me, I turned to an old source to calm down as an adult. My magic sleeping pill was a copy of "Cowboys & Aliens."

Don't get me wrong, the movie didn't bore me, but Jake Lonergan had inspired several works of my fiction. Well, your performance of him had. And the idea that he wasn't beyond redemption, and that he could be a hero appealed to me. The fact he loses two loves wasn't lost on me at all. But the way he was willing to stand up for a woman, well, let's just say that was a welcome respite from the flashbacks, which are panic and terror inducing.

I know you're not Jake or Bond or Mikail. But you're an artist plying your trade. I don't know your personal story, and in many ways I prefer it that way. It enables me to work my imagination to project onto a character that looks like you. I don't deserve to know what goes on in your private life. Tabloids don't interest me. I'm telling my story not because I desire some sort of reality television program, but because I want, for some reason, for you to know where I came from and how I survived and succeeded in the face of terrible odds. And I guess I want others, who might be in similar situations, to know that if I survived, so can they, and that this is one way to do it.

Your work did a lot for me. And if the universe turns further in my favour, maybe, perhaps, I'll get to work with you. As it stands, I am content to just thank you.

Sincerely,
Amy McCorkle

Dear Daniel,

So I've told you all about this heavy, dark shit that most people take to their graves. Or maybe share once in a lifetime. Me, I don't know, I think I have to share it for my own peace of mind. However, I thought I might change it up and tell you about the first time I produced a film. An independent film, produced on a shoestring budget.No way in hell am I ever going to let that thing see the light of day.

Let me start by telling you about my best friend and sister-from-another-mister, Missy Goodman. I met her while working in a bookstore, and I should just tell you now that you'll be hearing a lot about her. Not because we're dating, but because she's one of those kinds of friends everyone should be so lucky to have. She's the one who took care of me and bore the brunt of the hard stuff when I had two breakdowns in Texas (more on that in another post).

What we discovered at that bookstore was that we both loved to write, we both loved "General Hospital" (a soap), and we both loved television and movies and books, period. And when she came to me to write a romance novel, I said "Yes, let's do it for the money." That was in 1997. But this post is about "*Too Far From Texas*," our first foray into directing and producing.

In 2004, we had kind of fallen down on the writing end. Our writing partnership had petered out, although our friendship was stronger than ever. But, and I don't think I've mentioned this part before, I identify myself so closely with my work that it's hard to explain to people that, while I want a readership that enjoys my work, I think people confuse that with me wanting fame. I don't really desire fame and celebrity. You lose something when you get famous, your privacy. One might argue I'm sacrificing my privacy by doing this, but 'this' is just another form of self-expression for me. A way to address the kind of pain I've been through. I value my anonymity, and the computer and Internet give me at least a false sense of it.

Anyway, I've wandered off topic. In 2004, I was sitting in my therapist's office apologizing and crying over a car wreck I'd had, where I totaled Missy's car. It didn't hurt anyone, but she was justifiably upset with me. I'd been driving sleepy and hit the gas when the stoplight turned green.I also hit the caran inch in front of me that hadn't moved. Missy was there, and she told me it was okay, that it was in the past (a good year and a half in the past) at the time. Then I started talking about not writing and how I felt like that part of me had just died some kind of death and I was miserable.

I can't describe to you just how miserable I was. It was like I had deprived myself of food, water, and oxygen and then just watched that part of myself shrivel up and disappear. But in 2004 Missy did one of those kinds of things a friend who is more like a sister does. Or what a sister is supposed to do.

She'd been my writing partner and we'd once dreamed of making movies together. But somewhere along the way, my bipolar breakdowns and lack of money had stopped and robbed us not just the drive but of the kind of passion that drove me to write.

In the car later that night on the way home she looked at me and said, "*All right. Let's do this thing. Let's make a movie.*"

With those three sentences, she lifted me up out of my despair, and we began writing *Too Far From Texas*. Honestly, the hardest thing I ever did in my life was making that movie. Getting the money, casting it, directing it, and producing it.

You look up Murphy's Law in the film production handbook and there we'd be with that film. Everything that could go wrong did go wrong. First of all, we were so green and had never been in charge of anything business wise in our entire lives, which would later lead to much bigger problems. But young and driven, we were determined to get the project done.

The first sign of disaster up ahead was the casting of a diva. Didn't realize she was a diva when we cast her, but at the first rehearsal she was refusing to curse. She claimed artistic choice. We should have fired her ass on the spot, but not because of that, but because we don't need to be off book by shoot date do we should have been a big fat waving red flag that this was someone we didn't want anywhere near our production. But, we were green and didn't want to wait to make the movie so, dummy here pushed ahead. Then we hired an actor that she knew for one of the male lead roles. He was in the active service. We told him,"cut your hair." He calls up the Sunday before shooting starts and says, I went to get my haircut today but the barbershop was closed. Another big fat red flag. But again we pushed on. The other male lead? Well, his story is long, thorny and complicated and man it says it a lot about me and Missy and how we tried to hang onto him for subsequent productions.

He was charismatic, good looking, and had real, raw talent. But he had a drug and alcohol addiction too, and ultimately we had to cut him from pool of talent for our own peace of mind. He had good heart, but he was extremely troubled and he once told us, "I'll break your heart," which indeed he did, but not on that particular production. He had his shit together for Texas and it made the slide down that much more torturous.

The sound equipment we were using wasn't the most sophisticated in the world, and it picked up the sound of the air condition kicking on and off on location. We had to keep it off, so people sweated all day that first day. Just as it was cooling down at the end of day one, a hurricane-force severe thunderstorm knocked the power out. And the two male leads sat out on the patio getting drunk and looking at porn on the Internet after the rain had passed. While everyone else slept on location and just trusted these guys could handle it if some criminal happened upon us. Both of them had drinking problems, but the one with the talent was also the one who had the words "bang bang" tattooed on his fingers and had the kind of colorful history that allowed us to think he could protect us and the set. Ah, yes, youth.

In the end, we had to do 50 pages of reshoots with almost a completely different cast. We were barely able to edit it because two-thirds of the cast didn't know their lines and there was hardly any continuity. It is a shitty product and it's no wonder no festival will have it.

But, what it did do was reawaken my creative spirit. And allowed me to start writing again. To push past the damage of the mood disorder and tap into the parts of it that actually make me a better writer. I take my meds and my treatment seriously. There's a school of thought that if you're on medication, it inhibits you creatively. That's not so. Especially for me. Having been in treatment and relatively stable for the last 13 years, I know I am more productive on treatment than I was before it. Getting in treatment, that honor goes to another creative traveler, Maurice Benard. His courage to speak out about it in an industry that tends to sensationalize it or tell stories from the caretaker's perspective helped me walk through the doctors' doors in October of 1999 and seek help. I owe you both so much.

Sincerely,

Amy McCorkle

Dear Daniel,

I wish I could say my personal self-image was a healthy one. If I were honest I'd say in certain areas that it is. When it comes to writing, well, I have the success I've always wanted, even if it doesn't look like I always thought it would. I'm a small press success. You know? That means no advance except in rare cases, and a bigger cut on the royalty. The only story I haven't been able to sell on the pitch is this one. My memoirs, in a series of letters to you. Of course, in Frank's defense he hasn't seen it. As tested as I am in other areas, nonfiction isn't one of them. So I made this blog in the hopes that I would have a readership that might benefit from personal journey and that, maybe, when hell truly does freeze over, you might see it and know just how much you've inspired me.

Here's another way you've inspired me. I went for a walk today. So what's the big deal about that? I've struggled with my weight since I was a kid and have always thought I was ugly. I've believed I wasn't worthy to be liked or loved and had a real self- hatred thing going for the longest time. Not only was I victimized at home by most of the men in my family but also middle school was truly hell on Earth—I was the one they put the sign on, put stuff in my hair, got punched in the faceand called names. It was awful. I picked a high school expressly to get away from all the bullies I attended school with. Lori Joseph, Betty Floodand Robert Ford are just a few of the douchebags who liked to push me around and make my life away from home just as bad as could be at Jerry's on the weekend (that's my biological father).

Of course, I'm sure they're all grown up now and have no memory of being the jackasses that they were, but I had an eating disorder already without needing them help me to compound it. I try not to judge others with their own addictions. Some smoke, some drink, others use narcotics or prescription pills to escape the pain. Me, give twenty dollars and I'll spend 16 of it on Chinese takeout and still eat you under the table.

Some things have been moving to put me in a better place, and people would laugh if I told them a card reader has helped me to kind of embrace myself and go out there and get what I want. But there's an old adage in the program, (Overeaters Anonymous) and that is you have to be rigorously honest in order for any eating plan to work. It also helps not to go it alone. And by doing this it's like I have my hero cheering me on to lose this horrible weight, which seems to be holding me back.

You see, Friday I went grocery shopping, and I had what is called a moment of clarity. I've had these a couple of times about different things in my life. One, about my writing career, and two the last time I had true success in losing weight. I ran a marathon then. That's right, 26.2 miles. I want to do it again. But I have to take baby steps. And the first step is to be able to walk around the grocery store again and not have to ride around in one of those motorized carts. It's embarrassing at 37 years of age tootling around in one of those things. They're not meant for me or for people my age.

My moment of clarity came when I went up the Slim Fast aisle. You see, I'm on food stamps, and that stuff ain't cheap. But I realized I was working towardgetting of it. That's what the backlist is for of all of my books. So, I crunched the numbers and I devised a way to do the shakes and meal plan, lose the weight, and keep it off. That was Friday night. Saturday morning I got up and had a shake and went walking with my dad(my stepdad John, he's the one who introduced me to walking and running in middle school). Today is my second day on the program, and I have to admit I'm feeling really good.

How do you have anything to do with this? Well, I want someone to share my success with (not to worry I'm not under any delusions) and there is a guy who I'm interested in and I want to feel good about myself and worthy to be loved so I don't find myself in a position where I allow myself to be treated poorly. I feel like I'm worthy in my work and that has a lot to do with you.It's had the effect of making me want to better myself all around, and want balance in all of parts of my life.

I have two goals this year, health-wise. First, be fit enough to walk around the conventions and conferences enough to enjoy them properly. Second, to participate in a four-person marathon relay at my favorite park in Louisville, Kentucky, Iroquois Park. I have two others besides myself signed on for a little over five mile leg, my sister Brandy and my dad John (and he's had knee replacement surgery), interested in that fourth slot? Just kidding. My sister, Sara, says the only way she'll ever run is if someone is chasing her.

Anyway, I'll share a photo of me now so that you can get an idea of what 289 pounds looks like.

Sincerely,

Amy McCorkle

Dear Daniel,

I do this thing when I'm writing. I create heroes that I can fall in love with for 50,000 words or so. Of course, there are things about the fictional heroes that would make them impossible real life lovers or boyfriends. But, for a little while, I get to fall in love and be in love just like my heroine. I hope that doesn't sound silly. I know it does, but still, I hope I don't seem silly.

Do you remember that thing I said about learning the lesson that people will let you down, that they inevitably disappoint? I make heroes that may have disappointed at one point but the work ceaselessly to right their mistakes. And certainly the heroine is always much more forgiving than I am in these cases.

Forgiveness is hard for me. I know it's important because if you don't forgive, stuff eats you up inside. It leaves you raw, angry, and bitter. I should know, I've felt all of those things. Forgiveness is hard because it feels like you're giving your transgressor a free pass. But here's the thing: on the good days I know that's kind of bullshit. Forgiveness is for you and your own peace of mind.

So today is a good day, and I can forgive everyone who's ever hurt me. I don't necessarily have to break bread with them. Which is a good thing because many of the people I forgive or seek to forgive are guilty of some pretty heinous shit.

Let me say my mom and stepdad are no angels, but they are not the devil by any stretch of the imagination. They do a lot for those in their lives. I needed to move back in with them in order to be able(financially) to travel to these different cons and book signings, and they have not asked me to pay rent. Now, I have to clean up after myself and do my own laundry and stuff like that, but that's relatively simple. And that walking thing I was talking about? Dad(stepdad) introduced me to walking when I was 12 years old, and in order to encourage me to workout now he takes me walking. Of course, he and mom are also batshit crazy with issues of their own, which often drives me to my room to hide. But I know they love me without question, and that makes their transgressions easier to forgive than those of the others who have hurt me.

That being said there are others whom I have a more difficult time forgiving, such as my biological father. His crimes are different and I find my therapy is often focused on characters and villains I write that feature him prominently, at least his characteristics. And in "Gemini's War," I think I get my revenge in a very dark way. I certainly don't sit around thinking about it, but when I write antagonists they rarely have any redeeming qualities. Forgiving Jerry is hardest of all.

But forgiveness is a process, and when I think about all that the universe has given me in recent years it's easy to let things go for the most part. I'm happy with my life. I get to do what I love for a living fulltime. I'm more confident in myself than I've ever been. I wish I could say I got there all by myself, but I got here on the shoulders of other people.

My friends, my heroes, (yes, I have others, you are just the biggest one) such as Kurt Vonnegut, Ray Bradbury, Jane Austen, Sue Grafton, Scott Frank, William Goldman, Kevin Smith, Katherine Patterson, Judy Blume, and Douglas Adams to name a few. (Oh and Quentin Tarantino). You all made me believe there was hope and light at the very end of a long a dark tunnel. And even when it was just a pinpoint there you all were inspiring me, coaxing me, whispering to me that I could survive the darkness, that it would all get better if I just hung in there and didn't give up.

As I settle in to work on my self-publishing venture I hope one day you'll see this and now just how much I appreciate you and how you've inspired me.

Sincerely,
Amy McCorkle

Dear Daniel,

I have some awesome news. My post on body image and struggles with food addiction landed me a regular paying gig in Target Audience Magazine. It's an online publication that's featured my work on the cover and inside before. Once they reviewed two of my books, and the other time I penned an article about finding a small press. Both of those were free appearances.

And while I'm not being paid a lot, it's the first time I've been paid for something like that.

It's a way to chronicle my weight loss journey. As a writer, I face a lot of difficult things. Hell, as a human being I and many others like me face difficult things. Last night, as I lay in bed in the quiet of the night, my loneliness, pain and depression came bubbling to the surface. During the course of the day I'd had a heavy-duty argument most people fight over money. Missy and I have been best friends for 15 years, and we argue about the story whenever we're working on writing projects together. Trust me, we could give any married couple a run for their money. As it is, we resolved the argument and finished the first draft of "You're the Reason."

But as I lay quietly in the room, all the insecurities that I didn't think about during the day clamored up to meet me, and this triggered depression. During the argument, I sacrificed the need to be right for the desire to finish the screenplay. And in the process I catered to her need to be right. And honestly, I thought we were going to kill each other.

In her defense, I'm not the best collaborator. I like having control. I don't like having to share the leadership angle. I like losing myself in the story of the hero and the heroine; a multi-pronged approach isn't my natural voice. If you ever read my solo stuff versus my collaborative stuff, you'll see a marked difference.

Not that it's bad. Quite the contrary. Both types of my projects lend themselves to a level now that most people would consider them fortunate to have. I have a book series I'm collaborating on with Missy, called "Gunpowder and Lead"under my Kate Lynd moniker. It's a post- apocalyptic Hatfields-and-McCoys tale. We're fortunate it's a five-book series, and Missy just completed Book Two.

And under my McCorkle name we've collaborated on several screenplays. Some are not worth seeing,but worthy of burning, and someareso good they border on excellent. The two most recent,"City of the Damned" and "You're the Reason," are some of the best work we've ever done.

I'm fortunate. Even though I struggle with my emotions and insecurities, I battle with my need to control, and I have fears of being found out as an imposter, I know as long as I'm emotionally honest there is a better chance of me staying on track. Same with my eating right and exercising.

I didn't go walking yesterday, but I could already tell a difference from the three days I did go walking. In my regular movement, I wasn't panting as hard and my legs weren't cramping up as much. As a matter of fact, I think I'm tempted to get up on my stair-stepper for ten minutes. No doubt it will help me get ready for Fandom Fest even faster.

I so can't wait for Fandom Fest. But that's another post.

Sincerely,
Amy McCorkle

Dear Daniel,

When I was in high school, as I mentioned, I wrote my first screenplay. It was awful, it was dreadful, and, honestly, if it's ever found, I will disavow I ever dreamed up the thing.

But last night Missy and I finished a 14-year journey that started in January of 1999, well really, 15 years when we took a screenwriting workshop offered by Michael Hauge. He taught us the components and nuts and bolts of a screenplay. And we wrote many, many a bad screenplay. We even entered one of them into the prestigious Austin Film Festival. (It, too, was bad). The one thing I learned how to do really well at that workshop was pitch. Now, not too brag, but I have sold many books on a pitch alone. But screenplays, not so much. My prowess in the longer-form was not exactly matched in the form of movie writing.

There have been many drafts and many opportunities to turn "You're the Reason" into the real deal. Missy and I decided we wanted to make a movie, so we went to a filmmaking workshop where we learned a lot, and knew how to do just enough to be dangerous.

The first draft of "You're the Reason" was written in five days. Crazy, insane and full of disagreements. But what we produced got us the most heat from Hollywood that we'd ever gotten. Lee Daniels and Zide/Perry both showed initial interest on the pitch. But even though *You're the Reason* had a lot of promise, and when Lee Daniels 'passed' twice in the same year, he gave us a call the second time and told us it wasn't what they were looking for, but that we had talent and that we should keep working at it.

Since no one in Hollywood *ever* calls just to give you a pep talk, Missy and I were excited about the progress. That was in the early 2000s, right before *Monster's Ball* and way before *Precious*.

We've rewritten the thing too many times to count. But most recently after we saw a YouTube video of Kevin Smith's *Burn In Hell* speaking tour. He extols the virtues of "Why Not? Write the book, make the movie, produce the play?" (By the way, that's another thing I want to do).

Missy came to me and pitched the idea of writing *You're The Reason*. We started writing in late March, the day after Kevin Smith started *Clerks III*, and we finished exactly one day after he did. That means, well…Missy and I are always talking about signs and how things are meant to happen.

I never know how a screenplay is going to play to a reader. And, to be honest, I wrote *City of the Damned*(an adaptation of my series) with the idea that Missy would get a Michelle Phillips-like credit, which she does. As someone who has seen me through two emotional breakdowns because of the bipolar disorder, and gone to bed hungry and woken up that way, it certainly wouldn't do not to have her there for the good times as well.

That being said, *You're the Reason* is a joint venture, from start to finish. We've entered both screenplays into Austin. And although I do believe *these* scripts truly do have the potential to win it all, the only thing I am sure of is they are good enough to advance. It just depends on who is reading them.

City of the Damned is also entered in the Fandom Fest/Fright Night Film Fest screenwriting competition. Fandom Fest is going to be a lot of work, and, I hope, fun. With Missy there and other friends, I'm sure it will be regardless of how the screenwriting competition turns out.

Sincerely,
Amy McCorkle

Dear Daniel,

So, I suppose I should be honest. I ate breakfast this morning at 4:30 a.m. Real food, but I've been measuring my calories all day and will be responsible at dinner. See, I was kind of wide awake even though my body was tired. I hate that. My mania makes me prone to bad sleep patterns. Well, that, a shitty mattress, and sleeping most of the day before.

So what have I accomplished today? Absolutely nothing it seems. So I forced myself to sit down and write to 'you.' I get to do one of my favorite things tonight: I get to go to the bookstore. I know, I like to live dangerously.

Books have always provided an escape. And at different ages different authors were my shelter growing up. Judy Blume, Katherine Patterson, Scott O'Dell, C.S. Lewis. I read books like most people breathed air. As a high schooler who didn't change, I was into Ray Bradbury, Douglas Adams, Sue Grafton, Mary Higgins Clark, and the one who changed my life, Kurt Vonnegut.

I always dreamed of meeting Kurt Vonnegut and telling him how much his books meant to me. His writings were darkly funny and I loved his recurring character of Kilgore Trout, a hack who could only get published in porn magazines.

The ironic thing is some people would say *I* write porn. I don't write porn, but when you say "erotic romance," people conjure images of Fifty Shades of Grey. That is erotica, which in poorly skilled hands is porn. I don't write porn or erotica. Certain stories of mine are subgenre erotic romance and some are just subgenre romance.

I only have one straight dystopian tale and that's Breath of Life. And it ends with the heroine dying. It's dark and depressing. But then I was going through a very dark period with the 2012 elections and seeing the way one group played on people's fears and whipped them up into a frenzy over the barely concealed racism. It was just hard to watch otherwise normal and articulate friends sending me pictures of Obama in a turban, with him designed to look like a monkey. I feared we were about to be run over by these well meaning but misinformed people and it terrified me. It's the first in a trilogy. It's due out sometime this summer.

After I wrote Breath of Life I wanted to write something lighter. So I wrote Gemini's War. Here's an excerpt from it:

I ceased believing in angels when I was three years old; when the evil from which my mother so valiantly tried to protect me came and took her, plunging me headlong into madness.

Evil, I know your name. And it has always been Father.

Three times I thought I'd broken the bond for good. Three times I was captured and dragged, screaming defiantly back into hell. This time there would be no escape. There was nowhere to run. It was sure to end in death.

The fight had finally been knocked out of me by the time I was twenty-five.

My father was all-powerful. His name rang through the halls of justice when an undesirable need arose to service the dark pleasures of those same men. I was his daughter, and I was not immune. My short life had been written in blood. I could smell cigarette smoke and stale beer and heard the sound of raucous laughter as I lay there drugged and fighting to maintain consciousness.

"This is some cold-blooded shit. She must have something big on the old man."

"But…his own daughter?"

"Hey, it's not for me to judge. He pays me for this kind of work. I never said I was a soft."

"You have kids, don't you?"

I forced my eyes open as my heart still strained against the effects of the barbiturate cocktail they had injected me with a few hours beforehand.

"Yeah," the fat one said, "I almost regret abducting this one. She just wanted to be

My eyes were losing focus again, and it was hard to breathe. I spied a gun out of reach. I'd learned how to shoot one out of necessity. I stretched my fingers as far as they would go to no avail. My fingertips brushed the gun's grip. I knocked it to the ground, causing it to discharge.

The men jumped. "Goddamn it. Waste of a perfectly good bullet," the fat one swore. "Tie her hands and feet." The slender man hesitated. "Dammit, Johnson, if the old man isn't hesitating in rubbing her out, what makes you think he'll hold back on us?"

Johnson grabbed my hands without mercy and bound them together until the rope dug into my skin.

I was too weak to fight back. The will to survive overrode the pain. I saw men running toward us as they heaved me over the side of the Kennedy Bridge. Were those FBI logos on their jackets? I screamed as loud as I could. I prayed they would rescue me as I plummeted towards the water. I did not want to die.

Perhaps the law had finally caught up with my father and those he supplied with young women. Perhaps they would finally be brought to justice.

The water was freezing. I saw someone hitting the water beside me as I lost consciousness. Thiswas a force and a presence stronger and more intense than anything I had ever felt before, taking me and kicking towards the surface.

Lighter fare, lol? I don't really write comedy. I can write a funny line. I can be humorous around my friends. But you won't find me writing romantic comedies. It's not that I don't enjoy them when they're well done, but the only time I tried to write one it was dreadful, awful and not worth the paper it was printed on.

I ate responsibly but not exactly the way in my perfectionist mind I should have. But there will be good days and there will be bad days. Today, because I didn't overdo it, was a good day. Now if I can just sleep worth a damn.

Sincerely,
Amy McCorkle

Dear Daniel,

I wish I could say that the publishing world was devoid of the kind of cattiness and diva posturing one finds in Hollywood. That distinct brand of phoniness is just as pervasive in publishing as it is in the film industry. And since I tend to be an open book and trust that one is being genuine with me, it hurts my feelings like it would any human being when I realize one is just another jerk and douchebag.

I am not delusional, and I suppose my being the kind of geeked-out fangirl I am, I suppose it can come across that way. I suppose if I really wanted to be a bitch I could expose the ladies who are responsible for this hypocrisy but I won't. It would be a waste of time and energy and, trust me, their lives are far worse and empty than mine is. I figure that's the best revenge. In that respect, I suppose I can be catty too.

I think what sucks about the whole situation is that these ladies opened up to me and invited me into their lives and went through effort to make me feel like I was their friend. As a result, I'm always singing their praises to anyone who'll listen. Finding out they bad mouth me—and consider me delusional over my appreciation of your work—well that stings. I wish I could say that it didn't, but it does.

If I haven't made it clear before now allow me to say it now. I belong to geekdom's very sweet, very inclusive community referred to fandom. I love Star Trek, I love Star Wars, I loved the X-Files and Highlander. This summer I get to get my photo taken with Adrian Paul, the television series star of Highlander, and Gillian Anderson, Scully of the X-Files. I have never been so excited in my life.

Those shows were pivotal in my survival of insomnia during the years they were on and even though I'm not going to get the chance to explain that to them, my brief seconds with them will be the culmination of any fangirl's geek-out moment.

On a more serious note, I have not one but two screenplays that I co-wrote with my best friend Missyin competition. One of our screenwriting/filmmaking idols, Kevin Smith, will be there. Going to his Q & A with his best friend Jason Mewes is like a full circle moment for us. We're huge fans of his. As I said, we started writing *You're the Reason* one day after he started Clerks III, and finished exactly one day after.

I'm a huge romantic and see the symbolism in just about everything. As much as I dream about one day working with you, I realize my independent streak might keep me in the small press and indie filmmaking world. And even though you paid your dues there and cut your chops in the prestigious schools, that's not where you ply your trade anymore. You live in more rarified air.

Not that you think you're better than this world. As a matter of fact, from an interview I read once, I get the feeling you respect the Indies very much. You're aware of the fact when you become attached to a project money becomes an issue for a studio and with that comes creative control and you feel like the indie world is about people like me seeing my vision out to the end I want to see. And not what a bunch of suits want.

Not that that is a bad way to work, some are able to strike a balance in that world and work very well in that environment and create great work. Your friend Sam Mendes is a perfect example. I don't like everything he does, but I loved SKYFALL and it is clear he is a brilliant director.

In the end I suppose the fact I struggle with and live with a bipolar diagnosis, but deal with it and am in treatment for it and I'm not afraid to share that with people...I guess when people call me delusional, it upsets me. They're no better than the person who gives me the 'OMG, you're fucking crazy' look when I share that with them.

Let me just state for the record, I am a survivor. Of both abuse and mental illness. I have worked very hard to get where I am and where others have failed I have been successful. I typically have a profanity filled sentence for haters and doubters. So even though their phoniness has hurt me, I'll say to them what I have said to my doubters and others who've hurt me. A variation on Haters Are Motivators. They can, how is it people say? Oh yes, they can go fuck themselves. It seems I can be catty too. ;)

Sincerely,
Amy McCorkle

Dear Daniel,

When you have the kind of success I'm having (I know, I'm not the seller that EL James is but I have had a bestseller), to tend to be grateful for everything you've gotten. In two and a half years I've accomplished a lot of things I've always wanted to. But along the way you have to be given a chance. And the person in the publishing world who gave me a chance was Lea Schizas of MuseItUp Publishing. I've had lots of opportunities these last few years, but Lea was the first. And what I couldn't do in college and in my twenties, she helped me do at 35. She offered me a publication contract.

I had never been through edits before and it was brutal. Like boot camp tearing you down to build you back up. It was one of the worst experiences; being told your baby has big ears is no fun. But still Lea was there. I could call her anytime. She answered my emails. She was patient, attentive, all the things a neurotic tangle of nerves like me needed her to be. I submitted another piece called No Ordinary Love. While Another Way to Die had a fully fleshed out idea and character development, No Ordinary Love was much shorter. And was inspired by Cowboys and Aliens. It's nothing like Cowboys and Aliens, but it inspired me to try my hand at a sci-fi/dystopian piece.It was also an erotica piece. Now, I have written a lot of erotic romance, subgenre erotic romance and my first foray into it is actually one of my best sellers.

I have four books with MuseItUp. Those two and the first two books in the Gladiator Chronicles. I still have a third book to write in the GLADIATOR, ORACLE, QUEEN saga.

The person who gave me my break into print is Frank Hall of Hydra Publications, not the one in New York, but the one in Madison, Indiana. Another small press. The book is Bounty Hunter, a sci-fi erotic romance. Not erotica. There is a difference. There is no BDSM. I know some get the idea that erotic=dirty and that's just not the case. And it irritates me when people don't take the time to respect a genre that carries the entire publishing industry on its back. But that's another post for another day.

And Blackyrm, (Dave Mattingly) the publisher of Gemini's War, which I'm double launching at Fandom Fest with City of the Damned from Hydra, is offering to pay my way into Dragon Con. I really want to go to the Austin Film Festival, however, and am wondering how to swing both. Again, another time, another post.

But Fandom Fest is my first love. It was my first Con of any kind. And it has done nothing but yield good things. The first year I found Hydra. The second year I launched GLADIATOR. It reached as high as #43 in the Amazon free books sci-fi section. And in the guest list for last year it put me in touch with G.L. Giles, a book reviewer for Target Audience Magazine. That connection brought a feature about me and two great reviews into being. I posted about my love for the small press and the editor for TAM asked me to do a post about finding a good small/indie press.

This blog led to a regular feature about writers, emotional issues and food addiction in TAM. It pays and builds my brand. Promotion doesn't come easily for me. I tend to think in the big picture and miss small details because of film background. I'm good at planning parties and setting them up, but I am horrible at executing them. I tend to want to run away from my own gatherings.

I threw a Christmas party for my friends, and my family decided that they were invited. It became a huge deal and I just wanted to abandon everyone and everything and hide in my room. I have a bit of social anxiety. So, as much as I'm looking forward to Fandom Fest, a little part of me that gets louder everyday, freaking out. Because panic attacks like to hit me out of nowhere, and when I can't get away from the noise, it's really bad. I start to shake. Noise bombards me, I can't breathe, and I start to cry. It's not something I enjoy experiencing and if I can avoid I try to avoid stressful situations.

I can handle just about anything, but it's like I have a shelf life. And once the shelf life runs out, I'm caput. I need to go home and decompress. That's why events like Fandom Fest are such a double-edged sword for me. I have friends like Missy, Pam, Carla and Elise, and people who have touched my life in such a positive way, like Bertena, Ellen, Delilah, Tanjaand Greta. I'm lucky to have survived what I did growing up. I'm lucky to have a mom and a dad(John, not Jerry) who love me and through their actions show me how to follow my dreams, and not settle for something other than that. My dad (John) went back to school, got his law degree and became a public defender in his late forties. My mom has been a public school teacher for 25 years. Definitely not the highest-paying ventures in the world.

And to their credit, with the exception of when I was in high school, there was just an acceptance that I was going to build my career as I saw fit. Whatever that was. So, like I said, as shitty as my life was in some ways, I always knew they loved me. But Vonnegut, Bradbury, and Grafton helped me to survive my own problems. And I wrote. I always wrote. And thanks to some very generous people I got my shot at as a published author.

Sincerely,
Amy McCorkle

Dear Daniel,

Late at night, when I lay down to sleep, sometimes, okaya lot in recent days, a depression falls over me. A loneliness, and an ache, and I feel so isolated and alone in this world. I know I'm not, but I can't help it. I've never pegged myself as 'needing' a man to complete me or validate my existence. But I find myself at a point where I want someone to celebrate in my accomplishments with. Someone who I can appreciate and he can appreciate me.

I know, it all sounds very silly, but at night, a time when, in the past most of the abuse happened I'd like to feel protected. And in this world I don't feel very protected or like there's anyone who will stand up for me other than myself. I know this is a myopic viewpoint and that it's simply not true. I have friends who do it all the time. But I want someone to defend me, to love me for me and not be scared of the fact that I do have a bipolar diagnosis.

Of course, maybe I'm scared of the fact I have a bipolar diagnosis. Maybe I find myself unwanted or undesirable, and, if that's the case, why would anyone else want to take the chance? If I'm completely honest with myself, I know there's a lot of that going on. But at 37, I find I'm turning over a new leaf.

I've never been much for dressy clothes. My style has always been my own. T-shirt and jeans. A brush through my hair and I'm done. But I decided to shake things up a bit. I went out and got my hair cut and colored. I bought some new clothes, I even got make-up and some jewelry. I hate shopping. So I bought these wedge boots and wore them once. Dear Lord they nearly killed my feet and me in the process. But I felt good, I felt confident and I was ready to take on the world. I've even included a few pictures of me at Conglomeration (a small sci-fi Con here in Louisville).

This last year has been really great. The compliment I got from my publisher yesterday made me feel really good. And my writing is stronger than ever.

A guy even flirted with me and told me I was cute. And he was attractive and funny and smart. So you know, I feel more confident and sure of myself than I have in a very long time. I know I'm 37. I know I want to be in a relationship. But I also know I don't have to sacrifice who I am and what I believeto be in one.

Perhaps I am high-maintenance. But not in that diva, bitchy way where I think the world revolves around me. I need patience, kindness, and lots of love because, perhaps, my road hasn't been as smooth as some of the others around me.

I believe everyone has a story. So, put their lives on blast for fame and glory and get infamy in return, then complain about it. (I can't watch the Kardashians; I'm sure they're good people, but they come off as overindulged and entitled and that is something that I can do without).

Having gone to bed hungry and woken that way I can say what I have now has been worth it. And as I lose the weight and the emotions come to the surface, like late at night I just have to ride it out until morning when I can talk to someone. And my dad (John) is usually where I start. He recently lost 155 pounds. Even though he's quick to strikeout emotionally, he makes amends these days. And it allows me to be more emotionally honest with him than anyone else in my family.

And by emotionally honest I don't mean being a bitch, I mean sitting down and telling him he hurt my feelings and taking responsibility for my part in whatever may have happened. It makes for a better living arrangement.

I wish I could do that with my mom, but she's *always* right and there's no two ways about it. But then I guess everyone's mom is that way. But I know on a good day she'd give me the shirt off her back and anyone else's who happened to be standing there.

You should know I love my family, even though they're a dysfunctional lot and even though they've hurt me (as I'm sure I've hurt them), I would do anything for them.

Sincerely,

Amy McCorkle

Dear Daniel,

It's amazing. I tell you how my family was so great yesterday. My mom and dad(John) and then today they shit all over it and make me a liar. They know my Uncle Junior raped me, they know my Uncle Ron assaulted me, and they know Jimmy McNut, a church elder, did unspeakable things to me. Maybe I should back up.

Tonight we were watching television; the news to be exact. My mother is a public school teacher. She works hard. And her efforts are often under appreciated. But that being said we were watching a news story about what it's really like to be a teacher in the public school system. They were talking about how students with problems came in so angry and how sometimes it takes half the day before they can get the student ready to learn. Then they talked about the students as "in need" and this was an excuse for them to act the way that they were.

I said it was a cop out on both their parts. I explained I had been traumatized and that I was still an overachieving student. That I made excellent grades and participated in every academic and athletic sport under the sun. I earned a partial scholarship to an out-of-state college. Even as I struggled against major mania in college, I was a successful debater and the captain of the college bowl team that won the university competition.

My stepdad proceeded to say I had no idea what these people were going through. That I didn't know what it was like to be afraid at night or wonder where I would be living or worry about going hungry. I was flabbergasted. (Yes, I used a ten-dollar word) Actually, I should have said devastated.

His words and casual dismissive attitude about me and my life experiences punched me in the gut and even though I'm going to the bookstore and I'm starting a new series tonight I'm really hurting and feel like they don't even begin to grasp the damage the do when they talk like this.

Do they think I don't know suffering? Do they think I went to bed one night and poof everything was forgotten? That I haven't been in therapy since I was 19 years to undo the damage they helped to inflict? The damage they do every time they say something incredibly stupid like that.

So, right now I just want to cry and eat everything in sight. This is my first real emotional test. I mean, people being catty isn't really a test. Anger is hurt, but hurt that turns to anger is much more toxic. I really want to binge right now. To go to the Chinese restaurant at home and buy "happy family," Crab Rangoon, and fried dumplings and shovel it all in and wash it down with a Coca-Cola.

The problem is, I have the money to do it. Wow. They just don't stop. My mother just accused me of eating her cookies. I didn't even know they had any fucking cookies. Yet it makes me want to eat that much more.

Addiction is a beast. I suppose I should be grateful that it's food and not heroin or alcohol or (sorry about this, I'm allergic to the smoke) cigarettes. Of course there is my other addiction: caffeine. I prefer mine in coffee form thank you.

Damn it's so hard to be strong. I just wish my family would behave. It would make my recovery so much easier. And it would go a long way toward healing my relationship with them in this area.

Sincerely,

Amy McCorkle

Dear Daniel,

So, I'm coming to you late. I have my coffee and, here in a few minutes, I'll have to take my night-time meds for the bipolar disorder. After that, chances are I'll be too tired to write. But I wanted tell you, as bad my life can seem, sometimes the most beautiful things are born out of that ugliness.

My heroines have a theme. They are strong, they are lonely, and they've been fighting the good fight on their own for so long that when blessings come their way they're willing to go to any lengths to make sure the people responsible for those blessings know just how much they're appreciated. Yesterday I found out I was a semi-finalist in the 2013 Moondance International

Film Festival for short story with my chapter excerpt from my upcoming release, Gemini's War. I was elated, to say the least.

Unfortunately, I don't think I'll be able to attend the festival. My publisher is sending me to Dragon Con! They're paying my way and everything. And, at the end of the month I will be attending Night Risers Film Festival & Expo just a few miles from my home. My publisher wants me there too. At the end of August I will be attending Killer Nashville, a multi-genre writers' con. I'm entered in two of their contests: the Claymore and the Silver Falchion. One is for unpublished fiction and the other is for published books since last year's Con. But as much as I'm looking forward to all of that I'm going to be at the Austin Film Festival in October with two entries: City of the Damned and You're the Reason.

What else makes today so great, I had my cards read. I know, some people think readings are silly, but so far everything I've been told has happened. I'm a big believer in that what you put out into the Universe comes back to you. So, when it was suggested I make a vision board and put different goals, hopes and dreams on there in the form of pictures and words, I decided to take the leap and do it. And things have just been happening at really fast rate. I was looking for a project to put the fire in my belly about self-publishing, and now I have three projects I'm working on; the second book in the *Gemini Rising* Trilogy, and a long gestating project with *When Doves Cry*, and an eight- book gladiatorial epic that follows a young girl from the age of 14 to young adulthood at 28. According to the cards (like I said may think it silly but everything that's been told to me by this reader has happened), this series will start off as a self-publishing venture and gain enough success that New York will come calling. Some examples of her words include telling me I was going to sign a three-book deal for Gemini's War, which happened. She said this blog would bring me success. I have landed two freelance writing assignments and a spot on a local radio talk show. She said it would inspire people, and indeed people have contacted me both through the comments section and off-list to tell me how much my blog meant to them even after being live for only a short time. Her name is Bertena Varney, and she's also an author with me at Hydra Publications. Not the one in New York, the one in Madison, Indiana.

Today was a really good day, as you can tell. But what I think is so sad about this was that I hardly spent any time with my family. And that when you hold up the picture am I happy when I'm with them that it's like my bipolar disorder. They run hot and cold.

I used to expect them to be there at my events cheering me on in my proudest moments. But there are so many factors. In one particular family unit there are three nephews andtwo demanding sisters, whom they cater to. I love them all, but they're just so damn hard to be around. I'm always at odds with them. And maybe if I had kids I'd understand. But I don't have kids. And I don't ask my parents to pay for my bills. I get a $754 a month disability check and 105 dollars in food stamps, and I have to make that work.

I don't have rent right now, but I did know living with them might bring a shitload of heartache down on me. And, as you can see, it does. I did so that I could attend conventions and travel for a year, in the hope of launching the next level in my career. And yesterday and today have given me fresh hope.

I know the power to achieve these things in the picture of my vision includingprofessional actors and actresses I'd like to work with, awards I want to win, the attributes I'd like my special guy to have, if he's out there, and the different levels I want to work in. I'd like to produce a play on Broadway. I'd like to win a major award for my books. I'd like to write, produce, and direct an Oscar-winning film. I'd like to be on a bestsellers list like the NYT Bestsellers list so I have picture of a top ten list.

I know I'm 37, and the clock is ticking. The odds are not ever in my favor, but if work like they are then success will come way. It's just a matter of time.

Sincerely,
Amy McCorkle

Dear Daniel,

Tonight was the pre-launch red carpet event for my Gemini Rising Trilogy. It included a Booktrailer Film Festival, prizes for the participants provided by my publisher, Blackwyrm, my writing partner on *Gunpowder and Lead,* and me. We discussed flame-throwers, rocket launchers and the vision boards we had. And Dave Mattingly, the head of Blackwyrm, interviewed me and asked me about my path to publishing.

My audience was small. But they were fans. Missy says I like them best of all my cousins because they're my fan club. And in a sense they are. They look up to me. Two out of three of them want to be novelists and one I think harbors dreams of being a songwriter and writes poetry. I really adore them. They helped me at my launch of GLADIATOR last year. Well, two of them did. One was touring Europe with the Musician Ambassadors program through the University of Louisville, and her younger sister will probably be doing the same program her senior year.

They're chomping at the bit to read my books. Many of them are on the spicier side, so they have to wait until they're eighteen. But the one I was talking about tonight was *Gemini's War,* and I pitched that as "James Bond meets the Girl With the Dragon Tattoo."It's more violent than it is steamy, so they can read it. Which is odd. I'd be much more wary of the violence than the sex.

Only two of my three cousins were there tonight. But I was touched that they came. I got lots of hugs and congratulations on the book. I'm so used to people being nonplussed in family about what I do that the attention was jarring. Rebekah was nervous and tongue-tied. I told her it was just me, Amy. But she bought my book Bounty Hunter, and I autographed it for her.

I thought of her and how she viewed me and my status, and how I view you. Not that I'm anywhere near a fraction of the smallest negative you can think of successful as you. I would be tongue-tied around you, and I'm sure you would think, "I'm just me. I'm just a guywho acts for a living. This hero worship thing is unnerving and really has nothing to do with me."

I've been in Rebekah's shoes. I've met some of my heroes. I got to meet Maurice Benard of *General Hospital*, as he's been filming *The Ghost and the Whale*. He has bipolar disorder and does a lot of awareness campaigning for people to recognize the illness in themselves. His willingness to be as open as he is, is the reason I recognized the symptoms in myself, and sought treatment before I had a psychotic break. When I told him about that, he was very sweet and very nice, and listened. Even though I could see he was kind of in an 'up' cycle. So I got anxious, my throat closed off and I couldn't even meet his gaze. And he's someone I would love to work with.

But as with you, I'm intimidated by his success as I am with yours. I dream of working on projects with lots of different people. This summer I get to hear one of my writer heroes speak. Kevin Smith. I love his movies. Not all of them, but most of them. He's a funny guy. He's down to earth and he's accessible to his fans. His speaking tours are probably my favorite though. He's raw, he's earthy, he's inspiring, and he's funny as hell. I won't get to walk up to him and meet him, which is okay. I got to meet Scott Frank once, and Jamie Foxx/Denzel Washington. I say dumb things when I'm nervous. And I wasstar struck a lot when I met him. I told him I don't care that Out of Sight only made $30million in box office; I loved it. I was 23 and I was probably manic. But when I'm nervous I cry or I say stupid shit or both.

So when Rebekah was gushing and struggling in her first pitch, I told her she would be fine. No one told me what is was to network. It was just some nebulous thing. Cool fact I got my first Guest of Honor Author gig at the Mystical Paranormal Fair in Lexington, KY June 15th and 16th this year. I've actually gotten a continuing series in Target Audience Magazine from this blog, a feature article on my newest series I'm writing, and an article for the print publication The Book Breeze, which is a gladiatorial epic that follows a girl seeking justice and vengeance from the ages of 14 until the age 28.

I owe a lot to you Daniel. Like I said at the beginning. I don't know you and you don't know me. But I know your work. And it has inspired me to dream bigger than I ever thought possible.

Sincerely,
Amy McCorkle

Dear Daniel,

My dad(John) has a rule when it comes to the journey of weight loss. "Don't make perfect the enemy of the good." It's something I'm reminded of this morning when I can't sleep and the bar on my many years old day bed is digging into my back.

Tuesday as you may or may not recall I was told I was the recipient of a semi-finalist score at the 2013 Moondance International Film Festival competition. That was exciting. But as any addictis wont to do, I wanted to celebrate with my drug of choice: food.

I started down a slippery slope. On Tuesday, I went to Olive Garden; on Wednesday, I went to El Nopal; and last night I ate two burritos from Taco Bell, and then at midnight I ate a hunk of ham, two piece of cheese, and a piece of the cookie cake I had at my red carpet event. I know it sounds like I'm nit-picking, but the control freak part of myself who is going to be all on my own this weekend is yelling at myself and a certain amount of self-recrimination and self-loathing is going on.

But I've had some real milestones this week. I was able to walk around Wal-Mart for about ten to twenty-minutes before losing my breath. Then when I went and traded in Missy's mother's jewelry for cash, I was able to stand in place for about ten to twenty minutes more. And, so far, I've actually lost one pound! At 288 pounds, down from 289 pounds in the first week!

I'm reminded as my stomach gave me problems from the last couple of days to get back on track, because I've had some really good things happen.

But I'll admit, this weekend frightens me. Whenever I'm vulnerable is when I'm likely to want to eat even more. I eat because I'm happy. I eat because I'm sad. I eat because I'm bored. I eat because I have a bad habit of popping juju fish, fruit slices, and sour slices (jellied candies) when I write.

The one thing I've found I cannot give up, even though it hurts my GERD and I should take my Prevacid for it, and I never do (I know, I'm super-religious about my bipolar treatment.Ironic,right? Or just plain stupid). What I cannot live without is coffee. Caffeinated java. Lots of creamer. Lots of sweetener. Coffee. The elixir of everything creative that I work on. That is one addiction that I'm afraid I'm just not willing to give up, in the face of every other issue I face.

The food addiction is just so powerful. I tend to have an all or nothing personality. Either I'm all in or I'm not in at all. And that's a sword that cuts both ways when trying to change your health habits. I want so much to avoid the pitfalls of obesity. Type 2 Diabetes runs in my family on my mother's side, as does COPD. Heart disease runs on my biological father's side. Those are things I don't want to ignore.

So, since weight loss and changing habits is a long-term marathon, not an overnight sprint, I try to keep what my father says in mind. "Don't let perfect be the enemy of the good." I want to be good. It's good to be a perfectionist sometimes. Like say when I'm editing a screenplay or manuscript. But on the first run through I just want to get the words out on the page. I can go back once the principal story is down and carve out a brilliant tale from there. (Though I would hardly call my work brilliant, although it is nice that I can call it award-winning).

But the point is that if I try to make my work absolutely perfect I may never send it out for consideration. That being said, I don't want to make perfect the enemy of the good work that I do. For the last two weeks I haven't been perfect, but I have been good. And I've been rewarded for it.

Stepping on the scale and seeing 288 pounds has never made me so happy. I'm down a pound. I can walk for ten to twenty minutes, I can stand in place for ten to twenty minutes, which is awesome. I'm recommitted to my plan. And maybe I'll get out for a walk at the grocery store this weekend. I know it sounds goofy, but I walk at the grocery store. The food doesn't tempt me or mock me, oddly enough. But then I'm too busy thinking as I huff and puff along, whose bright idea was this?

I wish I could walk outside this weekend, but it's supposed to rain and storm on Sunday. I haven't heard anything about severe weather, but as you will see, I'm terrified of the T word. I don't want to speak it into being. And besides, that's another post.

As it is, if you ever decide to give up something that is bad for you, my suggestion is what my dad's is to me. Take it one day at a time and don't make perfect the enemy of good.

Sincerely,
Amy McCorkle

Dear Daniel,

Wow. All I can say is wow. Yesterday I was asked to be on a panel of experts for an Author Exchange by Target Audience Magazine. I'm still in a daze over it.

First of all, that anyone would consider me an expert in any category, least of all Author Promotion, and second…honestly, I don't know if there is a second. The idea is that I would read someone's work and give them marketing ideas based on the content of their book. Pay would be secondary to giving back as a mentor, which has always been something that I wanted to do yet has always seemed so frustrating.

I was called a marketing expert, or as you like to say, I have a shtick. Let me be the first to say to I don't really have a shtick. I only know how to be myself. I have only ever known how to be myself and the only place where this has seemed to be rewarded is in the small press. And that's okay with me. Right now it feels like my career is exploding (in a good way) and that it's all that I can do to keep up.

Other authors complain about how easy I have it. The thing is I've busted my ass for every single thing that I've gotten. I mean, the career fairy didn't just come down out of the sky and just say poof you spoke it, so it is so.

Don't get me wrong, the last two and a half years have been incredible. All the contracts, the events, the print books, the magazine articles, and the reviews, both good and bad. I once got a quote from the movie GLADIATOR on my Gladiator Chronicles series, but I've also gotten the one word review 'disgusting.'

The fact there is any book to review is the miracle in and of itself, so I try not to let the reviews affect me one way or another. But I'll be honest. The validation I didn't get growing up from Jerry coupled with the attention I got only when I accomplished something makes that sort of thing a slippery slope.

I want desperately for someone to be proud of me. I know I should be enough and that the accomplishment itself should be enough. I'm not one of those people who needs someone to bow down at their feet. That sort of thing is nauseating.

But the proud thing. Yeah, that sort of thing is important to me. I don't have kids like my sisters and brother so I'm SOL. That would be *shit out of luck*.

Just so you know here's how my family tree goes, it's kind of knotty, so just hold all questions until the end because well, it's like a damn soap opera.

Kevin Hicks (older half-brother)-{Jerry McCorkle, Sherry Williams} I might as a side-note say here that Sherry was my mother's friend until…

Brandy McMillan (younger sister)-{Jerry McCorkle, Faye Keough}

Sara Keough (younger sister)-{John Keough, Faye Keough}

Sabrina McCorkle (youngest sister)-{Jerry McCorkle, Doris} Sabrina is married, but I don't know her married name.

They all have children. I'm a cat lady. Sara, as much as she frustrates me in the way she lives her life, is the one I'm closest to, and she recently helped me out with a signing. She's also a huge reader. Her son Jonathan is a sweet kid who can't wait to go to Fandom Fest in order to be my costume contest judge, and go swimming at the hotel swimming pool.

Brandy and I have a complicated relationship. Her son Isaiah is a teenager who wants nothing to do with my career. He wants to play basketball and be popular with the girls, which is normal.

Sabrina and I bond over our mutual disdain for Jerry, but she still hungers for a relationship with him. If I were honest, I guess I wish he were a normal dad too. Her daughter Alyssa was just born. To be honest that terrifies me for her.

And Lyric and Ally are artistic types like Kevin. I feel for Kevin. Jerry is such a bastard he won't even acknowledge him as his son. And he sounds just like Jerry. It's spooky.

I wish I enjoyed big gatherings because, honestly, when we get together, the siblings, we get along great. Kevin is welcome and we acknowledge him as part of the family. I wish I could get them to come to my event at Fandom Fest. Kevin is a tattoo artist in training.

It's one of those things where I have to be enough. And my accomplishments have to be enough to fulfill me. And my friends' support has to be enough. Because if I count on my family being consistent I know I'll only be disappointed.

But on a great note I'm an expert in author promotion, which is something I'm still in a slight state of shock about. Anyway, I hope your day is as great as mine.

Sincerely,
Amy McCorkle

Dear Daniel,

I have dreams. Big dreams. Some might call them grandiose. But I really believe anything is possible if you just put your mind to it.

I dream of lots of things and I think it's important to dream because, sometimes, in the darkness, dreams are the only light you've got. They're the only things that keep you hanging on when you feel like you're about to come undone.

In October of 1999, I felt like coming undone. Less and less sleep every night. The inability to sleep. Throwing things at my best friend. Cursing her. Threatening her. At one point I knew who she was, but I didn't know my own name. And worst of all, I couldn't write. And when I did write, it was shit. The only thing I had was my dreams and her friendship.

My dreams and my friend were my touchstones. I don't know why they didn't vanish. Both of them refused to give up on me. I wanted to write screenplays. I wanted to make a movie. And, when I reached out for help, I saw my efforts to hang in there rewarded.

The first film I saw after being diagnosed was The Insider. Set in Kentucky and centered on the whistle blower Jeffery Wigand, I was introduced to the actor Russell Crowe in a leading role. I had seen him before in L.A. Confidential and he was brilliant in it. But that movie really pissed me off—cold-blooded killers don't miss at point blank range. But that's a story inconsistency and Russell and everyone else in that movie were superb in their performances.

The cool blue filters used on Insider were soothing to my jangled, recovering nerves after an emotional breakdown. As a result, I love that movie. And for all the talk of Kevin Spacey and Denzel Washington (they too were superb in American Beauty and the Hurricane), I thought Russell's breakthrough performance as an alcoholic, and a tightly-wound tobacco scientist was incredible. And, of course, it was set in the city I was born and raised in. They had been looking for production assistants on that film. Believe me, I was kicking myself when I realized what kind of opportunity I had passed up.

The thing is that it made me realize I could still enjoy a movie. It had been a good year since I realized just how much I couldn't sit and relax because of the bipolar disorder. But being on the meds was like night and day. However, the worst possible thing happened: creatively I went dry and for eight months, and I wrote nothing. Nada, zilch. Then, in May, the floodgates opened.

What happened? I saw a preview for GLADIATOR. Before I ever went to the theater, I had written a novella. It sucked. It was bad. It was an historical.

Now, I have no business writing historical. But it was a gift from the writing gods. I could still write stories. I was still passionate about writing stories. It was such a relief to know I wasn't dead in that area as I had ALWAYS been passionate about storytelling.

Missy says I've always got my head in the clouds and she's got me by the ankles grounding me so that I don't float off into the ethers. Which is sooo very true.

I often have a big vision and I can get things moving, like I did with the Red Carpet Launch for example. I made the plans for food, my publisher, the Booktrailer Film Festival, the promotion, the venue. When we got to the location, Missy set up everything including the books, the swag display, the food, and the ice. She's really great. Everyone needs to be so lucky as to have at least one friend like Missy.

I mean, it's not like I'm chopped liver. We've truly walked through the fire together. She's seen me at my worst and not walked away, and vice-versa. You don't find friends like that everyday. Hell, you don't find family like that everyday.

When you've eaten spaghetti five nights a week and hot dogs for variety the other two nights and meet with someone who understands what it's like to go to bed hungry and wake up hungry, then you know they're a friend.

I know it's crazy but the litmus test for the guy in my life won't be my mom and dad, it will be Missy. Mom and Dad will just want someone who will take me off their hands. I know I'm thirty-seven, but I believe it's never too late to find love.

Given my life often it is hope that keeps me going. Dreams that fuel my ambition. And I look for that hope and those dreams in my field of passion: the creative arts. But I know a lot of elbow grease goes into that ambition. That nose-to-the-grindstone approach is the only thing that works. And that success is in the eye of the beholder.

I have had success. And yet I dream of different things. I'm excited about THE LAST WARRIOR series I'm working on. Maybe I'll share more about it next time. As it is this letter is long, and I'm sure you and whoever is reading this understands dreams that don't just happen. Hard work is the only thing that leads to it, and even then it's not a guarantee. You have to be prepared when the opportunity arises and have a dash of luck for good measure. These last two and a half years I've been ready. I've been fortunate. And I've capitalized on opportunities that have presented themselves. I don't apologize for that. I've spent my whole life apologizing for the person I was. I'm sick of that shit. I have people in my circle who have a problem with that, and it seems, unfortunately I'm going to have to deal with them sooner rather than later. And it makes it especially hard when you're depending on them so much.

Sincerely,
Amy McCorkle

Dear Daniel,

The journey of a million miles, right? You were quoted once on how you handle your career and I thought it was brilliant. Not because of some abject hero worship thing, but because it was fucking true. When asked about your agent's other clients you said something to the effect that you didn't concern yourself with that shit. And to be honest, I laughed because you can't concern yourself with keeping up with those around you. If you do, you'll never be satisfied and you might run the risk of bitterness and some serious sour grapes.

That doesn't mean I don't reach with one hand to pull a friend up in their career while I'm reaching up to advance mine. It just means the only competition I'm really having is with myself. Unless, of course, you're talking about film festivals. Then I'm just happy to land on the board. But I won't lie. I love to win.

I've always loved to win. But this hasn't really had anything to do with the people around me. It hasn't been the *I must beat you personally* kind of thing. It was always more of the *I need that trophy/certificate/medal/plaque/medal* kind of thing because I'm so damn competitive. The only thing where I was more competitive about the work and not purely about winning was in Young Authors.

When I was thirteen, in 1989, (yes, I'm carbon dating myself to some degree here) I wrote a story called *A Candle In the Dark*. I had no idea who the Bielski Brothers were, and my story was set in France. But it told the tale of a young woman leading people through the woods and the French Underground to safety. There was a love story involving a strong, tough, and lonely girl and an understanding guy in a high-stakes drama unfolding around them. Sound familiar? I won Young Authors that year. I was extremely proud of the win.

My current projects unfold around a similar theme. Gemini's Legacy is book 2 in the Gemini Rising Trilogy. It centers on themes of family Mother/Daughter, Father/Daughter. But then all of my work seems to.

But THE LAST WARRIOR: SWEET SACRIFICE is about a young woman (a 14-year-old girl) who escapes a post-apocalyptic enslavement in order to exact a blood-soaked vendetta only to discover everything she has ever known is a lie. There are paranormal elements, and the theme of family runs strong throughout.

It's an 8-book epic that follows her as she grows from a teenage girl into womanhood. It's a violent tale and, in some ways, is very adult. But the sex and romance doesn't even surface until around book 3 or 4, though there are romantic notions. Dying for what you believe in and Kamikaze moments, I suppose, show the sense that the whole series is romantic. I'm a pantster as opposed to a plotter so I'm not even sure my heroine makes it out alive. But I'm not afraid to kill characters off if it serves the story to do so.

Those two stories are the ones I'm most passionate about, and there is a third book I wish to finish. When Doves Cry is a mob epic about two sisters who are the only survivors of a mob hit on their family. What makes this story important to me is that Missy and I have been working on it for

I love the fact I'm busier than I've ever been. I love the fact I can say I'm an award-winning author. I love the fact I can say I'm multi-published. But I feel like it's the height of arrogance to say it too long and too loud. I'm blessed to be doing this at all, let alone be successful at it.

I worry that those around me who will doubt themselves in the face of what I'm doing as opposed to being inspired by it. As opposed to me, I'm inspired by others' success. It makes me feel like I can do it to. They've traveled the road, then why can't I?

I have terrific team supporting me. My cover artist, Delilah K. Stephans, my content editor, Tanja Cilia, my line editor, Greta Gunselman, and formatters whom I will say nothing about because I'm not sure they want to be mentioned. My cheerleaders, Missy Goodman and several other friends, who know who they are and who are there for me in times of need.

Perhaps I don't thank these people enough, but I hope they know that I love them dearly as family and friends. They have done wonderful things for me to. Mom, Dad (John), are you listening? I know there's the chance they might read this blog and take away from it that I'm a whiny brat who doesn't appreciate the good that they do. Nothing could be further from the truth. I just wish I could protect myself a little better when they run cold and hurt me.

Sincerely,
Amy McCorkle

Dear Daniel,

I know coming to you twice today. But I'm hurting and I feel like no one within my vicinity can hear me or help me. I have good friends. Check that I have great friends. And my family often hates it when I put them in front of what they want me to do.

But you have to know, I was happy, for a little while to have them home from their vacation at the lake. Being alone for so long had gotten to me a little bit last night and it kind of fucked with me. I blubbered to my best friend Missy and she said,"You need to tell your mother they can't just leave you stranded like that all weekend. Either they need to leave you a car or you need to go with them to the lake."

You would have thought I'd unleashed the apocalypse, or perhaps opened the gates of Hell because I'm pretty sure my mother's head spun like a top and pea soup shot out of her mouth. As it was, her eyes bugged and she started yelling. Dad said,"You have your sisters." And the one I have the most complicated relationship with said, "Sara lives just up the street."That's not fair. What do you say to that?

I'm on disability. I love to write. And even that sometimes is affected by my bipolar disorder. But I'm prolific and I write very fast. I'm always promoting and I try very hard to give praise to those who deserve it who've helped me. So my income is $754 a month. Everything has to be paid with that. Mom isn't charging me rent in cash, but she sure is exacting her pound of flesh.

After Brandy and Isaiah left the argument continued. She slammed things while she was cleaning, and said I wasn't Missy's daughter. I said no, she's my best friend. And a lot of stuff, before it could get any worse I retreated to my bedroom where I could talk in peace to Missy. I chose to text her and talk on FB. I didn't want to escalate the fight to something more disastrous than it already was.

She talked to Sara, she got over whatever was making her angry to the point of rage and I told her Missy heard me crying about being lonely and cooped up for three days without a way of leaving at midnight and there wasn't much she could do and it made her feel bad for me.

I want to take a moment here and say I'm not asking you to feel sorry for me. I understand I made a deal with the devil moving in here last August. I knew what kind of people they were. And I knew it would come to her being mad at someone and her taking it out on me. Dad(John) being sick and taking it out on me.

Per the car situation, I don't have the money to support my fledgling writing career and save for a vehicle and pay for bills. I can do two of three. Barely. And I have to depend on kindness from others and it makes me feel like a mooch and a leech, and like I'm not paying my own way through life. These are my crosses to bear, and no one else's.

But it's lonely sometimes, and when people who are supposed to love and support you kick you while you're down, well, that makes it kind of hard. But when the successes do come they are admittedly so much sweeter.

Award-winning British novelist Victoria Lamb loves this blog and says she's jealous and thought it was a brilliant concept. Bold and the Beautiful and former General Hospital Michele Val Jean scribe agrees with her. When people like that notice your work, it makes the struggle feel worth it. It's like, hey, someone notices me. Someone likes my writing and I'm not doing this in a vacuum. A fan friended me on Facebook and is going to make it a point to see me at a signing that I'm doing next month. So, as bad as my mom and dad and everyone was making my life, these people spread a little sunshine my way. And I love them for it.

Sincerely,
Amy McCorkle

Dear Daniel,

I'm hoping I've recovered somewhat from yesterday. Confrontations like that take it out of me and my long form writing suffers because of it. I got maybe two pages done on WARRIOR done because of it.

I wish I could say my emotions don't inhibit my work. But when I'm that angry or hurt, emotions block me.When I'm ready to write again, I'm usually drained by the fight. Oh, they let me use the car last night to go to the bookstore. I spent the whole time talking to a friend on Facebook and just unloading a lot of stuff.

I don't mean to come off so negative sometimes. My family is just so screwed up. Don't get me wrong, I love them and all, but when the chips are down I should know better than to approach them with anything beyond the simple light lifting they desire.

I think they have a fundamental misunderstanding of who I am and a lack of ability to understand the adult I've become is a result of a lot of choices I was forced to make as a child and ones I chose to make as an adult.

One of those things I've always said is that I don't want kids. Even as a kid. But as a kid I was raising and protecting to some degree my two younger siblings. Ever since I can remember Brandy was in need of some kind of shield and at the time I was willing to take it up for her. In all honesty I think it was probably that sort of thinking that helped me survive the abuse at Jerry's on the weekends when he, his brother, or one of his guests would prey on me.

But I'm tired of protecting others to my own detriment. Is that wrong? I mean I'm extremely loyal to my friends. Pam, Missy, Elise, Carla. I'm making new friends and professional contacts, who treat me better than my own family does. The small press has kind of embraced me and I like it. It makes feel like I'm loved and appreciated. I wonder, am I so broken that professional friendships have to take the place of the blood bonds and those who say they love me more than anyone simply because of that fact?

How broken am I that I still want validation from my biological father who doesn't know me, abused me, and will never quite know how much he's damaged me? I wrote him a letter once telling him I hated things that he did to me and didn't do for me. As a practicing alcoholic who smokes, Jerry is also a Vietnam Vet. His mother was a cold woman. She once wrote my name on the picture of the fattest woman in a photograph and left it for me to find. His dad was married 17 times—that he can remember. He also thought it was okay to strike a woman down. The only thing I remember about him is that he was a drinker too and that he was sick most of the time I knew him with Cancer. And he had dog that bit. His teeth went through and through. Of course, in the dog's defense he was chained to the trailer.

That's Jerry's side of the family. He also had two brothers, one who abused me, and a sister whom we often went camping with. I think Jerry is the black sheep. But it's not like all of the McCorkles are worthless. He had an uncle named Houston and he had two sons, Doug and Leemont, who now goes by Lee.

The only reason I know about Lee is because last year at my launch for *The Gladiator Chronicles* Lee sought me out. He had his son Miller with him. We talked about *Star Trek* and how he and his brother used to travel the sci-fi con circuit together. I had a giveaway tote full of books from MuseItUp authors and Miller won the giveaway. And Lee bought my book.

Today has been a nice day, but again my parents haven't been here. I worry that one day even though I love them and they love me I will have to cut ties with them when they do stupid shit like they did yesterday. I certainly hope not. I love them very much. And want desperately to do right by them. They just make is so damn hard sometimes.

Sincerely,

Amy McCorkle

Dear Daniel,

So I had a slip last night. You know, like an alcoholic, only with food. I wish I could say I was an angel in this department. But I ate horribly from Saturday to yesterday. Being alone isn't my strong suit. As I've demonstrated.

Being isolated and alone and cooped up in a house for three days with nothing to do is hard to deal with for anyone, but for someone like me it hits all of my food triggers. Boredom and loneliness are really big triggers and Saturday I was alone a lot. I didn't eat my main meal in the middle of the day, and I ate a full order of Crab Rangoon, fried dumplings, and a large order of Happy Family from the nearest Chinese Food restaurant. On Sunday I ate an entire Digorno pizza. Monday, I gorged on Little Cesar pizza, had a venti iced café mocha and a blondie brownie blast. Yesterday, I ate an entire chicken parmesan meal from Encore with no sides, then had a grande iced café mocha. Then, when I couldn't sleep, I ate two tubs of Greek yogurt, four slices of processed Swiss cheese, two wedges of Laughing Cow cheese spread, half a can of Cheese Pringles, and the rest of a Cheetos snack mix.

A lot of food, I know. Ultimately I'm responsible for that mess. No one stuck a gun to my head and made me eat it. But being alone with forty dollars is risky behavior, and a slippery slope. But I'm determined to make it one day at a time. So it seems I need to recommit myself on a daily basis.

I understand that there's a huge difference between being alone and being lonely, and this past weekend I found myself at the crossroads where these two happened to meet. Up until about midnight I was okay. I found refuge in my work, but it obviously wasn't enough. I needed live human contact and my main source of support was either out of town or being pulled in different directions.

I depend on Missy a great deal by choice because we have truly walked through the fire together. Me with her issues, which I won't go into here, and her through mine.

My biggest issue in the past is my bipolar diagnosis, which, I think as an emotional eater, complicates my food addiction recovery. In October of 1999 we moved from Kentucky to San Antonio, Texas. We would have preferred Austin. We attended the Austin Film Festival for the first time. (This fall will be our second time there.)

To say we were fish out of water would be an understatement. To say the least, we wouldn't have said shit if we had a mouth full of it. We were commuting from San Antonio to Austin daily. We had producer badges but wasted them. Didn't know what the fuck networking was all about and were totally green on how to work a festival. I was 23. No one was there to show us the ropes. Everything Missy and I learned was through trial and error. The biggest examples of the disconnect between us and the main group was this, people were eating in the restaurants we were eating bologna sandwiches and pretzels we had brought from home while drinking two and half dollar soft drinks. Also one day we left the headlights on. When we came out at the end of the day the car was dead. When we asked for help, people said, "Oh I jetted in." And I thought do they know how they sound? They sound like the most disconnected assholes ever. When we asked to use the desk phone, they pointed us to a pay phone. We don't even have pay phones now.

That being said, we met a screenwriter by the name of Jim Vaughn. He was older gentleman, who was drinking gin and smoking cigarettes in the bar. (Things I'm sure that you can only do one of now) and he was the most genuine, real, kind and patient person there. He was 69 years old and I would love to run into him again. And if Missy and I were to win at Austin this year he would surely be included in our speech. There are just some people you learn from and use their knowledge to benefit your own career and trade on your own name and not on theirs. Of course, I think that's something you should do with everyone, and if your connection bears fruit then all the better.

My food addiction is such that I worry about Austin and I worry about getting around without gasping for air. So, I recommit myself to my efforts and I try to forgive myself of my eating transgressions as I look forward to perhaps victories in my professional life. So, I look forward to the next event where I am the guest of honor one day at a time. The Mystical Paranormal Fair in Lexington, Kentucky, and one of several Hydra Publication guests at Joseph Beth Booksellers on June 15th!

Sincerely,

Amy McCorkle

Dear Daniel,

Good day writing wise. Was almost done on WARRIOR when faced with an unpleasant truth. When you have success, there will be all kinds of people around you.

There will be those who are proud of your accomplishments, but not really see how hard you work to make it happen. Those people are my parents. I expect that from them. I'm in the small press. They have jobs with salaries, benefits, and a secure income. I'm lucky if I see $30 every three months in royalties. That's with me promoting my tail off. Using what I can afford via Facebook, Twitter, Blogs, websites, LinkedIn, and StumbleUpon. Then there's the out-of-the-box ideas like a prelaunch event showcasing other people's work, while promoting mine.

I know as a small press author my reach is to some degree limited to what I can afford to do to promote. When my efforts are stymied by an outside force, it can be very frustrating. It leaves me thinking, what am I supposed to do? Clearly I'm not an A-lister, a brand author. I mean, that's eventually the big-picture goal. But I don't even make the alphabet.

Other people are genuinely happy for me and just want to be successful for themselves. And, as my best friend Missy would say, 'me too, me too.' Others struggle with feelings of envy and jealousy, and are honest about it. Still, othersare just snarky and out for themselves. Tell me, how do you deal with this?

I don't particularly care what people think about me. In a lot ways, I don't concern myself with other people's actions. I figure what they do reflects on them, not on me.

I had a publisher tell me once publishing was a business, and writing is personal—until you hand it over to the publisher. It's still art, but it becomes a product at the same time. All I know is that writing is a personal act for me. Editing is not. I have to divorce myself from my work. If I don't, it's hard to look at it objectively.

Thus with the promotional efforts stymied, I find myself at a big crossroads. What to do to promote? I feel as if my hand has slapped hard and I'm being punished for being aggressive in getting my name out there when I see other authors doing the exactly the same thing in exactly the same place. Like there's some kind of secret code that gets them in but leaves me out.

I have never been one to let anything keep me down for too long. If I can't promote there I can't promote there and that's the end of it. All the wishing, and hand wringing, and tantrum throwing won't change that fact.

I mean, when I measure everything this one bump in the road isn't going to kill me or my career. I was just told "No," which is fine. I certainly didn't mean to offend anyone with my posts. And it isn't like it's the last time I'm going to be told no.

People have told me no in some fashion or another as I've grown into an adult. First they said, "You're book isn't good enough." So I wrote and submitted until I couldn't be denied access anymore. I found a publisher who would nurture me and my voice until it was strong enough to be heard above the din of all the other writers struggling to be heard. I have a piece of the pie. An admittedly small piece of the pie at the moment, but I know hard work and strong story win out over those who would sit on the sidelines and do nothing.

MuseItUp Publishing is a wonderful place, as are my other publishers. But Muse took me from a struggling writer and honed me into one who now has the courage to put her out of the box marketing ideas to work.

I have a voice. I won't be 'shut up' by those around me, whether well-intentioned or not. It's not my way. I've worked too hard. I feel like the girl in my *Last Warrior* series, Bella Morte. She is destined to become a trained assassin. She's only fourteen and the life she has led is a precarious one. She has survived against the odds. I have 8 books to figure out her journey. Maybe when it debuts in September I can send you a signed copy to show you what you inspire me to do when others hold me back. (Today wasn't nearly as bad as it felt. International Bestselling Author Alicia Bessette liked the blog, so I must be doing something right!)

Sincerely,
Amy McCorkle

Dear Daniel,

Never, never, never quit.—Winston Churchill

If you are living on the downside of advantage, and are relying purely on courage, it can be done.—Russell Crowe, Oscar Speech for GLADIATOR

Haters are motivators.—Kyle Busch

Today I graduate. In October of 1999, I suffered my first emotional breakdown, which led to my diagnosis of bipolar disorder. In October of 2000, as the doctors sought to stabilize me with a drug cocktail, the process, coupled with being fired from Children's World because I suspected a young girl was being abused, threw me into a manic episode, which led to a second breakdown.

Now, almost fifteen years later, stable and in recovery, I am proud to say I am simply under medical monitoring. I will continue seeing Dr. Rebek for check-ups and evaluations, but my team of brilliant physicians and therapists say I am ready to leave the nest and, should a crisis arise, I am more than welcome to return to the therapy fold.

Honestly, with the bullshit I live through every day, I wonder if leaving the protective fold of therapy is such a good idea. But it's been fifteen years. I still have nightmares to some degree, but they are no longer as intense or as many as they have been in the past.

Oh, don't get me wrong. I still dream in Technicolor and there are still nights when I'm watching Cowboys and Aliens, and wishing there was a hero out there for me. But if therapy and treatment has taught me anything it's that recovery and balance are possible.

Recovering from an emotional breakdown is truly the hardest work I've ever put into anything (except maybe that marathon I ran in January of 1999). Putting myself back together has been no easy feat and there are those around me who deserve a great deal of credit.

Let me start with the person at the top of the list: Missy Goodman. What started out as a writing partnership has turned into probably the best friendship I've ever had. When I fell apart, she was the kind of friend most people only dream about. If I could choose family, it would be her at the front of the line.

We've withstood a lot from each other and those around us. Now, whenever I need someone to have my back, I know I can depend on her more so than anyone else. The phrase "walking through the fire" applies directly to her, as friendship with me hasn't always been a cakewalk. In all honesty, I'm still not, but friends like Missy let me know that when I come through something, I won't have to survive my surroundings, but that I can get down to the business of living.

Then there's the group itself, which has been a great source of support as well. Often I am, believe it or not, cheerful, bubbly, and positive. It's just there are those around me who drain on that. These people, like Missy, have seen me at my best and at my worst. I leave nothing but best wishes and knowing that should a need arise, the group is there for me to return to.

Given the dramatics of the last few days, I am happy for a day of celebration like today. And here's what I like about the quotes.

As an endurance runner in the past, I knew if I just kept putting one foot in front of the other I would make it to the finish line. I never quit and that I had the courage at all to start was huge. Finishing was just the cherry on top of a really cool sundae. So I never quit.

I cried the first time I heard Russell's speech. And again every time I see it on YouTube. Because you see sometimes I feel like courage is the only thing I have.

As for the haters being motivators? All successful people have people I suppose who don't like them and resent them for having a taste of success. I can't worry about those people. They're too busy wallowing in their own resentment and unhappiness for me to worry about. I wish they saw life the way I did, with infinite possibilities. But some are trapped in a very dark way of thinking. So when people hate me, or complain about me I tell myself—work a little bit harder. Reach a little bit higher. Because in the grand scheme of things haters only hurt themselves and have nothing to do with me. Those that resent me and the way I do things? That's them. Not on me.

Sincerely,
Amy McCorkle

Dear Daniel,

I'm scared of storms. I mean terrified. Petrified. Mortified. Stupefied.Scared. Living in Kentucky, and having been raised in a trailer (a contraption that they say you're better off going and lying in a ditch outside in the storm rather than staying inside if there's a tornado) left me with a phobia of storms.

Today the system that has been ravaging the west is moving through where I live. How afraid am I? My parents have a house. My Aunt Debbie and Uncle Frank have a home with a basement. If there is severe weather, they'll let me stay with them. Aunt Jan is there too.

I've been trying to conquer my fear of storms. But it's just so damn hard. When I was twelve, my family and I were down at Nolin Lake and I got caught out in a severe thunderstorm. We don't have beautiful seaside or oceans here, so it's lakes and rivers. You know, I've been to Florida but I've never seen the ocean in person.

My cousin Corey and I had gone fishing. To get where we were going, Corey and I walked down an incredibly steep hill. Honestly, it looked more like a drop off. I was wearing flip-flop sandals and carrying a fishing pole. There were rumblings of thunder but, as any kid is wont to do, I charged ahead wanting to fish. But as we stood on the embankment the clouds rolled in, the wind kicked up and the thunder came more frequently. I was DONE at that point. Corey wouldn't leave, so I left without him. As I walked up the embankment the hook caught in my shorts (*great*) and I was forced to break the fishing line with my bare hands, which if you know anything about fishing line it's that no 12-year-old girl should be able to break it without something sharp. I was lucky that the hook didn't open up into my leg, and that all I got from it was a scratch.

As I walked down the road that was nothing more than rocks and dirt the rain started to come down in buckets. I looked to the sky and black raced over the white ones. My stomach was in knots and my shoes were getting slippery and hard to keep on so I took them off and started to scream for help. Keeping calm really wasn't my strong suit at the time. Eventually I stopped yelling and looked for a landmark. What I remembered was a large vehicle with a busted out window. When I saw it I still wasn't sure I was in the right place, but I was determined to at least get up the steep drop off and get around civilization. So up I went.

Fishing pole and sandals in hand I grabbed onto tree trunks and slowly pulled my way to the top. I stepped on thorn bushes, twigs, and God only knows what else. I was incredibly fortunate that nothing poisonous bit me and that I avoided poison ivy altogether.

When I finally got to the top I was flushed, hot, red-faced, and out of breath. And like a gift I was right behind the trailer we were staying in on the property.

Ever since then I've been terrified of storms. I have a shitload of storm stories. One from when I was five years old and a babysitter was watching me and my sister Brandy and me. We had a basement back then. One where I was at a pizza joint with a friend and we heard a funnel cloud go over ahead. And another still where there were some dumb-asses standing outside, while I heard a hitch wailing moan. Truly, the only thing scarier than hearing tornado siren, to me, is hearing the tornado itself.

Missy often says it's not the tornado that's going to kill you, but the heart attack you'll have when you see it that will. I'm pretty sure she's right. I wish I had a house with a basement. That's a dream you know. Nothing fancy, just a place that will withstand an F5 tornado. I'm not asking for too much, am I?

Anyway, I feel better now that the storm has passed and that I wrote this. I know you're not really there, but thank you for listening anyway. ;)

Sincerely,
Amy McCorkle

Dear Daniel,

I have a confession to make. Last fall while writing Gemini's War I bought the song *Skyfall* by Adele on Amazon. And over a four-to-six-week time period I listened to it on a loop (fantastic song) while I wrote *Gemini's War*. With ninety pages to go I saw *Skyfall*. Within a week the book was finished.

I adore that book. I adore the song. I adore the movie. For the second book in the series I've been listening to the Skyfall score. That is fabulous as well. *Gemini's Legacy* is so close to being done. Seventy-seven pages to be exact. I'm going to work on it first today. I've been kind of scattered as of late.

I meditated last night and this morning. I take issue with the words God and people shoving their religion on me, no matter how well intentioned they are.

My dad(John) once called me his little iconoclast. Here's what I do believe: the Universe is a large place and everyone has their place in it. I don't believe things happen for a reason or that God wills for people to be traumatized. I think that particular notion is bullshit. If you believe it, that's fine, there are a great many people who subscribe to it.

I do believe man has free will and such when a man, or a woman chooses to break the law they should answer for their crimes. Do I believe that people with mental illness deserve a free pass because sometimes they break from reality? No. But let me tell you why.

I have a mental illness and, ultimately, I believe you're responsible for your own actions. Because when I see these mass killers (the movie theater shootings) and Newtown do what they do, I have to look at the people around them.

Surely, they must've seen the warning signs. Those with serious mental health issues always have warning signs. Just because one thinks you should just suck it up and be a man or woman and 'deal' with it doesn't mean the Universe is letting you off the hook. The Newtown shooter's mother *took him to the shooting range and talked about the end of days.* I have an outlet for my emotions. My writing. The movies were my refuge. I watched television. Now it seems sometimes when these things happen the news starts bandying the words"mental illness" around, and painting everyone with the same stigmatizing brush.

They use pop psychology terminology, and get so-called experts who target one thing or another. First it's movies. Then it's television. Now it's video games. Here's the thing: back in the day it was Tipper Gore's insane crusade against rock music. Teenagers find outlets. These things aren't the problem. They are not the reason why people kill. These people are sick.

They need medication and therapy. But even then the way people are treated, and the way treatment is viewed, people often think they're trash, that they're disposable. And yes, often people break away from reality, and these tragedies occur.

But the legal definition of insanity is such, to know the difference between right and wrong.

I knew the difference between right and wrong.

I sometimes didn't know if I would live or die.

I read controversial books.

I questioned authority.

I wrote dark stories. I still do.

And I live with a bipolar disorder diagnosis in a hostile environment. But that doesn't give me the right to go and inflict my state of misery on someone else. It doesn't give me a pass to destroy someone else's life.

However, there are very real situations where self-defense pushes you to do the impossible, the unthinkable. Domestic violence is often the end result of broken people perpetuating a cycle of brokenness upon themselves. It doesn't give the abuser a free pass.

When my mom and stepdad tell me I didn't have it hard, or that my biological father had a bad childhood, only half that sentiment is true. Jerry had it very rough growing up. There was no warmth in his life. As a result he is filled with anguish and pain, and is dying a lonely old man filled with bitterness. But that doesn't give him a pass for what he did to me.

In my parents' defense, they don't know what Jerry did to me. But then, they're broken too. The ones who weren't broken were cold. There was love in their home, and, to some degree, I'm sure I clung to that.

I'm not perfect. Not by a mile. But I take responsibility for the adult I've become. I am not failure. In fact I consider myself a success, with both professional friends and close friends whom I hold very close to my heart.

When handling myself in my career I try to follow my heroes' examples. Like George Clooney, there are 'girls' as opposed to the boys. In that circle is my best friendMissy Goodman and my friend Pamela Turner. Each award-winning screenwriters and authors in their own right. They have been there from the beginning, and as far as celebrating it is they I want to always tell first when something good happens. I know they are genuine, good people who have my back.

The next level includes professional friends: Bertena Varney and Elise VanCise (she and I bonded over our mutual love for the Highlander television series and Russell Crowe movies).

Then, there are those who have helped mentor me: Lea Schizas, Ellen Eldridge, and Delilah Stephans. And there are many others I am failing to mention, but they should know the good turns they have done me have not been forgotten.

Like you, I choose to concern myself with my own career and not worry about who's doing better or who's doing worse. Because there is always that dynamic. My career is successful because I've worked hard and I've capitalized on certain opportunities.

I am a survivor of childhood sex abuse. I live with a mental illness. I chose right over might. I read banned books. I see violent movies. And I know there is a stigma talking about all of this. But I'm sick and tired of people blaming outside elements on what is essentially lack of treatment for a serious illness.

Sincerely,
Amy McCorkle

Dear Daniel,

I played alto saxophone for seven years. Sat first chair for six of them. And had I wanted to I could've gone to a Performing Arts School. But as good as I was, and as much as I loved playing music, I found it wasn't my passion. So when it came time to choose which school to go to, I was accepted into all of the schools I applied to, I chose a legal magnet high school. My mother's exact words were, "go ahead, break my heart".

I never became the professional musician she wanted me to become. But to this day I love music. All kinds. Classical to rap to punk to country to rock.

Music I've found speaks directly to the heart. It's pure emotion, and at its best it is both personal and universal. The best art always is.

That's why for me SKYFALL became like this beacon that kept me from going off the rails while making my way through Gemini's War. The tragedy and pain laced throughout that song is at once powerful and breathtaking. And the rebirth and strength and defiance to be bent down for too long. The song is tragedy and triumph and Adele, well, Adele was Adele. She's fucking brilliant every time out and if anything all the song did was cement her iconic status.

The idea of a flawed yet heroic heroine and hero could face the worst and still come out on top was born out of that. The assassin and the reluctant assassin finding their way to one another to find their happily ever after. (Gemini's War) Someone always dies in the Bond films. And to be honest, I like it that way. It gives Bond a tragic quality that I think serves the story well.

Whenever I was anxious or doubted I could finish the story I listened to it and I found my footing, I found my way into the novel. And wrote to be honest, the best book I've written to date.

Of course, I learned lessons on that book. And I write now hoping I'm writing better on those projects. At the moment I'm struggling through Gemini's Legacy, the end of the book is always harder than the beginning of it.

But the song was the birthplace of it all. The visuals it conjured swept me up in fast frenzy of 10 pages. I hope to have an autographed copy to send you in July.

What I find so powerful about the song is that it makes me feel not so alone. It gives me a voice where so often I feel voiceless. I think the best music always makes you feel that way. As a writer it inspires me to do my best work. When people read my stuff I want them to feel like they have a voice. That they're not alone. That they too, if they wanted to, could write an original story.

I know there's a whole world of fan fiction out there. And I'm aware of the fact people write it. I've tried my hand at it and I simply can't bring myself to write in someone else's territory. Not very well anyway. I like writing my own stuff. And making money doing it. I suppose I'm just selfish that way.

I've got seventy-two pages left to write on the second book in the GEMINI RISING trilogy. And I find myself listening to SKYFALL to write the final push to. And admittedly my hero, Aidan Wells, bears a striking physical resemblance to you. But the truth is it's my imagination at working on the character itself.

But the trilogy is told from Gemini's POV. Her life is a study in tragedy. But she refuses to give up and the end of this book I know what I have to do but I don't really want to do it. But then it serves the story best.

I write short, 50K-60K, sometimes even shorter. I have about 15K to go in Gemini's Legacy and I really need to start. So I've listened to SKYFALL many times, so it's time to go write the end of my story.

Sincerely,
Amy McCorkle

Dear Daniel,

I suppose I should say I'm on the wagon again as far as my lifestyle change goes. I seem to fall off the eating wagon more often than I'm staying on it. So today I am back on. In an unsteady world and a volatile household it seems it's harder than ever to stay on that wagon. Ultimately I'm responsible for my own actions, but like a junkie needing her fix when things get emotional around here I reach for food. The junkie, the carbier, the better. Really the worse but let's be honest here, with mostly healthy food in the house it's not like I can't find something to binge on there either.

I only say this because getting off of any hard drug is just plain crazy. And often in the beginning it's like a roller coaster threatening to go off its tracks at any moment. So today on this morning, because e shit insurance I'm on won't allow for my meds to be refilled until well this morning. I'm hopeful she was able over ride it as without my bipolar meds things are even harder to cope with. I depend on them to keep me stability but because this shit insurance I'm on, the company won't allow for my meds to be refilled until well this morning. I'm hopeful she was able over ride it as without my bipolar meds things are even harder to cope with. It's not like pain medication where I use it to get high or they wear their usefulness out. It's about stability and normality and functioning in the world around me properly.

When my meds are off I find it difficult to sleep, difficult to write, and I'm easily agitated and I'm more likely to pick a fight or am easily ensnared into one. I find my judgment is skewed and that mountains are easily made out of molehills and that even though I may be right I find it impossible to walk away and accept the fact the people I am arguing with will never see it my way. I'm likely to escalate a fight. I'm likely to scream, yell, and cry and nothing and no one can console me.

It's been awhile since my insurance company has pulled this stunt and when they do it I feel so voiceless and powerless I wonder if the new legislation will help me or hinder me. I believe in healthcare reform. And when I get to a point where I'm able to I will more likely than not be generous to NAMI and other various mental health organizations who work with the indigent and the poor. Because considering that I am one of them now, I am hopeful in the future that I won't be.

Don't get me wrong, most people without disability who are suffering from what I live with envy what I have, access to medical care. I wouldn't call it great. 23 visits for mental health is better than 3 but I've been in therapy for bipolar disorder since 1999. 23 visits doesn't cut it. So I have glitch. I need my meds. And chances are they're waiting for me at Seven Counties. The young woman who works at QOL is a real sweetie and she is always doing her best to accommodate the many clients there.

The old saying, don't shoot the messenger? It definitely applies to her. This world would be a much more harmonious place if it would just embrace preventative medicine as opposed to waiting until the shit has it the proverbial fan.

My meds have been off since Friday. I had to parcel them out in order to have medicine all three days this weekend. And when I pick them up this afternoon and take the prescribed dose I will more than likely crash and sleep the sleep of the dead.

That being said, I am of reasonably sound mind and body. And I will be able to get up on that wagon in both cases and when I take my bipolar meds I will be back on track. And maybe it will just be a kiddie roller coaster instead of those insane ones that honestly I'm too fat to be on right now but that I will never get on again.

Sincerely,
Amy McCorkle

Dear Daniel,

Growing up I never had an affinity for narcotic or alcohol usage. In fact part of me was terrified of taking that first hit/snort/or drink for fear that I would start down that road of addiction and lose all semblance of control of my life. But as early as five I remember waking up on Saturday mornings after my parents had friends over, and where they'd had White Castle or Taco Bell I would rummage through the empty bags laying all over the living room looking for leftovers. Now if that isn't the sign of an addict I don't know what is.

Honestly it seems like the food demon has me these days. I'm back on the wagon today, having my breakfast shake. But I wonder if it's only a matter of time during the passing minutes and seconds of the day before I mosey into the kitchen and find the leftovers of my binge last night.

I feel so weak in the face of food and my emotions. Like, if I'm happy and want to celebrate, I want to eat. If I'm sad and depressed, I don't want to feel this, so let's eat to that too.

I know I'm not alone in this. And that there are those who starve themselves in an attempt to control the food and what it does to them. It's the same thing that controls me and drives me to eat compulsively then feel the self-loathing that I do now.

Not that I wish it on anyone. Pain and self-hatred don't really serve any real purpose. Okay well maybe they do. Perhaps they drive you to be better, to treat yourself better than you have in the past. At least I can see that in an idealist's kind of way.

As it is I have several friends who cut, or have cut in the past. Some I went to high school with, some who are married now. Most no longer do it. But it wasn't as if I didn't understand the psychology of it. It made them feel better. They used the physical pain to control the emotional pain. Was it self-destructive behavior? Yes. But they didn't need my judgment. They needed my friendship. And most of the time an adult's reaction was just to scream and yell and compound their pain.

I never cut, but I sure could put away some food. And given the right circumstances I still can. For whatever reasons I want so badly just to give up on this front. To say I can't control this. Because I can't. I'm powerless on this front. I can no more control this addiction than I can the weather. And to think I can is ludicrous.

It's not the food but it is the food. It's not the food in the sense I'm an addict and in whatever I choose to do I have the propensity to abuse it. It is the food in that is the substance that makes me high when I use it. Yes, I get a high on food when I abuse it. Don't judge unless you've been there.

Some people use cigarettes and booze;my biological father certainly does. I use food. I find myself sometimes desperate to get my fix and I will do anything to get it. I'm not proud of that fact. It just happens to be my behavior when it comes to my food.

That being said my life today is much happier than it was yesterday. More stable thanks to my meds.

On a day when Sara just wanted to get her kids out of the house she was nice enough to stop and get my meds yesterday. After sleeping all day I pigged out and slept all night. Not exactly healthy behavior.

Of course today I choose to work. And I'm hopeful to go to the bookstore and knock out some more pages on Gemini's Legacy. Every day I'm closer to being finished with the book. I look forward to finishing the trilogy. I really want to work on BELLA MORTE but I really want to lose myself in the series, so I want to finish some of my work I owe my other publishers.

So it's Legacy, the third book in the trilogy and Doves before I move on to Bella Morte. Thanks again for listening, sometimes I just need to get the dark stuff out and these days there seems to be plenty of it to go around.

Sincerely,

Amy McCorkle

Dear Daniel,

Today I want to tell you about this guy. He's an award-winning actor who's also a mental health advocate. And as much as your work helped me breakthrough the ceiling of publication, it was his as both and an actor and as someone willing to share his personal journey of struggle and healing that salvaged my dream, and honestly saved my life.

You see, I don't know Maurice either. We are not friends. We are not acquaintances. But we share one very common trait. We both live with a bipolar diagnosis. We both have experienced it's darker grip of bipolar disorder and we have both come out on the other side of it because we had loving and supportive and brave people around us who, in retrospect might have been better off in their own lives at the time turn tailing and running away from us, but to our great fortune, did not.

Maurice is a Daytime Emmy Award winner for best Lead Actor for the role of Sonny Corinthos on General Hospital. He has also been the recipient of the PRISM Award for his work portraying a character with bipolar disorder. He has suffered probably in ways that even I can't fathom. But during a time when I was perched so precariously on the edge of sanity and madness myself in October of 1999, it was his story of vulnerability and strength that gave me the sense that I was not alone.

Maurice walked, stumbled, walked some more, stumbled some more in his journey of treatment and journey to healing. And what I've learned along the way by watching him is that to hide your illness in shame is to only exacerbate the condition. Maurice is the model that creative artists should strive to be like.

It took him a few times to get the gist of it but with his steadfast wife Paula beside him, and a great and supportive environment to work I've had the great pleasure to watch him flourish and know how to run my career.

He shares his story whenever he gets the chance. He listens to those whose life he has changed for the better with his advocacy. And of the younger actors on set, when he sees something special in them he seeks them out, and gives them advice, even mentoring them. The times I've met him whether it be as someone giving him a script or approaching his people about being the narrator of my books in audio format, he's been nothing but a gentleman, and when I was at my lowest, shattered and steal healing from second breakdown at a fan event I probably should've stayed home from he gave me his full attention even though I was in a room full of people vying for his very much in demand attention.

I am a million miles away from that person in some ways. What do I mean at my lowest point that he was 'there' for me and countless others without even realizing the kind of impact he was having?

When I was in San Antonio so disconnected and broken and lost without my own voice he was up for a Soap Opera Digest Award. I think for either Favorite Lead Actor or Best Lead Actor. When he won he got up on stage he said, probably in one of the most courageous acts I've ever seen say, 'for anyone with bipolar disorder, if I can, you can' or something very similar to that.

Now I know this is going to sound very corny, but I kind of had a sixth sense that he was going to say something about it or to that effect, or maybe it was more of something to the effect I needed to hear someone like him, that I admired so greatly to say it. But when he said I remember crying. Everything seemed so far beyond my reach at the time.

I had been fired from my job at Children's World because of my bipolar status and God bless Missy was the kind of friend everyone should be so lucky to have. I used to not understand the concept of someone being the kind of rock either as a friend or a husband. And while I do have that kind of friendship now I understand what Maurice says about his super woman wife Paula.

Missy knows me. She knows my moods. When I travel the Con circuit and sit on panels and sign my books she knows I have a shelf life and that when my limitations aren't respected it can really backfire. She doesn't see that as a weakness and she wants me to succeed to my highest level possible. So she helps me do things most people wouldn't. She is a successful author in her own right, but she is a brilliant human being and as I shine in her light, Maurice shines in Paula's.

Now, if only I could find a guy to sweep me off my feet lol. But that's another post for another day.

Maurice has travelled a rocky road in his journey, but like me there are those who are devoted to him around him that he draws his strength from. He is now in a feature film called the Ghost and the Whale. While I've only seen a trailer for it, it looks like fantastic film about love, loss, and mental illness. His performance looks really good and I'm curious to see it when it comes out.

I don't need him to be Sonny in everything he does, nor do I expect him, as a fellow artist to anchor himself permanently in GH's bay. As an artist you want to do many things, as I want to tell many stories. I hope he finds the success that you have, because he is certainly deserving of it.

Sincerely,
Amy McCorkle

Dear Daniel,

Different people have shaped me over the years. I think it should be obvious by now confrontational tones or people I don't do well with. It just exacerbates every negative attribute I have. But some people have had a dual effect on me.

When I was seventeen years old I think I had one of the most stressful jobs ever. I worked for Daniel T. Taylor III. He is a local attorney who'd argued before the Supreme Court—and won. He hired me as a runner. I had no car. Hell, I didn't even have a driver's license. It was my first summer job, and honestly, as hard as it was, and as crazy (in a good way) that he was, I learned a great deal. And when he paid me a compliment at the end of the summer I was touched. But man was I relieved when I walked out of his office for the last time.

That being said, I want to say I learned what the words 'work ethic' meant. I didn't know how to take shorthand. I still don't, but I fashioned my own 'short hand' when he would dictate memos. I was constantly screwing them up. And he wasn't the most patient man. But he taught me the meaning of the word professionalism. To address someone as Doctor when someone was a doctor, not as Mr. And to respect those around me.

I had me run errands on foot in an area that I was sure to get lost in. And I did. But I figured it out. He gave me enough rope to hang myself with and more often than not I was able to avoid that particular messy situation.

I answered phones. I went to court. On more than one occasion he made me want to cry. But

I don't hold that against him, he made his clients cry too.

Of course, while working for him I gained like twenty pounds. Which, at any age isn't good, and as seventeen year old is horrible.

Which brings me to this. He taught me a work ethic is invaluable. That loyalty is irreplaceable. And that respecting those in positions of authority can be a good thing as well as something you might question your sanity over lol.

And then there's that matter of the twenty pounds. I had field hockey practice and marching band to start with that year. It was horrendous.

Although, when I look back at those pictures now I see how pretty I really was. Funny how we see ourselves. I saw myself as this bloated, ugly, piece of shit back then. All of my sisters were thin, so I thought that equaled pretty. Not that my biological father did my self-esteem any good on that front.

So back on the wagon. I'm eating real food, not the shakes. And I plan on getting exercise. Real exercise. I've already built up and endurance. Not much of one. But it might make the walk to and from the Covention Center to the hotel during Fandom Fest/Fright Night easier to handle.

Talking to Mr. Taylor today (yes, the crazy old coot is still alive) made me reflect upon all of this stuff. He really was a great guy. Maybe not someone I'd want to work for again. And when I think about it I worked my first job as a server at a Derby party. The Kentucky Derby that is. He had rich people and important people there. Sometimes the same. Other times they were not.

And let me tell you, a bunch of rich, drunk people singing and playing the piano, *snicker. They went on and on about how great they sounded. From one of the few sober people at the party, the truth was anything but. However, that being said, they were all nice to me. Especially the Human Rights lawyers who took on pro bono death penalty cases. I was only sixteen years old and they listened to me like my opinion mattered.

That taught me a profound lesson. Everyone, no matter what their station in life. With money, without money, white collar, blue collar, or poverty stricken, we all mattered. I was fortunate enough to live in a house at that point. My family's trailer days behind us. But we didn't live in the best of neighborhoods. Honestly, I still don't.

Of course I dream of living in a nice neighborhood. In a nice home with a finished basement. I also dream of owning a car. Of any kind. But disability and thirty-five dollar quarterly royalty check ain't gonna make that happen.

So I do the one thing I know I'm good at. I work. I write. And I promote my brand. Eventually, if the story is good enough, I know I'll breakthrough.

Sincerely,

Amy McCorkle

Dear Daniel,

Holy Crap. *Holy Crap.* HOLY CRAP!

So what's the hullabaloo about? For the first time in my nineteen year writing career I am a finalist in a screenwriting competition in connection with a film festival. In this case the Fandom Fest/Fright Night Film Festival.

And the screenplay in question is Bounty Hunter. The adaptation from my sci-firomance novel of the same name is a finalist.

Jumping up and down wildly, doing the happy dance. Wishing I could tell all of my heroes I've just reached a career milestone. Winning would be awesome, but landing on the board is so exciting and getting invited to the awards ceremony in such a manner is just so freaking-fantastic.

I had wanted to enter a second screenplay but I missed the deadline. I didn't even think Bounty Hunter was my strongest work. Wow. I mean, *holy crap.*

It's like I'm having this fantastic dream and I don't want to wake up from it. Supporters come out of the woodwork. People who've had nothing to do with you and your work and then suddenly poof. They want a piece of you. I don't have the heart to tell them there's not a monetary award attached to this prize.

But there are those supporters who bear mentioning. As my Aunt Debbie, Uncle Frank, and Aunt Jan like to call themselves, my storm shelter relatives, are pretty awesome in this regard. Not that long ago my Aunt Debbie said she believed big things were coming for me. I should've listened to her.

Then there's Denise Macaulife, my cousin Greg's wife. Her daughters Rebekah, Bridgette, and Mary are what Missy calls my fan club, they'll be at the awards ceremony. My mom and dad I think will reluctantly be there. Neither of them like to miss church. To be honest the movies are my church.

I want to win of course. And apparently there are three categories, sci-fi, fantasy, and horror. (I qualify for science fiction). 15 finalists out of 270 screenplays, which by all accounts, are good odds. Considering I entered Austin and they get like 6,000 entries. My odds I feel like are good to advance, I just don't know how far.

Still I've never finaled in anything! So this is huge. *Ginormous* as Buddy the Elf would say. At least it is for me.

Another thing, of 15 finalists there were only two female writes on the list. Of course, if you'd heard the antiquated attitude of one male sci-fi writer he would have died at the mere mention of a 'sci-fi romance' making the cut in any contest.

But the nice thing about Fandom Fest/Fright Night is that in the (this will be my third year) time I've been going I've found the atmosphere to be very inclusive. And each year it does something to advance my career.

So here are the people to thank for my finalist status: Missy, my erstwhile and patient best friend and writing partner we have traveled a long road. Landing on the board is super awesome. I can now move on to the next thing on the list. Pamela Turner, for being a great writer and friend who turned me on to Fandom Fest. Stephen Zimmer, literary director, who's found space for me each and every year. And Ken Daniels, for making me feel like a total rock star this year.

That being said. As I wait to hear back from Sundance Screenwriter's Lab and Austin Film Festival and EPIC I celebrate this latest accomplishment with the joy and relish it deserves. And oh, tomorrow is my birthday!

Sincerely,
Amy McCorkle

Dear Daniel,

I know this is going to seem unrelated to what I do and the point of this blog but, for high school I went to a legal magnet. I thought I wanted to be a lawyer. I had my pick of schools. I could've gone to my home school, Fairdale, where most of the kids who tormented me in middle school went. I had no desire to endure four more years of hell. Especially when home wasn't going to feel all that safe and secure either. I could have gone to a performing arts school, but I have to cop to something here. I loved music, I still do, but it wasn't the driving passion that writing was. And I saw a girl with pink hair and it rattled me. (I'm not proud of that little nugget of information, but there you have it.) Another school structured like a college atmosphere was available to me too. But I was bust living out my dad's (John's dream) and determined not to live out my mother's.

As it stood I would attend Central, excel there in the legal magnet, and realize, thanks to a job in a real law office I wanted nothing to do with the legal profession. Dad wanted me to be Scott Turow or John Grisham. Lawyers who wrote. That wasn't my path.

Not that I didn't love music. I was in marching band, concert band, and pep band. I made first cut All-State. I went to one of the music colleges in the nation's band clinic for three years. It was always so awesome. Like a party with a huge concert every winter. It was fun, and there was someone who wanted to be a concert trumpet player. He idolized the best of the best.

Kind of like I do with authors, screenwriters, directors, and actors (women are included in those sentiments). Although I was given a stark reminder of things when I saw the list of finalists for Fright Night. Only two other women in 15 (and one of them was my writing partner) were on that list.

Given the current political environment things aren't so great for my kind. I was anxious about it I wrote a novel during the election season. It was a dark dystopian tale. One that doesn't guarantee a happy ending for everyone involved. I had little faith in the American Public to do the right thing.

I didn't think Obama was a god. But he was far, far better than anything the opposition put up. I mean come on, really? Mr. Liar Liar I'm Sooo ObviouslyA Man With His Pants on Fire Romney and Mr. I Need My Ass Kicked Into the 21st Century Ryan were not even fit to hold office. So even if I didn't want to vote for Obama, these jokes in positions of power made my decision for me.

I was in such a dark place Breath of Life was born. Really, a hero, a man full of grief and self-loathing and hatred for the world around him lives in seclusion in a post apocalyptic war in which the country, divided against itself fell apart. In his life before the war he was a hitman. As the world fell apart he fought for a time but soon tired of the disorganization and grew embittered by both sides. It's not until a warrior girl with a tattoo of the Constitution on her back on the verge of death comes, literally, crashing into his life that his world view begins to change.

Eight years ago the election of Obama brought with it, a great deal of hope and promise for me. I mean, why wouldn't it? I couldn't stand Bush's politics. And Obama seemed like a refreshing change.

His re-election last November seemed more like a bullet dodged. The IRS 'scandal' such as it is doesn't shake me up. Apparently these so-called persecuted political groups were operation for profit what applying for non-profit status. As far as I'm considered this is much ado about fucking nothing. You played fast and loose with IRS and they came down hard on you. Boo-fuckin-hoo.

As for this wire-tapping email reading thing. That's far more egregious to me. It's a total invasion of my privacy and is part of what compelled me to write Breath of Life. Stuff like that is EPIC FAIL. I understand there are some unsavory aspects to protecting this great nation, but shit like that really pisses me off. And when the deck is stack against you as it is, a bullshit Congress that does absolutely nothing to get anything accomplished. Well, I could go on, but as you can see I'm pretty passionate about politics too. But I'm including a mock-up of the cover so you can see how lucky I am to write such a thing.

Sincerely,
Amy McCorkle

Dear Daniel,

I feel like I kind of phoned yesterday's letter in, I did such a lousy job of getting it in front of anybody. And I don't really think of it as my best work. But I think, it was my birthday, and I did so much and I was so tired that it really compromised what I'm trying to do with it.

I have so many hopes and dreams. Some of them include having a signature series that I'm known for. And Bella Morte seems to have evolved into just that. And by signature series I think,

Harry Potter=Rowling. Mallorys=Lindsey. Hamilton=Anita Blake. I mean I want to write all sorts of things but that's why I have other pan names I write under. It allows me that kind of freedom. And of course, as successful as I see myself I'm under no delusion.

I'm successful in a small scale way. When people say my name few people even know who the hell I am. Hell, as great as I feel like this blog is doing I still am at the mercy of the lovely people who grace me with the time to even come and read it. Sometimes they even leave me nice compliments. Which always gives me a thrill. ù

With the finaling of Bounty Hunter in the film festival screenplay competition I have to pinch myself. I've never done that before. And I'm still on something of a high from that and it makes me cry those big fat happy tears. I honestly wouldn't know what I would do if I won.

I know, I know, it's not the Oscars, the Independent Spirit Awards, or the Golden Globes, or even the Critic's Choice Awards, but for someone struggling to get by it's huge. And for me, who's been happy to just land on the board up to this point it's a big step.

It's important to note I haven't won shit at this point. But finaling? It's like winning to me. In the life I lead it's like a bright, promising light at the end of a very long tunnel that you and my other heroes have been lighting the way of up until this point. It's validation of all the hard work and sacrifice I've been pouring into this screenwriting thing up until this point.

As for the signature series, Bella Morte seems to be gaining traction every passing day. I find myself wanting to write for it even as I close in on the finish of book 2 of the *Gemini Rising* Trilogy. So today I write about it.

I slept better last night than I've slept in quite some time. I do so much better with sleep. But I know sometimes I'm such a workaholic I'm thinking it's a time suck on the time I could be writing.

That might have something to do with my serious lack of a social life. But then, I'd rather be alone with my characters than be in a room full of people. Which brings me to Fandom Fest/Fright Night Film Festival.

July is so close now. I get to do so much fun stuff. Sit on panels and talk about writing. (I know, I know, I'll be lucky to get one person to show up in the room. People are there to see the actors.) But still, I'm passionate about what I do and it'll be nice to be given a platform to possibly inspire others the way you and others have inspired me to embrace their hopes and dreams in the face of maybe a lot of doubters, including themselves.

I'll be doing the double release party for City of the Damned and Gemini's War. Which will include, a rock band, LAME, light refreshment, a costume contest to be judged by my nephew (who will be turning seven) and giveaways from my publishers. Again, I know hell is more likely to freeze over than you and your family coming, but the invitation stands.

I get to get my photo taken with Adrian Paul, the Highlander. I was going to see Kevin Smith, but his tickets sold out before I could purchase them. Perhaps I'll see him at the festival roaming around. Otherwise, I'll have to wait for another time to meet that hero of mine.

And the final day of Fright Night/Fandom Fest I get to attend my first ever Awards ceremony where I'm 'invited'. Of course I'll have a table where I get to hang out with my friends and sell my books during the rest of the ceremony but that seems like miles away.

I'm so lucky these days in a lot of respects. And I just wanted show you how a little thing can keep me a float. Although in some ways it seems like such a big thing.

Sincerely,
Amy McCorkle

Dear Daniel,

How do you deal with the anxiety of being the draw when your gut tells you maybe you shouldn't do something? Not because the people who have signed you up for the appearance or draw are bad. In fact the people in question are really great people. I've never been *the* special guest of or for anything in my life.

But I have a really bad idea of being swept up into something that sounds like a really good idea at the time only to have my limitations rear their big fat ugly heads at the worst time possible when I pushed. Especially when my boundaries weren't respected by well intentioned folks.

Right now, my stomach is in knots. I want to be able to fulfill my professional obligations if only because I don't want to let people down. But when I spend three hours on the phone having a complete and total breakdown it makes me wonder if forging ahead is such a wise idea.

I want to go but every physical symptom in my body is screaming not to. My stomach hurts.

There's tension in my neck. I want to eat everything in sight. And I'm constantly on the verge of tears.

Part of me tells me to suck it up. I can do this. Yet another part of me knows better. A part of me knows after years of therapy and medication management that when I don't respect my boundaries, and when they are aren't respected bad things happen.

When someone, very well intentioned presumes to know me better than I know myself well, then there's friction and trouble. I tend to be quiet and passive-aggressive. Articulating my own needs becomes incredibly difficult and secondary to making sure my own mental health is taken care of.

The last time I took a ride to a place where I was going to be without Missy it was at Concave it was a disaster. Ijust fear a repeat performance.

I feel like it's a professional obligation and that I'm fucked. That something really bad is going to happy and that each time I try to articulate this to my contact to the event they aren't trying to be cruel but that something bad is going to happen.

So I'm going to try something different. I'm going to try and meditate. And try to deal with the fear and reality that is my bipolar disorder.

Sincerely,
Amy McCorkle

Dear Daniel,

Today is one of those days where I could just curl up in bed and pull the blankets over my head. When you spend two days arguing with someone over a trip you didn't want to take to begin with and they keep coming at you even after you've agreed to keep the professional obligation and they tell you that you use your bipolar disorder as a crutch and that you'll never be successful well you have no choice other than to cut the cord.

My therapist, because of my (her words) remarkable success in conquering bipolar disorder has asked me to present my journey to an official board. She says they find it helps with maintaining balance in giving service back on the part of the client.

So to have someone who claims to know me better than I know myself and that she's 'just being honest'. And the thing is I don't think it was anything malicious on her part. She's really good at what she does and I respect her a great deal for it.

I feel as if I've been through an emotional war of contrition and it's hard to do anything. I have projects that need finishing and this bullshit ain't gonna cut it.

You know how you have family, friends who are like the family you should have had in a fair world (lol), then friends you make through work in the beginning, and then people, who prove to be only worthy of acquaintance status?

. I have a really small circle of friends. I can count them on four fingers. You've heard me talk about most of them already. There's Missy. Really, there hasn't been much we haven't faced in our friendship together. Starvation, the struggle to sell our work and gain representation, paying bills, heartache, my mental illness, our past abuse survival, each other(lol) and fight to put our name on the film and publishing maps. We've shared cross country trips, endured film festivals as green horns and have been the odd man out in several competitions. We both love film and books and music. We love soap operas. We cast our stories whether co-writing or working on separate projects. And yes we fight from time to time. But we've known each other for 17 years. And I know of the people I want in my corner she's number one on the list.

The next person on the list Pamela Turner. I've talked about her too. She is one of the kookiest, most talented, hardest workingwriters-screenwriters-filmmakers-artists I know. I met her in 2001 when she auditioned for a film Missy and I were putting together. She stepped in as cinematographer with her equipment when another cinematographer backed out 2 days before filming. She's taken me to the emergency room and watched me puke my guts out. She's taken me to the emergency room when I thought I was having a heart attack and no one else would or could. She's taken me to countless therapy session and doctor's appointments because I don't own a car. I read her work and love it. Not because I'm a yes person, but because I genuinely like her work. She's one of the most ambitious and hardest working friends I have. And, next to Missy she's the best friend I have. Yes she makes me crazy sometimes, but all friends do that to each other. I'm sure I do it to her.

Then there's my out of state friend, Elise VanCise. If there ever was a hard luck case it's her. But she doesn't sit around moping. She's also an author and blogger and graphic artist and a single mother who works ceaselessly to give her son a good life and a safe home. We bonded over NaNoWriMo and a shared love of the television series Highlander and Russell Crowe movies. If there is any justice in this world she will succeed further than her wildest dreams.

The same goes for all of my friends. I should've said one hand. Carla Deal is an extremely talented artist and when she gets out of her own way she writes incredible stories. She's a wonderful cook, a great mother, and when I hang at her place we always watch YouTube videos into the wee hours of the morning. It's one of the few times I'll drink.

Finally there's the Marr family. Mary and Paul. (Their son is adorable but I've hardly gotten to see them in recent years). Mary was my friend when I was 19 years old. When I was struggling to establish boundaries with my family. And trying to know who to trust and who not to trust. Paul was the first Alpha male I ever knew who was also funny as hell and a big softie once you got to know him. To this day whenever I call their house he says, "What are you wearing?" He's such a perve, but in a harmless way. He was the first guy to say string the bastards up when it came to my attackers. And he was always trying to protect me from the instability at the time that was my family life. That's another thing, they're coming in for Fandom Fest. Mary and Paul are regulars on the Con circuit in the southwest and have family in Kentucky. I'm really looking forward to their visit.

Really on a day when you lose your friend and it's never any fun when that happens, it forces you to sit back and reflect on all that you do have. And what I have is a lot. I was told I would never be a success, that I use my mental illness as a crutch, and that I have poor taste in friends and that they are enablers.

As Pam said, I have fans who love my books, I have awards, I have a successful blog, I was asked by my actual therapist to present my story before an official board because it is such a model of success. I have made new friends in the professional world and feel like things, though they feel hurtful and withering now, will only serve to make me stronger in the future.

Sincerely,
Amy McCorkle

Dear Daniel,

I think I can say truly, without reservation, you are a fucking genius NOT to be on social media. I am not famous. I don't have a lot of money. So Social Media is the main way I promote and communicate with my readership. But there are perils to it as I've learned very recently. Someone, as I have related, I believed was a friend will not stop attempting to contact me. And frankly, apart from the emotional drain it has put on me, I've had to block them on every social media outlet I'm on. They texted me negative messages about my long time friends. I had to block their phone number to my phone.

Friends have told me if this behavior continues I need to contact the police. Please, at this point, allow me to take a moment to say, this blog is more about me telling my memoirs than it is about anything else. I picked you, as a hero of mine to frame the blog in. I hope I never make any actor/director/writer/novelist/artist of any kind feel the way I feel right now.

I have a book signing this Saturday and they are going to be there. Part of me is like, I can't let the state of fear they've got me keep me from being able to function in my profession. And the other part of me is like, stay home, hide do not do anything to rock the boat.

Not that what I'm experiencing is anything like what someone like say, you, would experience at all. But for the last few days I've had knots in my stomach. I haven't been able to write much and I have several deadlines.

It's odd being in this situation. I would have never thought I would find myself in a position where I wanted to retreat from the world because of something like this.

I don't think they realize what kind of position they're putting me in. I've had several friends tell me I need to call the authorities. But I just want it to stop. So far today I haven't heard from them. So I'm going to take it a little bit at a time. Unfortunately this blog, where I've felt relatively safe to express myself in the past I know they could very easily follow me that way.

I don't like the paranoia they've managed to stir up in me. It makes me cranky, hell, it makes me a class A bitch to everyone else around me. And that's not fair to them.

But the nice thing is I've written this blog over the course of two days. I'm starting to feel safer. To feel better. But there's that little part of me that thinks Saturday is looming and I shouldn't have to feel awkward or fearful at all. The nice thing is, I'll be getting there with a good friend earlier than this other person and I can hang with some of the nicer people who are a part of one of my publisher's.

I'm looking forward to clearing the deck of my work. And there seems to be so much of it. Four books, three I'm juggling, one that I need to write and a screenplay adaptation. I know a lot of people would envy that mess but I stress out and I had this person saying hurry up, hurry up, hurry up. And now it seems it that I will simply wilt under the pressure.

And taking on too much is a mistake. I should've ignored this person. They gave me some incredibly bad advice and I just followed them like some kind of automaton. But if I sit down and make things in a linear fashion I might be able to finish my projects after all.

So right now I'll be working on GEMINI'S LEGACY until it's done. Then WHEN DOVES CRY. Then BELLA MORTE: SACRIFICE. Then GEMINI'S REVENGE. Then the screenplay adaptation. I am going to finish this all by the end of the year.

I just have to pace myself. My mental health depends on it. I'm not a lazy person by any stretch of the imagination. I just have to take care of myself. And that includes shielding myself from undesirable situations. As such I'm bringing my Aunt to Fandom Fest. She can run the table and keep unwanted persons away from me.

This is my Aunt Debbie. She's my 'tornado shelter' relative. And while my family is far from perfect, my biological father and his side could give a shit about me anymore, and my parents are often controlling themselves, I know if I say back off or do something to put a boundary down they aren't going to react violently.

I don't know this person that well at all. Just two things, don't ever let anyone talk you into creating a social media presence. Second, I hope I never make anyone feel the way I've been made to feel the last few days. And if I do that to you please let me know, that is not the point of this blog.

Sincerely,
Amy McCorkle

Dear Daniel,

Tell me, is there something in the water? Have all of my acquaintances suddenly taken a crazy pill and decided they get to control what I put on here as well as tell me how to run my career? Because at least as fucked up as my family is they lay of me professionally. I know I have attained a certain amount of success. Thanks to people showing me the way, helping me out, not all of them get mentioned. If I named everyone who ever helped me out with grocery money this blog would be never ending. And even though the person probably deserves an obligatory mention, which means I would have eventually gotten around to it, I will NOT be bullied into doing something out of guilt or perceived obligation.

I've helped a lot of people out. They thank me at the time. Some have parlayed that help into something bigger. Do I get the credit for it, no. Does it bother me that they don't freaking sky write it for me to be noticed by the public at large? No. And in the end all I did was make the initial meeting possible. They did the hard work of nurturing the relationship and parlaying it into something pretty awesome. All the credit goes to them.

I mentioned in an earlier blog that I knew what it was like to go to bed hungry and wake up hungry. I was accused of lying. I was told this blog was nothing but a pity party and pure fiction and that I didn't know the truth from fiction anymore.

My life much like the bipolar disorder is filled with extreme highs and lows. Which can make it difficult to sound happy. I never expected blow back from a blog I sat down to write as a thank you to you and use it as a way to from my memoirs. The person I speaking about is my ex. And out of respect I have not broadcast the tumultuous details of the journey we've taken from couple to good friends. He wasn't great boyfriend material, but I was a batshit crazy untreated bipolar 19 year old. I'm not even going to mention his name. Because well, I'm big on paying it forward but I'm pretty private when it comes to that sort of thing.

Does it piss me off that his wife wants to take credit for it all? Well, I'm only human, of course it does. She didn't write the books. She didn't edit the books. She didn't write the screenplays. Or enter the contests or submit to publishers or publish. They paid for one $40 advert and one $25 haircut outside the groceries.

I hate to say it, but HATERS ARE MOTIVATORS. And she wanted a thank you. So thank you. For the above mentioned things. One thing I will not do is give them any more space in my life.

But like I said highs and lows right? I mentioned other professional friends, right. That I've earned the reputation as being something of a marketing whiz. I honestly don't know how it happened. But I was taught everything I know by the likes of Christine Bell, Lea Schizas, and the film industry as a whole.

I was asked today to be the marketing director of a new epub company. And the series I'm working on BELLA MORTE has been accepted for publication there. ALL 8 BOOKS! So as hard as the week has been I have only one more stressful event to attend to. The signing at Joseph –Beth. After that clear sailing.

Sincerely,
Amy McCorkle

Dear Daniel,

I took some time yesterday to relax and heal up from last week's turmoil. The situations have resolved themselves. Both to my satisfaction. I was able to save a twenty year friendship with one and able to co-exist professionally with the other.

There are people who helped me who haven't been mentioned on the blog or in the letters not because I don't recognize what they've done for me, but because in some ways I wish to keep that part of my life private. And while I want to take this chance to thank everyone who has ever helped me in whole or in part, I want those who live out of state to know sometimes your distance from me simply puts you out of my frame of reference from time to time. Kind of, out of sight out of mind. But that doesn't mean I don't appreciate all the wonderful things my friends have done for me.

It's just when people are less than positive in how they approach me I get angry, defensive. I think sometimes they mean one thing but their words say something else entirely. But a twenty-year friendship isn't something I let go by the wayside so easily. And I love those involved. (Not romantically, the only thing I love with a passion is my writing time. Not even the career. The actual act of writing.)

I don't have a lot of friends, and to throw the ones who've, yes, proven themselves to be there for me at times emotionally when others haven't well, one misunderstanding isn't worth throwing the baby out with the bath water.

There aren't many to celebrate with. And they won't be able to come for the awards ceremony of Fright Night but they will be someone I call and tell first thing. Although, this may be a place where I come and jump up and down and squeal if my miracle of miracles I win.

One thing I'm super hyped about is this marketing director position. To be honest I'm a little nervous. It's a lot of work. I don't do anything halfway and I don't want this job to be any less so. I really like and respect my boss and co-owner and I'm excited that my best friend is on board too. It's something apparently I'm good at and I hope to do the owner and founder proud by the work I do.

And by taking the time off that I did yesterday I think I'm going to get a ton done today. Which is awesome. Finding balance is so hard for me. I tend to burn the candle at both ends and then something bad happens and I crash and burn. I plan on doing some marketing work for all of my houses today. Some simple things like sharing my covers for Hydra and Muse. And some more extensive work for the new house. And looking to list my Bounty Hunter book on some free sites for a July 15th and 16th giveaway my publisher has planned.

I'm really proud of the time taken off yesterday. Even if it only was four hours. I ate dinner out and hung out with my best friend, Missy and it was just a nice relaxing evening until about nine. Then I wrote and at ten I watched *The Nanny* with my mom.

I know, exciting, right? I like it when my life is uneventful. The most exciting I want it to get is when positive, fun, loving things happen in my life. Like finaling in contests, or maybe even going far enough in the competition to win. Like signing contracts for books I've written. Or seeing them in print and fan mail or a positive review.

Something last week definitely brought home. You can never be humble enough, or happy enough when dealing with success at any level.

And as for those who don't understand. Or are bitter and jealous and want to lay into you, or perhaps even want to ride on your coat tails of success. As much as I say HATERS ARE MOTIVATORS, I know there is nothing I can do to control that particular element of the reading and writing population. All that I can do is control how I react.

I know as alone as I feel sometimes there are those out there who make it better, who do things to help ease the pathway of struggle. But it's still hard. And I've been through a lot in my life. Which makes the success I'm experiencing now all that much sweeter. The fact I get to share it with my friends makes it all that much better.

Sincerely,
Amy McCorkle

Dear Daniel,

I'm excited. Really, really bursting from within excited. Missy was able to get tickets to the Kevin Smith Event at Fandom Fest. I know this is going to sound corny and lame but as writing partners we kind of pegged him as one of our heroes.

We came into this screenwriting gig a few years after he hit it big with CLERKS. And if you've ever worked in movie rental place or worked a stop 'n rob (convenient store) then you know why a certain generation kind of glommed onto him the way that they did and made him a cult hero.

He's actually a talented guy and gifted storyteller. I've read several of his memoirs he's funny, empathetic, and has an incredibly strong voice as a writer. I think he's sorely underrated in the industry, but I think he proved his worth and guts with Red State. And my personal favorite movie of his, Zach and Miri Make A Porno. Which they do, but it's actually a warm, romantic comedy wrapped up in his signature bawdy style.

Some people are offended by that sort of thing. I'm just not. When you're doing something because you have a passion for, it shows. Now, Zach and Miri isn't actually one of his box office successes. He'll tell you it broke is heart opening weekend. For an interesting take on this read his Tough Shit memoir it's an eye opener on this business and how the person you thought you could trust can change in devastating heart beat.

He's a fascinating guy and even though I'm not going to get to actually shake his hand and meet him I'm going to get to see him to do what he does best. The movie he will be screening is produced with his best friend Jason Mewes.

Theirs is a long and tested friendship, fraught with Jason's battle with addiction and when

Jason was struggling to stay clean Kevin opened up his huge heart and they produced this film together. At the end of each screening of the film they do a podcast and it's like therapy and it helps Jason stay clean. That's love, that's friendship. And all the reason more to admire a man like him, and admire Jason for travelling the path to sobriety and being clean.

I know from experience with my best friend that the path to sanity has not always been easy, and for a while I laid down my screenwriting and filmmaking dream and explored novels, novellas and short stories for a while.

And then I saw his *Burn in Hell* tour on YouTube. He was inspiring and although I had written Bounty Hunter with no pressure. From March to April Missy and I wrote two more scripts. Which we promptly entered in Austin. And with *You're the Reason* we took a snowball's chance in hell and entered it in the Sundance Screenwriter's Lab competition. We're hopeful, but standing out amongst thousands is no small task. But I'm pleased to say to say I feel inspired and like I can stand tall where once I would have wilted. Everyone who reads this please cross their fingers for my upcoming competition, Fright Night. If you so choose that is. Nothing compares to the thrill of finaling. With the exception I think of winning, which honestly is just the icing on an already delicious cake.

Sincerely,
Amy McCorkle

Dear Daniel,

I have several victories to report. One, GEMINI'S LEGACY is done and awaiting edits. Two, WHEN DOVES CRY, the second short novel I was working on is finished. That means, since February, I have completed a novella, CITY OF THE DAMNED, two feature length screenplays, and the two short novels. All I can say is HOT DAMN. I have never been that productive in my life. And did I mention I'm 17K into book 1 of my BELLA MORTE series?

All of this on the heels of my BOUNTY HUNTER screenplay finaling in the Fright Night Film Festival makes the hard stuff all worth it. All of the books are contracted for publication. And I'm waiting to hear back on the Claymore competition at Killer Nashville for LEGACY and

Sundance and Austin for YOU'RE THE REASON and Austin for CITY OF THE DAMNED screenplay.

I have never felt so blessed in my entire life. Finishing projects used to be my Achilles heel. When I was in high school my Aunt Rosie, my first official fan said I'm not going to read anything else by you until you finish it. Then it became I can only work on one project at a time.

And then thanks to a wonderful person who put up with my incessant need to read my cards gave me the message, the Universe favors any idea you start now. And boom 4 projects all finished. BOUNTY HUNTER was written last year over a period of four months (the screenplay). Breath of Life was written from August to September. Gemini's War was written from October until the middle of November.

It's been an especially good run creativity wise. And now that I'm onto book 1 of BELLA MORTE I can really focus and lose myself in the story. It may come along faster now that the other books are finished.

Of course, I have two other projects in the queue waiting to be written, the conclusion of GEMINI RISING and the screenplay adaptation of Gemini's War. Then of course the rest of the BELLA books.

Some say I'm fortunate to be able to do what I do full time. And I'll admit, they're right. But when I organize my day a ton can be get done. And the marketing gig is going fantastic. I have lots of ideas. Some that can be implemented now and others that have to wait. I'm kind of in a holding pattern right now. But that doesn't mean when I get the green light I won't be off like a shot. Hell, I think I'm bombarding my boss now with ideas.

At some point in my career I would like to help the people who have helped me along the way. Whether we've fought and made up or fought and not made up. At some point people are helping me.

As you've seen my life is like a roller coaster. I don't want a roller coaster. I want balance. Harmony. Joy. But I know anything worth having comes with the good and the bad. And right now I'm blessed with a multitude of ideas. But book 3 in GEMINI RISING is still unformed in the back of my mind. And I'm too exhausted with the story to contemplate writing the screenplay my publisher has asked to see. So I'm working on my passion project at the moment. BELLA MORTE.

As I've mentioned Fandom Fest is going to be off the chain for me. Kevin Smith, sitting on panels, a dealer table, a sanctioned event I'm putting on to launch GEMINI'S WAR, a photo with one of my other heroes, Adrian Paul, and the icing on an already delicious cake, and awards ceremony where I'm a finalist.

I wish I had some kind of crystal ball where I knew whether or not I won. But to be honest my weekend is so jammed packed full of cool shit I should be able to distract myself until the big reveal as to whether I go home with hardware or not.

So as I close out this letter, I want to extend the invitation to Fandom Fest for my launch to you and your family, I know I've already invited you once, but I think it bears repeating just how much your work inspires me in my work.

Sincerely,
Amy McCorkle

Dear Daniel,

I don't know what the weather is like where you live, whethertornado weather is a mainstay. But I hate spring in early to mid summer in Kentucky for a lot of reasons. I don't officially live in tornado alley, honestly I don't think my heart could take it if I did. I mean nothing good could come of a place where 'tornado' and 'alley' are synonymous with each other. I mean severe thunderstorms are bad enough.

Wednesday my home was hammered by two rounds of severe thunderstorms. And in retrospect I'm grateful that the first round came through early in the day, around four in the afternoon. It took some of the energy out of the atmosphere for the second round later that night. What I didn't really bank on was that second round going late into the night.

I was at Missy's house and it was raining hard and it was putting on quite a light show. So as it began to die down I decided I would drive home.

Yes. You heard me right. Miss Chicken Little herself when it comes to bad weather decided at the tail end of a severe thunderstorm it would be a 'good idea' to get out and drive in that shit. I'm telling ya' I'm a fuckin' genius for making that move.

There was a flash flood warning out. And as I drove home listening to the AM station for weather, I got to listen to the same system that had just passed through my area was now spawning tornados to the south of Bullitt County.

I was driving across the county on a back road. Really the only way to get to Shepherdsville from Mount Washington was the back road and it was dark, mostly unlit and each time I hit a large pond of water the car jerked, giving me a heart attack several times over.

I don't like to drive in the rain, and even clouds give me the heebie-jeebies if they look dark enough. I've set under a wall cloud before in the middle of gridlocked traffic and that's an experience I NEVER need to repeat. Fortunately nothing snaked its way down from there but a gush of relief washed over me when it began to rain. And that weekend I ended up staying at my aunt and uncle's house. You know, the ones with the basement and a landlady from hell? Well, no you wouldn't know that but they are my safe house in a storm.

When I got home I was tangle of frazzled nerves and jagged edges. I went in my room to work and quickly realized I was tense and when my night meds kicked in I was emotionally drained and the thought of anymore work getting done while I was awake was an ephemeral dream. I crashed and burned and slept from 11PM to almost 5PM uninterrupted. Which these days is unheard of. Usually I sleep until 2AM get up set up to work and around an hour or two later fall asleep.

I know I need a new mattress but I don't have the kind of money it takes even to buy a $99 one, but with Fandom Fest/Fright Night coming, Killer Nashville, Night Risers Expo and Film Fest I have no extra money. It's not like I blow my cash on irresponsible items. But I'm hopeful that one day this small press success finds mainstream success and can afford a new bed. A new mattress and a house with a basement to put them in.

Sincerely,
Amy McCorkle

Dear Daniel,

I finished book 1 of Bella Morte and am looking for my next project and find myself wanting to produce, create, and write an indie soap. I know, some look down on the medium but

I think it's an underappreciated one. Of course, on television it's almost impossible to break into that line of work. But in a web series it's wide open. I want to put together a series bible. A damn good one and go to New York for the indie soap awards and pitch it to some possible partners. I know I'm good on the pitch. I'm damn good at it. But getting people to get on board with your dreams isn't necessarily the easiest job in the world. And balancing that with commitments with my marketing endeavors with my new press and my series I'm working on in the publishing world seems like a lot.

The truth is, I love storytelling, in whatever medium it's in. And I cut my teeth on soaps. I know, people don't take you seriously when you work in soaps. But honestly, I write subgenre romance, to my mind I already work in the medium. And there is no shame in it. In fact, I feel like I've toiled on some hallowed ground.

I love the idea of a mob soap. Stories of a family that perhaps is falling apart because of the decay from within. But then, what do I know?

I have to sit down with the other half of my Hollywood brain, Missy and come up with the indie soap. I can write books on my own just fine. And even then I consult her.

I wish I could say I had this high minded look at art, but I just want to tell stories. And I suppose to that end, I am an artist. I wish I were more comfortable with that label. But I guess if I don't respect my place in the world of storytelling no one else will.

Of course I could just write a series straight out of my series I'm writing for my new series. I think I might. But first I have to write the second book in the continuing series.

I am inspired to be sure. Funny that it took this letter to focus my energies to take the courageous step to write the second book in the series. I'm going to pitch it to ICM at Killer Nashville. It would seem I have a great deal of work to do.

I have no idea what the second book will be about. And since the second book belongs to the new house as does the other seven books, I feel like I have some freedom there that I wouldn't have at a larger house in New York. Of course that doesn't mean if I wrote longer I wouldn't give the series a chance there.

The reality is I write anywhere from 25K-40K usually, but to garner that elusive print contract in New York you need 80K and the longest I've been able to write is 60K and even that needed some paring down.

Bella Morte casts the proto-type character I usually have for you as father/mentor type as opposed to the romantic lead. I feel kind of silly telling you that, but the heroine is fourteen in this series. I can't say much more for fear of giving away spoilers of the series. So I'll stop there. But if you're interested in reading an excerpt in its very rough form, here it is, https://facebook.com/BellaMorte8.

The indie soap is still very much on the table, but the idea of Bella Morte as a television series is just to delicious to contemplate. It would take a young actress with considerable acting chops to pull it off.

I'm a huge fan of Revolution on NBC, but Charlie, the daughter needs a little more seasoning. However Billy Burke is wonderful. As is Esposito. Both command the screen whenever they're on it.

I want my series to sing like LOST did. Well, anyway, I need to get to work on the second book. And the pitch for the series and ICM. It's not every day that company comes to the southern region of the United States.

Sincerely,

Amy McCorkle

Dear Daniel,

I know it's been awhile since I posted last. Recovering from such an onslaught of personal attacks against me personally and the blog itself really took a lot out of me. I wondered for a time if I'd even return to it at all. And then I realized, this was my fucking house and I can pretty much say what goes and what doesn't on it. Let's start with the beginning shall we.

As with any mental illness I deal with a lot of anxiety. And the controversy stirred up by well meaning but ill advised friends generated more of it than I realized. It paralyzed me from returning to my beloved blog. In the process I have neglected it. And myself to some degree. Even with the great news and the good time coming up this weekend (I am sooo going to rock Fandom Fest/Fright Night) my anxiety had gone up to levels I hadn't experienced in a long time.

Anxiety at its worst has cost me jobs, because I simply could not function in regular work environment. My physical health deteriorated to such a degree I had to train myself to have enough endurance to conquer Fandom Fest. And I isolated myself in the house because I did not want to deal with any kind of crowd. They are projecting over 30K people at Fandom Fest/Fright Night. While that's good for business it was starting to freak me out. Then Hydra is rearranging, so that means previous contracts are jettisoned because they can't afford to put them out. Which is fine I had another home to take them to. Bounty Hunter, on the other hand, which hit #9 on the Amazon Bestsellers list this last week remains are part of their stable as do Gunpowder & Lead Book 1 and Set Fire to the Rain. Bounty Hunter is the book I adapted to screenplay format and is a finalist Fright Night.

So all of that is taken care of and my tally of 31 contracts remains intact. But my anxiety was robbing me of much needed sleep, and instead of happy Amy there more negative attributes of my bipolar disorder were heightened. Irritability, anger, nastiness. Just crap people shouldn't have to deal with. With Fandom Fest days away I went to the doctor and begged him for help.

He said the only thing he could do was place me on an anti-anxiety pill. Which, if you know me, and you don't, I have resisted for quite some time. It seemed I was taking a lot meds as it was for the bipolar disorder and I didn't want to have to take any more medicine. Now I know some eschew medication, claiming it's harmful for you, and in a since it's physically hard on your body. But I remembered what I was like when first diagnosed with bipolar disorder and lithium saved my life. Eventually the side effects were too harsh I was moved off of it to Depakote ER which saved my life a second time. In time the doctors found the right combination and I've been able to put my life back together.

As it was I was sleeping one hour, waking up and trying desperately to go back to sleep unsuccessfully all over again. Until finally, desperate at the anxiety I was feeling light of recent events I let the doctor give me the lowest dose of Adavan he could. The result has been miraculous. I sleep better, I'm more relaxed, and I'm writing again.

I know there's this terrible mentality that some in Hollywood perpetuate psychiatry is the devil's playground, and that all you need is love. And while love is part of the formula for sanity if I didn't take the meds I would be a lost soul. I have been so depressed in my life at times I didn't get out of bed. Or worse, wanted to die.

Abuse of any substance is bad for you. But I am closely monitored by my doctor. Where I once required weekly therapy and 4 week intervals with my doctor. I no longer need the weekly therapy and I now see the doctor every 12 weeks.

Fandom Fest and Fright Night are going to be huge and I have my doctor, my best friend Missy, and yes, watching Cowboys & Aliens and Casino Royale to thank for getting me through my latest crisis. Thank you and once again you are invited to GEMINI'S WAR release party. There will be a rock band, a costume contest, giveaways, and light refreshment in the Brown Room on the second floor of the Galt House in Louisville, KY. I know, I live in the real world. You don't know me, and in reality you have no idea this blog exists. But a fellow artist, and yes, fan, can always hope, right?

Sincerely,
Amy McCorkle

Dear Daniel,

Yesterday was the best of times it was the worst of times. Walking the pedway between the Galt House and the Kentucky International Convention Center and back… hell on earth to a big out of shape girl like me. But here's the beauty of it. I made it. Gasping, heaving, and sweating like a state fair pig I made it. And while resting in the bar area on the way back to my room I saw Grant Wilson of Ghost Hunters fame. He now does graphic novels and games. Well, Missy and I went back to our hotel room and had dinner. Jimmie Johns is wonderful when you're on a budget and you don't want to walk anywhere else.

Having cooled off and gotten some nosh in I started getting antsy but wasn't especially hip to going to the exhibitors' party. If only because standing up after the walking we'd done earlier seemed like a real chore. Instead we went back to the deli/bar area and sat down and chit chatted down in that area.

That's when Grant Wilson made his appearance again. A group of fans wanted his picture and I have to admit. I wasn't any different. These other girls were very forward and it was hard to get his attention at first. And when I first spoke I found it difficult to do so. But a funny thing happened.

His kindness and sweetness allowed me to talk about the fact I was an author at the Con and then the conversation led to graphic novels and the fact he had a series of them. Which led to him asking me if I would be interested in writing for them. I said yes, he said he knew a bunch of guys at Marvel looking for writers and he gave me his card and he told me to shoot him an email.

The icing on the cake I got my picture taken with him. Of course, I know nothing is a fate accompli in situations like this. That this is simply an opportunity presenting itself. It's a path I'll wander down and see where it leads but when someone breathes the words graphic novels and Marvel in the same breath, it kind of makes you stand up and take attention.

That notwithstanding, Grant Wilson, was kind to me. Generous with his time and stood a long time just speaking with me and my screenwriting partner Missy Goodman and another woman whom gotten lost, named Dana. I want to say Grant's friend was named Mike, they were all awesome. And if this is any indication as to what this Fandom Fest holds in store for me it means good things are ahead for sure.

Sometimes things seem so dark, Wednesday I was featured on the front page of my local newspaper and I still couldn't get my mother to and father to say they'd come to the awards ceremony. But I guess sometimes you take the bad with the good, and that you have to find validation elsewhere. Knowing you've worked hard has to be the reward and even though you want Mom and Dad to love you for the effort you put forth sometimes you just have to know sometimes they're so busy taking care of everyone else it can't matter whether they clap for you or not.

But here's the facts, they offered a celebratory dinner should I win the screenwriting competition, Fingers crossed.

Sincerely,
Amy McCorkle

Dear Daniel,

Stan Lee Ate My Food,
Well, I don't know if he helped himself to it, but certainly everyone else did. Let me explain. For the most part Fandom Fest was a success for me. My table had great placement by the celebrities. I sold a total of 33 books. 15 of Gladiator Chronicles, 6 of Gemini's War, and 12 of

Bounty Hunter. I met Grant Wilson, who knew how to make it not weird for a geek to talk to him. We ended up talking writing and graphic novels and he gave me his card and he told me to shoot him an email after Fandom Fest. Which I've done. I also gave him complimentary copies of Bounty Hunter and Gemini's War.

I met and had my picture taken with Brian O' Halloran, Dante of Clerks fame. I had my picture taken with Jim Cornette, a local wrestling legend. All three of them gracious and kind and just so happy to make a fan happy. And then I met Adrian Paul. I don't think he knew what to make of me, I handed him my books and I think he thought I was a fangirl giving him fan art. But I wasn't. Those books were written and hard won into publication. One was a bestseller and the other an award winner. I'm not sure he liked being there. Which is understandable, the organization of Fandom Fest left much to be desired. Which brings me to my book launch party.

Directly before me was the Stan Lee Meet and Greet. Stan is a legend and far be it from me to besmirch the man. But I paid for a room party and got pushed from an 8 o'clock start time to 9:30PM. The food meant for my party had been eaten by the people in the Stan Lee Meet and Greet. We finally get in, the band sets up and rocks the house for three songs before the hotel threatens to cut the power to the room. Cops close the doors to the crowds coming in and the ones there step out. Leaving me with a busted up book launch.

That being said, my guest authors were wonderful, Sb Knight, and Pamela Turner helped me put on one heck of a Q&A panel and I managed to sell two copies of Gemini's War to an almost empty crowd. Thanks to Dave I had a beautiful cake that was also delicious.

And the icing on the cake? The awards ceremony was cancelled due to death and illness by the organizers of it, the winners will be notified over the next several days. I still have my fingers crossed and oh, by all the walking from the pedway to the convention hall I lost six pounds.

So I wait to hear on this festival, the Claymore, and Austin and Sundance. And from Grant Wilson. I also found a PR person to take my brand to the next level. Hopefully you'll be hearing from me soon professionally, and not just from this blog.

Sincerely,
Amy McCorkle

Dear Daniel,

Sometimes you wonder if your career will ever take the jump that people dream of it making. Well, I feel like I'm doing my best to make that happen. Last night I signed the paperwork that made Alicia Justice of Jitterbug PR my first block in the business side of my writing career. I met her at Fandom Fest and she was ebullient and full of energy and seemed excited at the prospect of working with me.

She plans on adding publicist and literary agent to her name so I look forward to perhaps growing my career with her as time goes by. Still no word on the film festival. Although I feel like I'm good enough to win I wonder if me being vocal about my dissatisfaction with my launch party and how it went. But like I said, I had some really cool shit come out of Fandom Fest.

I'm already planning for next year. Mysticon is on the horizon and I'd like to launch my Bella Morte series there. Right down to wearing a costume, ala Comic Con as a character from the book. I just wish I had some guy friends to dress up as the male characters Shane and Sam. Shane is the long lost parent who mentors Bella in book 1. And Sam is her friend turned romantic interest as the series progresses.

I have to admit, Fandom was such clusterfuck in some regards that I'm glad hell didn't freeze over, you would've had no place to hide and I would've been embarrassed at the way my launch turned out for someone I admired so much to see firsthand.

But here's the thing, I'm working on a novel I hope to take to the Big 5 in New York should they still be standing via an agent. And I need to send the query letters out that I have for my screenplays with Missy. All signs are telling me it's time to take the next step up. And I have to admit, I'm a little scared to do so.

I have to wonder was it like this for you when your career was budding and you had to start getting people to do certain things for you as opposed to doing everything yourself? I recently landed on the front of the local newspaper because I arranged it. The interview went fantastic and it was a wonderful experience. I know one day I won't want that attention. But it's one of those things that I want people to know about my books, and let's face it, authors are not afforded the same attention by the media that rock stars and actors and movie people are. And I'll be honest, part of me is grateful for that.

The anonymity it affords me is wonderful. I'm allowed to kind of develop at my own rate and the success, hard won, is sweet. Perhaps one day we will get the opportunity to work together. Although I'll be honest, there's a part of me that fears true social interaction. And you're just a person I know but your work has been influential on my career. And I can't really overstate that enough.

I have a question, one I don't really expect an answer too, but it's more rhetorical than anything else. What do you do when someone you know, or even a fan takes a dangerous turn and you start to wonder about their sanity and your safety?

Sincerely,
Amy McCorkle

Dear Daniel,

Truly good things are coming my way. I kind of wish I would have signed up for Context instead of Night Risers (different little Cons that aren't even on your radar) but Night Risers is closer and perhaps great things will happen there.

I decided not to go to Killer Nashville. I'm not really prepared. Most of my books are already with publishers and the one I am working on isn't anywhere near finished. I don't particularly care for coming off as half baked when I've worked so hard to build my brand and have recently taken steps to build my Amy McCorkle name as Kate Lynd seems to be establishing itself quite well. Having had two Amazon bestsellers under that moniker that sold like freaking hotcakes at Fandom I think it's clear which name needs work.

So I have a publicist now. Which is really weird. I'm not used to it. Of course, I don't sit back and let her do all the work I come up with ideas. Like a party celebrating the release of Bella Morte where I dress up. Of course I have no idea where to buy costuming gear. Or where to buy decorations for the room.

I wish I knew how to direct sci-fi action films as that seems to be where my passion lay. Of course, with Missy I write other more…indie flavored films that favor the Sundance scene. Mysticon makes me want to adapt my Bounty Hunter screenplay to the big screen from the screenplay we wrote.

Missy is much more romantic drama. Of course, I love romantic dramas too. But I love sci-fi action romances as well. The books I'm writing now are three entirely different tales. One is *Avenging Gemini*, the final installment of the *Gemini Rising* Trilogy for Blackwyrm. The other one is Bella Morte: Shattered, book 2 in the 8 book series for the new press I mentioned, and the third is a personal challenge, it's currently titled Big Blue Nation, but I want to hit 79K. The furthest I've ever gotten is 60K.

Of course I have three screenplays I need to pitch. One is the finalist which I am *still* waiting for news on and the other two I'm simply waiting on Austin and Sundance. Those are much more likely not to do anything, but one can hope, right? I know in my gut, however, they are great scripts and the best work Missy and I have ever done. But it's a matter of the right people reading it at the right time.

August is Sundance announcement to see if we advance to the second round. Honestly, I think Austin is the better bet for us. But we won't know until we know.

However, Claymore was a bust for me. But that doesn't really matter, that book now has a publisher and that's what really matters, right?

Well, I hope each time I come here I have some great news to share. I met some cool people at Fandom Fest like Joe and Sarah at the Kevin Smith and Jason Mewes event that kicked off the whole thing.

Now on to Night Risers. I plan on getting a hotel. Driving back and forth will be a real pain in the ass. Oh well, as it is I hope to sell lots of books. But you never now, it's a smaller Con, and the accent is on horror and I don't know if I'll be able to move Gemini's War. But here's to hoping for the best.

Sincerely,
Amy McCorkle

Dear Daniel,

You ever have one of those wholly craptastic moments where you think this is it? I really did it. I climbed, I fought and they're really giving me a reward for it? Well the winners of the

Fright Night Film Festival were announced really late last night. And maybe it's a little late. And maybe nobody is watching, but we did it! Me and Missy really did it! https://www.facebook.com/pages/Fright-Night-Film-Fest/63772024471 Bounty Hunter, the book I was inspired to write after seeing Cowboys & Aliens, which inspired me to call on Missy to help adapt it to screenplay won Best Sci-Fi Screenplay!

I know the reality is you're not watching this or reading this, but I owe so much of this particular project to you Daniel. Your talent allows me to project my imagination onto what I need the character to do. If you were a limited actor I couldn't do half the writing that I do. I tend to 'cast my work. There are other actors but I do have preference for your style of acting so it's easy to cast you.

Don't get me wrong. What I do isn't fan fiction by any stretch of the imagination. What I do is hard work. I like casting Eva Green and Kate Winslet in the female leads as much as I like casting the men. Cate Blanchett is another favorite. Jennifer Lawrence. Constance Towers. Maurice Benard.

I digress. I WON! And it's because Cowboys & Aliens reignited my passion with all things sci-fi, dystopian, and western. So I really have you and a splendid cast, crew, director, writers, and producer to thank for that.

I cried last night. I know, it's just a competition. Failure isn't fatal and success isn't permanent. But when you work hard and see it pay off it's one of those things that makes you want to keep going.

It'sfuel for when you're feeling down and thinking the whole world is against you. When you think everything's a clusterfuck…and it makes you turn and see things aren't all bad. That someone, professionals, people who work in the same arena as you do respect your work and it lets you know that even though you live in a nowhere town that somewhere thinks highly of your work and you're not working in a vacuum.

I need to submit my screenplays to agents and production companies, I have the credits now, but I'm waiting to hear from Austin and Sundance. I'm sure that will impress people more, but I've never won a competition and it feels good to get one under my belt.

You know, I can almost forgive Fandom Fest and Stan Lee for eating my food. And I was on the cover of my local newspaper the Wednesday before we left for Fandom. It just feels like everything is going my way.

Not that I'm assuming that it always will. And if you've read this blog at all you know that isn't the case. But right now it is. My dad even made me a celebratory fried egg and cheese sandwich.

He's a little crazy right now, he has a big trial coming up. So it's basically duck and cover but he was sweet enough to indulge me this morning.

I wonder if I'll ever meet all my heroes. But until then I'm content to come to this blog and 'write' letters to 'you'. I'm sure you're not reading it but I can't help it, you have no idea how your work and your work ethic has shone the light on at times what has been a very dark path for me. Here's a picture of my stepdad that I call dad. Truth be told as hard as he and my mother have made it from time to time I love them very much, and they have helped make me the person I am today.

Sincerely,
Amy McCorkle

I'm one of Amy's publishers for several books contracted with us and would like to conclude Amy's Letters to Daniel by saying the following:

I've witnessed Amy grow and struggle through her writing career because of who she is: a hard-working writer who is a perfectionist, one who has to overcome daily struggles within herself and overcome the desire to simply walk away when the world seems to caving in on her.

These letters were a way for her to continue fighting these battles, and also to show others who may be inflicted with bi-polar, that anything and everything is possible.

I am truly proud of all that she has and will continue to achieve.

Lea Schizas

Part II

Dear Daniel,

I went to the movies today. Shocker, right? I mean I write stories for a living. Novels, short stories, screenplays. I'm thinking about tackling an indie soap, or television series bible, or even a graphic novel. Right now I'm waiting to hear back from Random House-Alibi imprint to see if they want more than just a pitch query letter when it comes to CORNBREAD. I'm proud of the short novel. It's unlike anything I've ever written. I mean it has thriller like elements but it's more of a character study.

Anyway, back to the movie. Missy and I went to see Lee Daniels' 'The Butler'. Lee Daniels assembled a top notch cast. Each person playing their role to effortless excellence. It got a little long at the end. But for that it can be forgiven, and the impact of the father/son relationship wasn't lost on me, nor was the emotional moment that the father and son shared as Obama was elected president. I cried.

Rich performances by all. Forest Whitaker and Oprah especially moving as the struggling but loving couple who stick together even through human failings.

Fun fact: Lee Daniels gave us our first shot at being read by a production company. We sent an early draft of *You're the Reason* to his company in 2001. He came back to us to pass on the screenplay twice in the same year. The second time he called us and told us it wasn't exactly what he was looking for, but that Missy and I had talent and that we should stick to it and hang in there.

Now we're waiting to hear back from Austin Film Festival. We could hear back as early as next week. We're hopeful to stay in the running for the Bronze Typewriter. As you never know what could come of such a career coup.

That being said, the last couple of days have been hard. Emotionally that is. So depressed, then up, then the computer hard drive crashes, then hunting for Microsoft Office 2007, getting the computer to where it would accept it. Arguing with Missy because I want to eat out so badly. Then being depressed again.

My mood has been all over the place. And getting disconnected from the manuscript makes things harder than anything. But here I am plugging back in the best way I know how.

I am not a victim. I have overcome a great many things. I have worked hard. I have earned my success and hope there is more to come. I hope the same things for my friends and family who have supported me in this long journey. Even when it feels like I am all alone in this fight I have to remind myself that is not always the case.

Because even when I struggle, I have pets who love me unconditionally. Even when my loved ones who have me starve ;).

Sincerely,
Amy McCorkle

Dear Daniel,

Today was a bad day. It's one of those days where being human catches up to me and I have to realize, as far as I reach in my treatment sometimes it exceeds my grasp. And the fact is some days the depression can not be faked out. Can not be tricked into submission. And can not be left behind by some willful act of aggression on my mania's part. People are going to be unhelpful, not by any act of malice, but by being consumed by their own exhaustion or previous commitments and I'm going to be left alone with thoughts of why won't they help me. I ask for it from strangers and friends and most times they go out of their way to give it. But tonight I get nothing from those I live with.

I put on dinner. Instead of making burgers for myself and Missy I gave them the meat to put in the spaghetti sauce. I could dwell on all the bullshit they do and stay in the name of pushing my career forward or I could move out and make it infinitely more difficult.

In some ways I have it very good. I live rent free in nice home, well, in a room with my cat, with pictures of inspiration all around me. Including a Skyfall official poster with you as Bond standing next to the Astin Martin. Effective gun porn. I have a vision board of all that I hope to achieve one day. An autographed photo of Adrian Paul, the Highlander. An official film poster for Going Under, short movie that Missy and I co-wrote, co-directed, and co-produced.

My crutch during times of emotional pain, Captain Oreo and his co-hort Private Doritos are also at the ready should I choose to numb myself up.

I wish I could articulate how lonely and isolated this house makes me feel sometimes. I have to force myself to think logically in the middle of emotional turmoil, the kind that threatens to suck me under from time to time.

Even in the face of such good fortune bipolar disorder doesn't discriminate. These last two and a half years have been an exhilarating ride. From nobody in the middle of nowhere to small press sensation (in my own mind of course lol) and film festival winner with a small cadre of friends, the kind that God sends when you're in need of the best kind. Special shout outs to Pamela Turner and Missy Goodman.

Each have their place in my heart. Each feed my imagination. Each do their part to keep me sane. And as I watch Mother I am struck by your talent and just how far you're willing to go for your work. Again Daniel you inspire me, well your work does, to help me come out of the deepest and darkest of funks and depressions. Makes me feel safe when indeed there is every reason to fear what is around me, and gives me hope as I wait to hear from the Austin Film Festival and pray somehow to make it at least to the semi-finalist round so that we can actually afford to go.

Sincerely,
Amy McCorkle

Dear Daniel,

I know it's been a while since I checked in. I've been hiding from the world. I got some bad news. Not life ending or life altering just news I would have rather not received. You're the Reason and City of the Damned didn't make it to the semi-finalist round of any category of Austin.

I mean, the odds weren't in our favor. There were over 8600 entries. We have a better shot at finding an agent through a cold query or just attending a film festival. But here's the harsh reality. Fandom Fest was when Missy could get off. She blew her entire vacation time on it and really it kind of paid off. All those books sold, meeting Grant Wilson, meeting Adrian Paul, meeting Brian O'Halloran. Making a possible contact in Grant. Selling 34 books. Winning the screenplay competition. It was incredible. Success is not final and failure is not fatal.

It took me a little while to recover from the rejection of the contest. The real let down is in not being able to attend Austin in and of itself. The knowledge we have now in how to work a festival would serve us much better. But perhaps that isn't our path to take.

As part of forcing myself out of this depressive funk I submitted two query letters, one for each of the screenplays Missy and I penned to a literary agent. And I submitted CORNBREAD to Random House Alibi, Blackwyrm, and MuseItUp so when I hear back I know I'll be okay. I'm not really thinking about those things at the moment I'm juggling several projects all of which are interesting enough to me I'm not worried about contracts.

Still, I really wanted to attend a film festival. But the reality is I'm attending Context, a literary con at the end of this month and everything I have is put towards that. A table, a reading, I'll be moderating a book to movie panel, and somehow I managed to land on a make 'em laugh panel. And while I can produce funny moments, or have my characters sat funny things a comedic writer I am not. I don't have that timing that some people are innately born with.

I'm a serious writer and I write about dramatic or sometimes melodramatic things. Not to say that's somehow better or superior to comedic writing. As a matter of fact I think comedic writing is harder. And I'm not even particularly good at it.

But in order to recover I'll be doing basic signings. One at A Reader's Corner, one at Bullitt County's Author Fair, and one at Half-Price Booksellers. And maybe even Joseph-Beth.

Next month I'm off. I need a mattress so that I can get more than four hours of sleep. I have to pay my publicist. But next month I'll be purchasing books and going on a shopping spree at NaNoWriMo Store. They are single handedly responsible for my slavish discipline and why I write so much every day. Okay, so maybe mine and Missy's friendship and my decided lack of a social life has something to do with it too.

But in order to recover I watch Casino Royale, Cowboys & Aliens, and Skyfall. These movies, among others make me feel better and give the sense that if I work harder enough, don't give up, and just believe bigger things will happen for me and Missy.

I want to thank you for that. I recently wrote a graphic novel and a play based upon my bestselling Bounty Hunter. I don't see much coming of them but imagining you in the lead of the play or the screenplay makes me dream big. And maybe one day I'll be fortunate enough to work with one of my heroes.

Sincerely,
Amy McCorkle

Dear Daniel,

I was listening to a favorite song of mine. The Story by Brandi Carlile. I feel like this is my story. I know this is going to sound incredibly goofy and corny and lame but I think of how you handle yourself professionally with your work ethic and those you care about in such a fierce way. And in the end I think about your body of work and how these things have inspired me in my own battles and struggles.

I still reside in a room at my parents to enable myself to travel to film festivals and conventions to sell my books and in hopes of finding a literary agent for my screenplays and teleplays. The thing about the song The Story she sings of the sun shining on her in one way but of how the world knows nothing of the deep pain she really is experiencing with the absence of telling them her tale of how she got where she is.

There's a line in the song that goes 'even when I was flat broke, you made me feel like a million bucks', and truly that is what your work makes me feel like when everything is falling apart around me. When those around me don't respect how hard it is just to get where I've gotten and threaten to throw me out at eleven o'clock at night because we've been at odds over me being sick and them catering to siblings who haven't the first clue about hard work of sacrifice for something so outrageous in its imaginings.

Don't get me wrong, my sisters are great mothers, but the manipulate people to get what they want instead of just asking for it straight out. My life is pretty separate from theirs but when I say I landed a publication contract (I landed my 32nd one recently for the upmarket thriller CORNBREAD, a story about a former bootlegger and war vet who gets drawn back into the nasty business of it all in the name of protecting a young woman).

I just finished scripting my first television pilot for the Nashville Screenplay Competition and extending Bounty Hunter for it. And now I'm working on a screenplay called Cold Dark

Morning for the competition. I'll enter City of the Damned too and Missy is working on another script. Then there's NaNoWriMo to consider in November.

See, as long as I'm writing I feel whole. The same way watching great films or cheesy ones or reading a great book. Home life swings hot and cold. My mom and dad don't want me around. I'm sure it has more to do with them wanting some privacy and private time just for the two of them. But it doesn't make the sting of rejection any easier to take.

The Story is a love song. And when I say it makes me think of you, I don't mean it in the crazy stalkerish way. I mean it creatively. You have the kind of presence and acting chops that make it easy to imagine you in the different roles(characters) I create. So, I love your work, and blessed through your talent to be able to imagine my best work.

And when life gets to be too hard emotionally all I have to do is pop in your work, usually Casino Royale when I'm writing thrillers, Cowboys & Aliens when I'm writing scifi or dystopian. And none of it is YA. No love triangles. And no vampires that sparkle (although I respect Stephanie Meyers for coming up with her own story and not ripping off someone's else's work).

So as the song goes, 'these stories don't mean anything when you've got no one to share them with'. So I share my story and my work with you in hopes that maybe one day you will see them. Or someone else will see my struggles and triumphs and be inspired to write their stories down. Or aspire to their greatest dreams even when no one else thinks their possible. Daniel, you're work makes me believe if I just work hard enough, if I just hone my craft enough, and get my name out there enough anything is possible.

I conquered bipolar disorder and abuse, surely I can set myself free from poverty. As Duane 'the Rock' Johnson once said, I may be broke, but I won't be broke forever. And you and your work and your view on how to handle your career, light the way whenever things seem their darkest for me.

Sincerely,
Amy McCorkle

Dear Daniel,

I'm proud to say my memoir has garnered bestseller status. It hit #2 on the Amazon Bestseller List and that makes three bestsellers in just under three years. To say I've been fortunate in my profession in the last two and a half-three years is an understatement.

Of course over the last few weeks I've been struggling with the ups and downs of my mood fluctuating. I see where the stress of living with other adults who are not my friends or significant others makes it difficult to cope when my mood does go off track.

They take it personally and have no way in which to gage it against normalcy since they're broken too and when I'm depressed or off the tracks they do things they don't realize just how much damage they do when they yell at me.

Of course I don't think at 38 I should be scared of my family but the reality of the situation is I'm terrified of them. Not that my mother is going to punch me with her fists or my dad (John NOT Jerry) is going to truly abandon me. But they sold me on the idea that I would have use of the car and I wouldn't be alone as much.

Which has all pretty much born out to be a lie. My mother takes care of my baby sister's kids and is so afraid she's going to boomerang back into this house she'll do anything to keep her and her boyfriend together. I.E. the man who doesn't want my sister to leave him but refuses to put a ring on it.

I know, I know, I shouldn't be bitter, I shouldn't judge. It's just that it gets lonely sitting in the house by my lonesome. But as I write I know I'm writing my way out of what can be my own personal hell.

Whether it's those around me who are unwittingly inflicting it upon me or my own mercurial nature where I can be as high as kite and irritable or depressed and blocked as a writer which in turn makes me irritable I know I've been through a lot.

Which makes watching your movies such a pleasure. Some I would like to view for the first time. I'm going to send your management team a copy of Letters to Daniel in hopes they get a grasp of what this blog is all about.

Sometimes I think I wander off topic. But then, what are blogs for. These last few weeks have been productive writing wise. I wrote a treatment and character bios for a television pilot, a drama. I wrote the pilot. I added ten pages to an award winning screenplay, Bounty Hunter. And I've started the adaptation of Gemini's War to screenplay and am prepping for NaNoWriMo

(National Novel Writing Month) in November with a piece called Tragedy Square.

But I've struggled with my mood. One minute I'm fine and the next day I'm sleeping all day long. The weather has been known to affect all of this.

I think it's odd that at this time last year I was writing You Know My Name, which eventually had its title changed to Gemini's War. After NaNo I think I'll take Avenging Gemini, the conclusion of the trilogy. Now I'm writing the film so that I can enter it in the Nashville Film Festival Screenwriting Competition.

I plan on entering 5 screenplays total into the competition and also into the Indie Gathering in Hudson next year. Wish me luck,

Sincerely,
Amy McCorkle

Dear Daniel,

Sometimes even adults get too big for their britches. Now I say this with the caveat that my mother is one of the world's worst customers. I say this because I've been in more than one place with her and seen her pull some serious attitude on some poor hapless worker just trying to get by and doesn't deserve the bullshit she's about to dump on. I think identify with them because my mother has dumped on *me* like that for no apparent reason and I think no one deserves that kind of abuse from anyone.

Well today got off to a rocky start. I had breakfast. A good healthy one. Multigrain Cheerios and 1% milk. Measured of course. I tried to write this post before leaving but I had no energy or focus to, then parents mention they're going to get their hair cut. I ask if I can go along.

Listen, I know a 38 year old grown ass woman riding around with her parents seems childish at best but I needed to get out of the house. And since all my money goes to my career and building it I have no car. (I have never owned a car) But I got static, they assumed I wanted them to pay for my hair cut, which couldn't have been further from the truth. I just didn't want to be alone, although, after what happened at lunch I questioned myself as to why I wanted to be with them in the first place.

I bartered my three books in print for a cut and style. I love talking to Keith, although as long as we stay off the topic of politics we're fine. He's like one of my biggest fans so it was awesome to catch up with him while he snipped and cut away.

So far, so good, right?

Then dad asks do you want lunch now or do you want to wait? Well, my seven year nephew said now and since my parents let the grandchildren make the decisions we were off to Wendy's. Which is where everything turned sour.

We go in and stand in line forever. It's lunchtime so that's to be expected, but given it's right off the interstate people stop there too. We order. My mother wants a skinny vanilla latte. It's on the menu on the wall, but it had been taken off the menu where they make drinks, sandwiches, whatever so they charged my mother for the latte and give her a small regular coffee. Did I mention she ordered a medium?

Since my mother can be a real bitch when it comes to getting things right when they charged her for the latte and gave her the coffee you can imagine the eruption. My dad, who counts his calories religiously was ready to *eat.*

So, like in the film Gravity the incorrect order created a catastrophic like chain of events which resulted in a yelling match, first between my mother and father and then between my father and the rude cashier behind the counter.

The cashier was clearly in the wrong, *but* having run into that problem before my mother would have been better off *just not ordering the damn drink.*

I will admit, I'm a high maintenance ordering kind of gal, but only at sit down restaurants. And as long as my food is hot and my drink stays full I'm pretty easy to please. I admit I've had my moments, where I've been tired or hungry and the service hasn't been bad it's just not been all that great and I had a shameful moment or too. But nothing on the level of today. Of course my Aunt Sue brings shaming the server to a whole 'nother level.

Sincerely,

Amy McCorkle

Dear Daniel,

If there was an immediate escape hatch to this house I would access it and use it at this very instant. I know my ship will come in, but waiting for it is painful, hurtful, and sometimes I feel like I'm drowning in the sea of my mother's judgment, her need to control, and her shocking lack of empathy at times.

No, Amy, you're eating well, you exercised? Well, you didn't do it right. Can you afford those calories? Did you walk far enough? Is your corner clean enough? No, Amy, no gratitude for you eating your own dinner and cleaning up after yourself.

I know I'm an adult and reinforcement for this shit isn't really needed but complaining about your life to me when you've kind of made that bed for yourself does little to make me feel bad for you.

Yes, I know your sister came closer to death than any of us are comfortable with. It shook me to the core too. Only I got the message. The road you're on leads to the same place as Debbie's. Heart attack, diabetes, insulin, poor kidney function, flirtation with death. I don't want that. I've started on the path back several times since our initial heart to heart over this, Daniel. Yet I've never been more determined to stay the course.

I don't want the health complications before 40. As for that I already suffer from acid reflux. I'm 38, I weigh 299lbs. I may not have the health problems but I'm certainly at risk for stuff that will kill me sooner rather than later.

As for my mother, she's at risk too. Maybe more so now than at any other time in her life, but as much as she wants to lecture me and Debbie she is in as much denial telling me why she can't do anything about her weight just yet. And why she's not as bad off as me or her sister.

You can't make people stop doing something they are getting a payoff from. It took my aunt almost dying to get the message, you're on a dangerous path. Your dreams you so aspire to? If you don't change your ways that television you want so much to create and write for? Will never happen. Those trophies you covet so much from the Emmys, the Golden Globes, and the Oscars? You will never have a chance to dress for them, get an invitation from them, be nominated by them.

And lastly, those heroes you want to thank in person, you'll be six feet under and they'll never know just how much of an impact they made on your life.

So here I am, at day four, hoping my family does not sabotage me in my attempts to take control of the one part of my life that seems to have eluded me. My food addiction. Because when I do finally take that stage I want to be Cinderella at the ball with her significant other on her arm and writing partner at her side, triumphing over every bad thing that has ever happened to me in my life and be able to smile and feel joy instead of the pain that sometimes suffocates me in my present day life.

Sincerely,
Amy McCorkle

Dear Daniel,

Today is a good day. A little static from the mom, but other than that I have to say that I feel good. I've been eating better, exercising, strict about my medicine, and been doing what I can to advance my career.

Yesterday was hard. And since mom had stayed home today because of my aunt's major health scare (she's a diabetic, and she went into renal failure after major heart surgery and almost died) now she's heading home. At my weight and age I knew where my 301lb body was taking me. And it terrified me. So I'm back on the horse and I've lost 4lbs in the last week. So today is a good day.

My dream is to one day to be able share my life with someone who understands and gets me on a very basic level. Someone who supports me in action as well as word. Someone who loves me and can understand why some days might not always be the best for me and loves me anyway.

And to be 129lbs in a gorgeous gown on an awards show stage saying thank you to everyone whoever lifted me up to the sky whenever I fell to the ground unable to go on.

Today is one of those days I can hold myself help. Today is one of those days I can write and I feel the words as if they won't stop. Today, at this moment I don't need to be lifted up.

But there are days, like yesterday where I needed lifting every step of the way. While family provides me with a roof and supplemental grocery money there is little else they do. I love them for this. There are few families in this world who would let their 38 year old daughter pursue her passion without a timeline hoping for the big break.

Recently I wrote a television series treatment based on a series of books I've been contracted to write for a relatively new press. Hekate Press. I'm its interim marketing director and I would definitely say its owner/publisher Delilah K Stephans has lifted me up professionally and been a sounding board personally. I pitched the idea and she commissioned it.

Here is the television series (as registered with the WGAw).

BELLA MORTE is in the vein of those great epic gladiatorial films such as *GLADIATOR* and the successful television series *REVOLUTION* and *GAME OF THRONES* set in the not so distant future after political unrest and a second civil war.

Like those films and televisions series BELLA MORTE is an epic tale about shifting political and magical alliances and allegiances where family and old loyalties conflict with the demands of realities the heroes and heroines are faced with in the now.

BELLA MORTE is about a young woman hell bent on revenge, but a prophecy about her keeps getting in her way.

It is about heroism, integrity, and self-sacrifice in the face of temptation and evil.

BELLA MORTE is about a young woman, JUSTICE, a member of an ancient group of mystics referred to as the Order. Twelve years ago was forced to watch the brutal execution of her mother and father. Enslaved and brutalized from that time on she has been sold from owner to owner. Each time they fail to 'break her' they sell her off again. She lands at the plantation of Cyrus and STEPHANIE WILSON. During an especially violent encounter Justice fights back and murders Cryus, she manages to escape and runs to the point of exhaustion.

The queen, ELEANOR OF KE'LAN represents the worst of the Dark Forces. She is the most powerful magic wielder, she is evil in its purest form. When she is alerted to JUSTICE'S escape she dispatches her loyal savage mercenary, KRAVITZ to find her and bring to her.

The only thing ELEANOR desires more than to crush humankind, is to have the love and loyalty of her favorite enslaved gladiator, DUNCAN XAVIER. She appeals to his basest of desires and the two do enjoy a sexual affair, but for him it goes no deeper. He loathes ELEANOR and himself more and more with each encounter. When she comes to him with an offer of freedom naturally he is suspicious. When orders him to kill the possible prophet and go free or face death with her, he is left conflicted. He was once a good man, but fighting to the death has left him without a true compass. WILLIAM SHEPHERD a fellow gladiator demands that he save the young woman. That if JUSTICE is who ELEANOR believes her to be JUSTICE has the ability save the nation from the dark forces that eat away from its former greatness every day.

KRAVITZ is a monster who takes what he wants and destroys the rest. He is the man responsible for JUSTICE'S lot in life, and when he finds her collapsed in the desert he brutalizes her once more before brings her in.

JUSTICE is then thrown into DUNCAN'S cell and at his feet. Close to death's door already, his decision is now. It is then and only then that WILLIAM reveals himself as a Conduit Warrior raised by a Crone who served the Order and that he has the power to heal her. DUNCAN relents and once she is healed she commands to the elements as he has only seen once before. His long missing and thought dead wife. They escape. Enraging ELEANOR OF KE'LAN and setting in motion a long constricted battle for JUSTICE, WILLIAM, and DUNCAN between the Dark Forces and the Order.

JUSTICE doesn't quite have the control or experience over her powers that the QUEEN does, and when they battle sometimes it appears the all is lost, but JUSTICE always finds a way, even at great mortal cost to save her, WILLIAM, and DUNCAN.

BELLA MORTE is about what JUSTICE wants, which is to bring death to House of the QUEEN and KRAVITZ and all who ever wronged her. Versus what she has to come to grips with is that more than she can possibly imagine rests upon her shoulders. And what that is isn't always quite as clear for her as it is as it is for those around her.

Action packed, and full of adventure and special effects, each episode of BELLA MORTE will contain the continuing arc JUSTICE'S struggle to do what is prophesized for the good of the former United States of America versus answering her emotional need to quench her thirst vengeance. Layers of story of the supporting characters story will carry the weight of the self contained arc within the episode. i.e. the QUEEN has a son who may or may not be that of DUNCAN'S.

Other core characters of BELLA MORTE are:

QUEEN ELEANOR OF KE'LAN- Once a fierce and loyal member of the Order an unrequited love for Duncan Xavier led to her turning against the very Order that trained her to master her power over the supernatural. Beautiful, poisonous to everything she touches, she rules with an iron fist. Obsessed with Duncan Xavier she will do anything to destroy his first born daughter, the much prophesized about Bella Morte (Justice), and win his love. The only good that may remain in her is her love for her seven year old son Henri.

DUNCAN XAVIER- Justice's real father. He just wanted to be left alone to live his life with his family. The second civil war didn't allow for that. Strong, rugged, and resigned he's the gladiator referred to as the Legend. He is undefeated in twenty years of battle. The queen is his release. The reason his wife, her sister, is dead. He wants to mend the rift between he and his daughter and teach her to battle with thought and skill and not just on raw instinct. He wants her to reject the prophecy and embrace a peaceful life. But when push comes to shove and they go into battle he is at her side, sometimes even if she doesn't want him there.

WILLIAM SHEPHERD- a conduit warrior schooled by his mother, a crone who served the Order. Upon finding his mother murdered he learned that his brother and sister were complicit in her death. Beaten savagely by his brother he is sold into slavery. He escapes and finds love on to have it ripped away by Kravitz and a queen serving the vision of the dark forces. Enslaved as a gladiator he comes to be known as the Mad Hatter for his 'insane' fighting style. When Justice comes into his life he must decide, hold out hope for his wife, or do as he's been raised, protect Bella Morte and teach her mastery over her supernatural gifts and teach her to embrace her destiny.

KRAVITZ- a violent savage warrior engaged in a lustful affair with the Queen. Drunk on his power and lust he enacts a brutal form of dark force justice. Raping and pillaging at will and doing whatever the queen orders. The only soft spot in his heart is for a mystery woman being 'turned' by the dark forces will. He will do anything to protect her, even from the queen, even at great risk to his own life. He is the one Justice seeks to make suffer the most as he has destroyed her life at every turn.

NERO- the head of the dark forces council. He seeks to control all women, even the queen, but finds out that perhaps he has bitten off more than he can chew.

CAREEN XAVIER- a powerful member the Order, Eleanor's sister, Duncan's missing and believed dead wife. She may or may not be alive.

LUCINDA SHEPHERD- William's missing wife he cannot seem to give up on. May or may not be alive. May or may not be serving the dark forces.

THE ORDER- an ancient body of female mystics who have risen up in the darkness of the second civil war to save the former United States. They prophesized of an supernatural assassin whose beauty is rivaled by no one. Referred to as Bella Morte, it is believed Justice Xavier is Bella Morte.

THE DARK FORCES- evil supernatural entity embodied by men who seek to wipe humankind from the world over and rule over an enslaved race. They fear the Prophecy more than anything, but want to see if the prophet can be turned to serve them.

As BELLA MORTE unfolds we will learn that the path for Justice is not always clear, and those she thinks she can trust sometimes let her down at the worst of moments. But it will be in these moments that she finds her true strength, her mettle, and what she is made of. Most of all Justice will be forced to learn how to forgive those who truly love her. And by the end of the series true love will have found our heroine, evil will have been vanquished, and a sense of family, which at the beginning had been in tatters, will be formed and in place, although loss will be faced, her family will be stronger than ever.

BELLA MORTE

Whoever is reading my blog if you like the treatment and wish to read the pilot, please contact me through my contact form or at amyleigh07@live.com. I hope you like it.

Sincerely,
Amy McCorkle

Dear Daniel,

I have the best kind of friends. They're all batcrap crazy, but still they're better than the dysfunctional, batcrap family that I have. Allow me to explain.

Last night I had dinner with my mom and dad. Recently, my sister Sara lost her job, due to a 'personality conflict'. My youngest sister is a total redneck. Not in any negative sense of the word. She's loyal even when perhaps the person she's loyal to doesn't deserve it. But at the same time she's a manipulative person who will go out of her way to get what she wants.

So as I was saying, I was at Bob Evans for dinner. Mom gets the call on the way home. Yes mom, I know I have a truck and a boyfriend who could get off his ass and go get and do the running that the family needs to do, but instead I'll ask you to go to Wal-Mart and pay for everything.

Listen, I've seen pictures of you smoking. But I'm not a smoker. And there's no way in hell I'm paying for someone else's habit. Mom justified buying all this stuff for them and keeping us out until 8:30 at night while Sara and her family sat snug in their apartment.

I used to eat out with my mom and dad A LOT. And they footed the bill. I try not to do it as much because they've made it clear on more than one occasion they don't want to. Which is fine. But they don't do it nearly as often as they used to, yet I get the same lecture every time I go with them. Order off the cheap end of the menu. Get water to drink. They treat me like a child yet they bend over backwards for Sara and her family and Brandy and her son.

I suppose that's their prerogative, and given I live in their home so that I can pursue my passion I should count my blessings and let it be at that.

But admittedly it's difficult. I'm eating better and exercising so the negative emotions, and the old wounds reopen much easier now that I'm not covering them up.

At the table, even in the face of me ordering the cheapest dinner, they tell me I'm hard to live with. They tell me I'm the most sensitive to my own feelings. And all be call me their most demanding child.

What do I actually ask of them? Something they want desperately to give to other people. Their time. They complain when I work and want to talk when I've completed a real full day. When I have news, like industry people giving me invaluable feedback on my work or said industry people possibly showing said work to those I couldn't possibly reach from where I am currently they give me the equivalent of an emotional shrug.

Meanwhile my friends know that for the kind of work I do these things I do are huge and have the potential to get me out of a place where the appreciation is little and the ignorance of what I do is vast.

So why do I crave their validation when it's obvious they want no part of this life? And will likely only stand up and cheer when the actual ship comes in. My friends appreciate and love me for who I am and what I do. My family's eyes simply glaze over when I talk about what my life is without them.

I love my family, but my friends have been the collective on which I depend both personally and professionally. Pam and Missy, they are without a doubt batcrap crazy, but then so am I. I understand their crazy and for the most part they understand mine. And for that reason I'll be able to switch gears and finish my NaNoWriMo word count.

Sincerely,
Amy McCorkle

Dear Daniel,

I know I often write of the hardships I'm facing. And though I'm well aware of people having it worse than me I want to share with you some of the really cool stuff that is happening. And there really is some cool stuff going on. Nothing that screams 'you've made it', but stuff that inspires me to keep going.

Let's start with the simple stuff. I've been contracted by Hekate Press to pen an 8 book series called Bella Morte. I've already talked about this on my blog here, but it bears repeating. I sold it on a simple pitch. The idea came out of a reading I had done for me by a gifted woman by the name of Bertena Varney. She said a lot of things but only one that I ran with, that it was a character that was tough and had been through a lot and knew how to fight. She said it would be a 4-8 book tale. And that I would be 'known' for it.

Justice Xavier is the character that was born out of those suggestions and the series took shape from that point on. I wrote a fast 25K draft that although good, was limited in that it was told from the first person. I decided to do a massive overhaul and double the length for my NaNoWriMo project. I pitched the series to cover artist extraordinaire and new publisher/owner Delilah K Stephans. She liked the idea and took it on. She got the concept and when I told her my plans to overhaul and how I was going to overhaul it she liked the idea even more.

Now, you know, as in Hollywood relationships are key and Delilah was my cover artist with MuseItUp Publishing for almost three years before she decided to venture out on her own with this company. And when Hydra Publications went through a reorganization I asked for the rights to two of my series back and Delilah agreed to take them on at Hekate. So as Hekate opens its doors on November 15th for new submissions, I am proud to say I am the Interim Marketing Director. Another blessing.

In the process I decided I wanted to develop Bella Morte into a television series. So I wrote the pilot. Now I know I'm bragging and it's bad form, but the pilot totally kicks ass. The treatment, however, took a lot more work. So here is another place where I am blessed and lucky.

As I have mentioned previously I attended (and won at) Fandom Fest/Fright Night Film Festival this past July. While there I got to see some of my heroes (Kevin Smith, Adrian Paul) and meet some really cool people (Brian O'Halloran and Jim Cornette). While there I had the pleasure and good fortune of connecting with Grant Wilson of Ghost Hunters, we spoke about writing and ghost hunting and other some other things and he was impressed with me (I was squeeing on the inside) and he gave me his business card. We exchanged emails and when I asked about how to break into television he told me I needed to start with a treatment.

I had earlier in the year via another writer come into contact with Tom Sawyer, showrunner, Emmy winner and bestselling author of the Murder She Wrote series. I asked for some feedback on my treatment. And he gave me some blunt, but wonderful advice and was kind enough to send me some examples of television treatments he had done. My treatment improved a hundred fold.

Now I have a Facebook contact that I don't want to overwhelm with requests so I'll keep him anonymous, but suffice it to say he is a television and stage actor who was able to trouble shoot my treatment further. I have sent him the revisions and I await his further feedback.

I have also entered the Nashville Film Festival Screenwriting Competition in several categories, the Indie Gathering Competition and ScriptPipeline's First Look Competition with several screenplays and the pilot and treatment for Bella Morte.

Honestly, I don't know how this will all pan out, but I'm nothing if not hopeful where it comes to my writing career. I have faith and believe and I am always writing. If not a book then a screenplay.

NaNo is cooking right now and the fact I had the energy to do a blog this late at night says something about what the competition does to you. Blessed beyond measure in my career, I take the lumps in my personal life, as my daybed I sleep on is literally falling apart and I have no money to replace it. LOL. Such is the trade off I make. Hope all is well with you and yours,

Sincerely,
Amy McCorkle

Dear Daniel,

I want to share something with you and those who read this blog. The handful who've graced me with their readership know that my recent trajectory is nothing short of mind boggling. I've been writing since I was five. Been watching t.v. and going to the movies before then. One of my first memories is being in a let down hatchback of a Pinto. Yes. I said hatchback and Pinto. And my mom, dad, sister Brandy and I were at the drive-in. And yes, I realize I said drive-in. The movie we were seeing was The Empire Strikes Back. I can't remember if I made it through the whole movie since that was 78 and that would make 3 at the time. But the experience I remember distinctly.

The speaker you hung on the window. The warm night air. The way you had to walk *all the way back* to the concession stand. The stickiness of the floor. Honestly one shouldn't probably eat *anything* that came out of that place. Every now and again we had the money for it but ultimately we had large paper bags and this was before the advent of microwave popcorn. We popped our own popcorn. When I got older my aunt and uncle did this, brought a cooler of cokes and lawn chairs and we sat outside the car and watched the movies that way. It was a cool and special way to go to the movies.

Growing into adulthood I found I wanted to be a part of the magic. I wanted to write movies. But being in the middle of nowhere when it came film (I live in KY) and being part of a blue collar family I didn't know anything beyond NYU and USC and UCLA film school. And the competition for those scholarships it seemed was way out of my league and my parents didn't have the money to send me anywhere. I went on a partial scholarship to a theatre arts program school where the focus was on acting. My mental health problems were already raring their ugly little heads so I dropped out after the first year.

After a brush with cult called Amway and bouncing around to several nothing jobs, I began to write. Not particularly well. But I played in my sandbox alone, playing around with the kinds of stories I wanted to tell. No one told me what I was doing was right or wrong. I was pretty much allowed to develop on my own. Reading books, going to films of all kinds from Batman to Muriel's Wedding.

For the longest time I resisted moving out of my family's house, funny, right? I'd been on my own, living with a boyfriend and his problematic family. I loved him very much, but I couldn't handle being cut off from everything I'd ever known, and after 5 months in New Mexico I moved back to Kentucky.

My voice was allowed to develop freely. And when I met Missy she approached me about writing a romance novel together. I, in my arrogance and ignorance told her sure let's write a romance novel for the money. She loved the romance genre, and what I found was that love stories are hard to craft. Especially ones that demand happily ever afters where I had a penchant for killing off one or both of the lovebirds. Nicholas Sparks likes to blather and blither on that he writes love tragedy. The reality is he writes women's fiction. Where romances don't always end happily ever after. Honestly, I read how he treated a female write for even suggesting this and I think he was just being jerk.

That being said, my twenties were filled with learning the art of the pitch, which I hate tobrag but I'm really good at it. And co-writing scripts and shooting short films. Some of which I would never show the light of day. But here's the thing, my voice was developing over that time. And in my early thirties I exercised my novel writing muscle. I needed a break, and Lea Schizas of MuseItUp Publishing gave it to me for my romantic suspense short novel, Another Way to Die. (Yes, I know, I stole the title from Quantum of Solace's Bond Theme. Bad Amy.) And proceeded to go through the most grueling edit ever. I now have five books with them. Each better than the last. I was 35. It was 2011. I am now 38, and have books spread out across three other small presses.

Then last fall I got the itch. I wanted to write a screenplay again. Just to see if I'd gotten any better. I hadn't gone near a screenplay in 5 years. They say it's a young person's game, but at 38 Missy and I, women, no less, scored our first win ever with Bounty Hunter. This past spring Missy and I watched Kevin's Burn In Hell tour. She asked me if I wanted to start down that path again. Why not? What did we have to lose?

In the span of 4 months I penned two short novels and co-wrote two screenplays. Since as you may have noticed I penned a pilot and developed a treatment. Wrote another short novel and now I'm working furiously towards a 70K length novel. My first one that I can actually take to agents.

For what it's worth I know drive-in's are dying. That New York will look vastly different on the publishing landscape, but I already have found an agent to submit to quite by accident. But first to finish that book, Bella Morte.

Sincerely,
Amy McCorkle

Dear Daniel,

Here I am 25K+ from my goal on NaNoWriMo. For those who read this blog don't know, NaNoWriMo is National Novel Writing Month. And I'll be honest Daniel, you don't know me, and the reality is will never know me, by that's not what this blog has ever been about so I'm going to talk about my current state of mind and my mind's current state is this. It is *exhausted.*

Let me explain. NaNo is 50K in one month. However, I am attempting 70K overall. I've never done that before. Ever. The furthest I've gotten is 60K and that was after trying to get out of it, several times. It lead to my first advance, which I gave back because they wanted to strip my voice out of the manuscript.

Don't get me wrong they were nice people and it's a fabulous indie publishing house but it wasn't the kind of fit I was looking for. It meant turning down a 500 dollar advance. Which in this world was very hard to do.

But as I said it's a year later and I know 70K is within my grasp but I'm very, *very* tired. When I tell my parents I'm toast after a day's work they think I'm nuts. Point is after all the tweeting, FBing, and blogging one should be sick to death of even being on line, yet, it's part of the daily grind.

Now, I love writing. Penning tales is kind of my thing. I feel like something's wrong if I'm not writing. Like maybe I'm fidgety and my skin starts to jump. I'm restless and without direction. I wonder if it's like that for other artists, that is you're not creating you feel like perhaps something is just *off*.

Which brings me to the flipside of that, the exhaustion. My parents are tolerant of my pursuit of my creative endeavors. In my dad's eyes my mother is a saint. And to some degree she is. But no one is perfect. Especially her or me. Dad is pointed in his assessment of this. He says living at home bothers me more than it bothers them. Of course it does. I spend two thirds of my time in that room. Partially because it's conducive to writing and partially because it protects me from whatever particular mood they're in that day.

Back to #NaNo. I struggled in the beginning. I thought, how am I going to make it to 50K? And then I realized what was blocking me. I had never written an EPIC before. A book with varying viewpoints. Flashback fully realized. And characters, even the bad ones, could have humanizing qualities. Innocents turned bad due to circumstances beyond their control. Heroes who are inherently flawed making them more anti-hero than hero. And with only one true heroic character, the heroine, I suddenly realized somewhere between 5K-15K that this book could go the full 70K distance. Which truth be told was still a little too short for NY but it just might wiggle through if it was good enough.

What makes things so awesome is I have my own personal cheerleader in someone I will not mention because I don't know how they feel about me using their name. Of course there's a part of me that doesn't want me to share her. She simply too awesome.

Sincerely,
Amy McCorkle

Dear Daniel,

Started my day to the greatest song EVER. Skyfall by Adele. It lets me know that the need to write romantic thrillers is just as deep in my bones as Bella Morte is. I saw a photo from GWTDT that allowed me to think of you as a professor. And listening to Skyfall lets me know I can have the freedom to write whatever it is I please. I just need a great agent and good IP attorney to make sure I don't get screwed in the process.

Dear Daniel,

On dreary, icy cold days like today and the tired creakiness is just so bone deep all you want to do is sleep. For me the reasons are many that I sleep on days like today. My mood disorder is linked to the weather at times. I've been extraordinarily happy these last few days. When an actor or actress you admire says they desire to play a part in your work you're trying your damndest to the television screen it makes for a delightful day. They give you a name of someone they want you to send the treatment and pilot to makes for a joyous day. I had one of those days yesterday for BELLA MORTE. But if you want to read about it just follow the hyperlinked Bella Morte and see where (hopefully) I'm starting to get a buzz going for the work. Another actor, Jon Lindstrom, favorite a tweet of mine which said I thought he would make a perfect Kravitz. So huge strides. An agent discovering me? Not exactly. Still waiting to hear back from two others with the treatment and pilot.

No, what has me happy today is the fact I've lost 10 pounds! Down from 302 to 292! The steps, the fruit, the vegetables, the meals. All started around Halloween means in a month's time I've lost 10lbs.! The holidays always prove to me to be the hardest so Thanksgiving, I know the British don't celebrate this holiday and I wonder what my ancestors on my father's mother's side think of all of this really think of it. Full blood Apache my great grandmother was and my great grandmother on my mother's father's side was biracial. Part Cherokee, part African American.

But boy do my modern day relatives cook up a feast on my mother's side. How can I say this politely? A friend of mine, his family plans fell through, I won't give names and I won't give details because well, this blog is essentially about me and my trials and triumphs. I figured if I asked my mother if he and his wife and daughter could come she shocked me and said no because my Aunt Debbie's kids were coming. This angered me to no end. I wanted to eat to it. So instead I said I would make dinner for him and his family at home. She immediately asked sarcastically who's going to pay for it? I scoffed there was an extra turkey in the freezer that would feed four just fine. Missy was making me some of her grandmother's cornbread dressing with chicken livers. And I could get green beans and a pumpkin pie and cool whip with my EBT card.

The long and short of it, I invited him, he had others volunteer faster and I'm making dinner for my friend whose daughter has an extreme form of autism that doesn't really allow them to celebrate the holidays like everyone else. And by only making three things with one dessert and one cocktail (white zinfandel and sprite zero) I keep the caloric splurge to a minimum.

Besides, if truth be told big family events bother me and crank my anxiety levels up to sky high levels. And then what do I do? I do what my mother did after our conversation about Thanksgiving I'd grab a bag of chili cheese fritos and down the puppy to its crumbs.

I simply went to my room and wrote. I had a word count to get and I simply didn't have time for her hypocritical bullshit. I understand my aunt almost died and it has freaked my mother out in a big way. It freaked me out. It gave me what many would say was a 'coming to Jesus' moment. Where my aunt was (open heart surgery, her kidneys shutting down, her coming thisclose to death) was where my habits were taking me. I didn't want to be on that path anymore. I think of where I want to be and that's what I'm going to do. I couldn't continue eating late at night. Snacking and sneaking and grazing and pigging out to the point of sickness.

My mom's not there yet. And I suspect she has her own mood disorder issues as both my sister Sara and I have bipolar disorder, and Brandy deals with depression. The only common like dna wise that we have is my mother. My mood disorder isn't her 'fault' it isn't anyone's fault, but there's a lot of anger in me. I feel it stir every time I write an emotional scene in a book or screenplay, or the teleplay I wrote for Nashville based on the book I'm writing.

I've stripped the excuses away. Yeah, I had a crazy, dysfunctional childhood, and mom and dad and Jerry are a good part of that. But the point is, and my mom likes to think she knows me (she doesn't) and she thinks she knows my mood disorder (she doesn't have the first clue) and she tries to command me not to face those issues, not feel them. But the reality is, if the weight is going to stay off I'm going to have to face those emotions that I've covered up. The pain, the anger, the anguish, the fear, the rage, it's all to going to come to the surface eventually, I just pray for the strength not to eat to it.

Sincerely,
Amy McCorkle

Dear Daniel,

This post is late. Not only in that it's 9:59PM as I sit down to write it but in that what are you truly grateful for and thankful for sense I didn't really have a post for that in that in some ways I feel blessed beyond measure and in others I feel like God is dumping the good on it to make up for some stuff that's not so cool that I got stuck with. But let's be positive. What I'm truly grateful for in my life right now is my recovery. And my recovery is three fold. I'll break it down.

I am a survivor of childhood sex abuse. It was severe and stranger than fiction and my mother and stepfather while they know some of the details I choose not to share most of it with them. In fact I've shared more about the abuse and my recovery from it on this blog than I have anywhere else save my therapist's office. It took years to do the work and it wasn't easy. Confronting those particular demons dredges up all kinds of dark and powerless feelings. And I was always supposed to be gentle with myself, but my mom and dad(John, NOT the predator(s)) didn't always make it easy.

Coming out of one of those sessions I almost always felt raw and vulnerable and they almost were always cranky or mad at someone else and I became a convenient target. When I tried to put my boundaries in place with them they made it very difficult. While in many ways they are supportive, i.e. letting me live in their house rent free and supplementing my grocery bills while I pursue my creative endeavors, they have no true comprehension of just how damaging their carelessness or anger can be.

In the long run the lesson I've learned in coping and dealing with them is that they *don't* understand the first bit about what I'm going through and it's best if I tell them nothing of my recovery process. They fail every time I expect them to act a certain e.g. they zig when I fully expect them to zag.

As it is, I have more interest in pouring my heart and soul into my work than into a romantic relationship. I like the love stories where I can control them. On paper. LOL. But the nightmares have for the most part have stopped. Although last night I had one so vivid I had to wake myself up several times to make sure I wasn't being raped again.

So, I'm thankful for the demons that have haunted me in that arena have receded for the most part to the background and only seem to bother me when I'm especially tired, or have faced an especially trying day the parent units.

Secondly, but I think of most importance to me, is my mental health recovery in regards to my bipolar diagnosis. If I'm honest with myself high school was when the symptoms started, first with the depression, then with the mania. In college the lack of sleep started and the night terrors were horrendous. Over the next five or six years I cycled like clockwork, but I didn't really start to lose my grip until I was 23. I was sleeping an hour a day. Every little thing set me off. And said awful things to the person who was in the thick of it with me: Missy.

My writing suffered as a result to the point I wasn't writing anything. And when I was it was crap. Flat. No real life in it. I didn't write on my own anymore. As good and as great as it was to work with Missy I had effectively crippled myself to only writing *with* someone. As my recovery progressed I realized my mojo had left me. And in my desperation to get well I had turned my back on the one thing that brought me more joy than anything else. Writing. And it was Missy who noticed an ad for a contest in 2003, NaNoWriMo 50,000 word book in 30 days.

I took the plunge and HANDWROTE the novel. It took me until the beginning of February to do it but I did it. And boy did my hand ache when it was all said and done with. Was it a great book? No. Was it going to win any awards? Certainly not. But it proved to me that I could do it.

In 2004 Missy and wrote, directed, and produced a movie, one too messed up to be edited. Half our cast were divas the other half couldn't wait to get the hell out of there because of it.

These steps among others helped in my healing process. And then, a breakthrough. In 2011 my sleep cycle righted itself. I scored three publication contracts and won an award. I kept writing. I kept getting better. I kept racking up contracts and in 2012 I had my first Amazon Bestseller in GLADIATOR: The Gladiator Chronicles. More awards followed. In 2013 I appeared the front of the city newspaper and my screenplay adaptation of my bestselling Bounty Hunter won the Best SciFi Screenplay Award at Fright Night. More than that I graduated from therapy to case management. I have been asked to present my recovery to the board of directors. I find that to be an incredible honor, and even when my memoir based on this blog, and Gemini's War became bestsellers on Amazon I find that it is what I am most grateful for. My recovery. Because without my recovery I would have none of the success that I have now.

I am fond of saying I wrote my way back from the brink of madness. But it was with the help of Anita, Rose, Ronnie, and Missy and Pam that I can sit still long enough to enjoy a television show, a movie, a book, and even yes the ability to sit down and write any of these is due in no small part to the roles these people played in my life over the last twelve years. It was a long road. But somehow I made it back to tell everyone else who may be at different points in their road to recovery that it can be done. Because if I can do anyone can. And that is truly what I am most thankful for this year.

Sincerely,
Amy McCorkle

Dear Daniel,

So 'tis the season to be…jolly. Yes. It is official I am happy. Typically I struggle around this time of year. I'm depressed. Or in a funk. Don't get me wrong, I love the holidays. I have a decorated 4 foot tree on a small cabinet next to me. I love giving and getting presents. Especially for my friends. I know them and they know me. And then of course there are my three cousins, Rebekah, Bridgette, and Mary Jo. Missy calls them my fan club. And I've kind of taken Rebekah under my wing as a writer. And another girl online Nicole. I write 'with' them via Facebook. We 1k 1hr it. That's one thousand words in one hour. Sometimes it flows easy. Other times it's a struggle. Given I've been either sick or sick on the antibiotics this last week I haven't felt much like writing.

But writing with Nicole and Rebekah who face similar challenges to myself (I won't say which ones, they both come from great families) and they need a little encouragement. I give a lot where Rebekah is concerned because her collegiate path so mirrors my own, only in that I was trying to get away from my house, and that she had a better support network than I did at the time. I'm proud of her. I gave her the simplest of goals. Write 150 words a day. It is the same missive I gave Nicole. That amount will give you 54K in a year. That's a short novel. Or a good chunk of longer book. And sometimes you'll get more, and sometimes you'll get less. I told them to be gentle with themselves and not to measure themselves to me or anyone else. She even has a blog Confessions of A Coffee Crazed Writer. In her most recent blog she talks about her mental health battle and how it doesn't have to get you down. I'm incredibly proud of her for her bravery and honesty.

On another front. I chose to go small press with Hekate Press for the Bella Morte series. Have garnered interest in the television series treatment and pilot from the acting community. Cady

McLain, Robin Strasser, Steve Burton and even Ricki Lake and Jon Lindstrom have tweeted their support. As a result a connection I made at Fandom Fest told me to send the treatment and my accolades on and he would forward them to agent/producers. But you know how Hollywood is, it might go, it might not. I'm hopeful though. If not the series is eight books long and will keep me writing until February of 2015. And to be a paid working author is awesome.

At the end of next month I find out if any of my scripts finaled in That Book Place's Author Fair's writing competition. Halfway through February I find out the result of First Look's contest results. And at the end of February I find out if I advanced in the Nashville Film Festival's Screenwriting Competition.

And on a sadder note my kitty of almost 13 years may be ill with something incurable. And it's dawning on me that she may not be with me much longer. And this realization right before the holidays threatens to break my heart.

Sincerely,
Amy McCorkle

Dear Daniel,

I usually have a reason to say thank you. First for my sanity, second for my friendships, and last of all for an abundance in my career that a few years ago seemed out of reach.

I have siblings who claim I'm the most selfish one in the family. Honestly, I'm not too worried about what they think. They done little to nothing to show me they care one iota about my sanity. They're too caught up in their own lives and drama to engage me on any meaningful level. I got them presents, mostly because I wanted to. But a conversation with my sister showed me just who was selfish between us. I suggested she stay and take her family home to help mom and dad home and she explained how inconvenient that was to everyone. And that I just wanted my fast food. I'm recovering from diverticulitis. My appetite isn't what it could be. She then got her panties in a bunch and stormed out of the house—but not without her Christmas present. I would say I unbelievable, but this sister has the habit of blaming everyone else for problems she creates for herself.

As for people I'm grateful for. The first friend on the list is Missy Goodman. No one is a saint.

No one is an angel. But Missy is the kind of friend everyone should be so lucky to have. Do we argue yes? Do we sometimes say hurtful things in anger? Yes. But does she show the degree of insensitivity of others who claim that blood is the strongest determining factor in any given relationship? No. Has she walked through the kind of hellfire with me that would make most people weep and send the toughest guy running? Yes. Is she a big part of why I'm enjoying the success I am today? Yes. Her love and friendship and forgiving nature has been a huge component in my healing process that my sisters just have a fundamental lacking of. Not that my sisters aren't facing issues of their own. I love them, and I can be selfish as can anyone, but Missy has been the kind of friend movies like Beaches are about. Although she is definitely the Barbara Hershey character, we made a deal a long time ago, that no man is worth us tearing each other apart over. Even her hero is different. George Clooney is who she hangs her hat on. She looks to his work as I look to yours. Although she is fortunate enough to have 2 pages of ER script signed by her hero. As for me I must be content allowing this blog to do what it has grown into. An outlet as a memoir of sorts.

That being said the next person I'd like to thank is Pamela Turner. Pamela is the one who gave me the practical tools I needed to grasp onto success. She pointed me in the direction of the small press. She told me to not look down my nose at ebooks (which face it, I think a lot of people did and still do). She told me to go to Coyote Con. A free online writers conference. Where I participated in MayNoWriMo and wrote Another Way to Die. She then pointed me in the direction of digicon by Savvy Authors. Another online writers conference. I pitched every publisher guesting. Three of them said yes. One said not what they were looking for. And another said not the right fit but go to this publisher and tell them I sent you. I went with MuseItUp Publishing. She then pointed me in the direction of Fandom Fest, where I linked up with Hydra, which would eventually sign me for my first print novel, Bounty Hunter. The next year I launched my Gladiator series there and handed out a ton of free promo. And this year I sold 34 books, won the screenwriting competition, launched my Gemini Rising series, and met Grant Wilson whom I've turned into a valuable contact. Without Pam, my career doesn't take off. Not only that, next to Missy, she's the best friend I've got. Taking me to the doctor. Going out for lunches. Paying for my meds when I don't have the cash. Paying for my cats meds when I don't have the cash. Sure she's a bull in a china shop. But she's loyal, and when I'm struggling with my mood she is right there for me.

Other people have helped me. Tom Sawyer, Rich Ridings. My various publishers. Some of whom have become friends as well. Lea Schizas of Muse, Frank Hall, formerly of Hydra, Dave

Mattingly of Blackwyrm and Delilah K. Stephans of Hekate Press. Have all helped me become better writers.

Authors Julie Butcher and Christine Bell have benefitted me with their time and wisdom.

Bertena Varney and Suzie Wright and proven to be invaluable in the guideposts along the way.

And my little fan club of my cousins, Rebekah, Bridgette, and Mary McAuliffe have all given me so much in getting to know them. To know that anyone loves my work or admires me the way I admire you and your work tickles me to no end.

Sincerely,

Amy McCorkle

Dear Daniel,

For all the noise they make, my parents haven't got the first clue how to handle a child or an adult child with bipolar disorder. Which is sad considering they have two of them. My mother thinks a pill is a panacea of sorts. Take it and things are automatically all better. Which just simply isn't the case. Even I have trouble coping with my illness at times. Not the pill part. I don't have trouble with the idea of taking medicine. It's like brushing my teeth or taking a shower. Or doing my steps. I just do it.

Am I still prone to hypomanic highs and crashing off of them? Yes. Staying balanced is a constant battle which requires you to be ever vigilant, and on the lookout for symptoms that could sneak up on you without you even knowing it. Which happened to me.

I've had a relatively GREAT year. Lots of contracts, 4 books out, 3 bestsellers, two festival awards. Wrote 5 books. Wrote 2 screenplays. 1 teleplay, and a treatment. Graduating from therapy. Speaking before the board. Starting a group writers blog about mental illness. By The Seat Of Your Pants. Mentoring young writers struggling with mental illness. And a possible television show? GREAT friends. My first 70K novel. This list goes on and on.

But stress is stress. Good or bad I'm affected monthly and by the weather. So, when I got sick and couldn't get better Pam stepped up and took me to the doctors three times in 2 weeks.

And then it happened, the bottom fell out. I was overwhelmed. The third trip to the doctor's was enough to do it. Here's the thing, yesterday all I wanted was tlc. What I got was a decidedly mixed bag. On the one hand there's Missy.

She had a day planned with her mother. She wasn't able to come over. But she took every call. Whether I was crying, normal, or just a mess. She called my mother who had no clue as to how to handle the mixed episode and ran serious interference. I needed my mother to kind, tender, and nurturing, what I got was 50 shades of crazy. I woke up at seven and decided to do a movie marathon and I kicked it off with my favorite Bond movie, Casino Royale. I dozed on and off through it. Took it out, put Polar Express in. Dozed on and off throughout it. Woke up for the last twenty minutes. My mom announced we were having Christmas at the church reception hall.

Because nobody has the balls to stand up to my cousin who invited two more people to an already overcrowded house for my family's Christmas. If I'm not careful my mood and Brenna are on a collision course. My mom offered up candy that I bought for the house to the church. Told me Christmas would be at the reception hall at church and when I told her I was giving the girls their gifts at church she asked how I was going to hide it from Brenna.

Excuse me? I've got a relationship with Rebekah, Bridgette, and Mary that I don't have with any of Brenna's children. I made overtures towards her kids that she could have picked up and ran with. She thwarted it at every turn. She only has herself to blame.

My kept telling me when I cried that she didn't want *her* Christmas ruined. I wonder if it occurred to her there was a reason I don't particularly care for spending time with my family on Christmas. She doesn't care about anything other than the 'perfect holiday'. She really doesn't.

I mean she loves us but if she had, she wouldn't have dragged me out of the house with a tornado watch on when she knows how deathly afraid of them I am to spend time with people I don't necessarily feel up to being around.

I needed her to choose me. But she couldn't be bothered. Her initial response was, take her to the hospital. She wants me to helpless or healthy and gone. It is true what they say, you can't go home again, and after Nashville I plan on doing something about it.

Sincerely,
Amy McCorkle

Dear Daniel,

Christmas time is upon us. I don't know what you do to celebrate the holidays but this holiday season has snuck up on me and I have to admit, I don't feel as Christmasy as I would like. Full of good cheer and happiness, especially when my friend needs me to be. Missy is coping with feelings of depression caused by the death of her father in December of 2010. She needed me to be strong yesterday. Unfortunately, my hypomanic crash was and is to some degree still in full effect.

I'm okay now. But who's to say where the roller coaster will take me one hour from now, two hours from now, maybe five minutes from now. Being alone makes me cry. At least initially. An irrational fear will grip me and I'll feel abandoned, and as if no one loves me.

Yesterday I fell asleep when Missy needed me to make her laugh. I couldn't make me laugh, let alone make me her laugh. She was angry. Resentful. And when she told me as much I felt betrayed and as if she didn't understand that I wasn't functioning in a way that I was having too hard a time to help anyone.

So I told her I would put the load elsewhere so that I could help her. It was the best I could offer. She got upset and told me that she felt guilty when I said that. That, in reality is on her.

Under a clearer mindset I see that. But I also understand as much as I need her, my crash was in direct conflict with what she needed from me. She needed me to be strong. So I leaned on Delilah and Pam yesterday. Each helpful in their own way.

I think what people don't understand about the roller coaster of a crash is that it plays with your sleep cycle, it makes you cry, and as much as you try to fake it out it can make you its bitch. Which doesn't always make you the most reliable of friends.

It's not that my problem was more important than Missy's. You can't quantify something like that. We each felt like the other was letting them down. Which simply wasn't the case. We were each just needing something more than the other could give. Which when you're as close as me and Missy are, and have been through as much as we have, it just really, really, sucks.

I mean, I desperately *wanted* to be there for her, I just wasn't capable able. I had like, zero perspective on the matter. I needed people around me and everyone else had their own agendas. Which is exactly how life is. I did NOT want my family to leave last night. And when they did, I did NOT want Missy to go. But they left at the same time. Which upset me. I thought, *how dare they! Don't they see I'm suffering! I'm alone all the fucking time!*

Granted Missy is a nurturer. And she picks up a great deal of slack where my family really fucks up in dealing with this bipolar thing. And as much as I'm bitching right now Missy gets an A+ in how she copes with this shit as a friend. As a best friend.

I mean, there's a lot of good stuff that comes with me but it's times like these that really test both of us. I think sometimes she doesn't care enough to understand I can't help how I'm feeling and I'm sure she thinks I can control my emotion enough for one day to help her through some tough shit of her own.

So, Christmas can really suck a big one. But the reality is, I can't wait to give Missy her Christmas. I went nuts shopping for her at Big Lots and on Amazon. And a special gift I had Delilah design for her. The only ones I can't wait to give their Christmas even more are the girls, Rebekah, Bridgette, and Mary Jo. I mean, I got Jonathan a box set of my favorite mysteries as a kid, Encyclopedia Brown, but the others I could really be meh over.

Christmas is hard, and now, that it's hard for Missy too, I'm just going to have to learn how to cope without leaning on her as much at this time of year. This morning I will call Seven Counties and talk to Anita about getting in for a group meeting. Help me get some perspective. I love my friends and family but none of them know what it's like to be the ones with the illness raging in their bodies and brains. They just know what it is to deal with the result of it. And it's like when you have it, the whole family has it. And sometimes they get it and sometimes they don't.

So Missy, thank you for all that you do. Because even when you are human and feel resentment at my need for a great deal of your understanding and strength, I know you get me, I know you get my illness, and I know 9.999999 times out of 10 you are going to be the kind of friend I long for and maybe don't even deserve.

Sincerely,
Amy McCorkle

Dear Daniel,

Christmas Eve has come and gone and the reactions of Missy and the girls were exactly as I'd hoped they be. Excited, exuberant, and appreciative. Now I'm experiencing some of the other effects of the bipolar roller coaster. Sleep deprivation. I've had all of an hour of sleep. I don't wish that kind of shit on anyone. It makes for one hot mess of an emotional human being. I'm including a picture of me and Rebecca from Christmas Eve, she's the tall excited one holding the Gears of Golgotha book cover/poster I had designed for her by publisher/cover artist for Hekate Press Delilah K. Stephans. She absolutely loved it. As you can see in the picture. She and her sisters gave me a nice wallet, when I opened it—per their instructions there was a Barnes and Noble Gift Card in there. A very nice gesture, one that they didn't have to do and one I didn't prompt them for.

I got Bridgette a 3 Disc set of K-Pop music, and Mary a book with believer/skeptic viewpoints on the paranormal. They were all engrossed in their gifts, utterly appreciative and next to their reactions like I said, other than Missy I was rather meh, over the whole thing.

So tonight, as I drifted off to dreamland I day dreamed a little bit on what it might be like to win at Nashville. I've entered other contests. I'd like to win those. I'm a bit of a glory hog and moving forward in Hollywood is a much different game than say…being queen of the hill in the small press world. I mean things professionally got even sweeter the 23rd when I received a letter from a July con in Indianapolis that told me unofficially I had been excepted for the dealer's hall AND the panelist's list. Professionally things just happen for me in a way that some would say is luck.

But what is luck other than preparation meeting opportunity? Christmas with Missy was spectacular. She got me movie candy, A Christmas Story Fudge, A Christmas Story mug, a soft kitty warm kitty t-shirt, 4 books, the authors, Sherrilyn Kenyon, JR Ward, and Veronica something of Divergent fame. She got me a hollow wooden book with the streets of California on it, a pretty hat box, with a golden horseshoe she's been waiting for to fall out of my ass, wine glasses, a journal and a really cool picture that starts off with the phrase today is the day.

But the day dream. I think about winning at Nashville and then I think about meeting my heroes professionally and I wonder, given my personality, could I hold my shit together?

Like you. I mean you're super talented, and your acting, your style of acting is one I like as a writer. It affords me a wide berth in imagining you in different roles. For my first 7 books I imagined you as the hero and romantic lead. In my memoir you were the quiet witness to my life story. And in the Bella Morte series you are the title character's father who wants her prepared to meet her destiny, but reluctant to let it come to her for fear it will take her from him once again.

I don't know you, Mr. Craig, but I'd like to think I could keep my shit together if I met you. But here is the reality. I, am very much, a grateful person for the blessings that have come into my life. And meeting someone who inspires me to my potential the way that your work does I might indeed lose my shit. Not that I scream and act a fool. But I might cry happy tears and want to let you know that during my dark times. Like now when I can't sleep and am struggling to keep my head above water, I can pop in Skyfall, or Casino Royale, or Quantum of Solace, or my fave, Cowboys & Aliens. I would love to see some of your smaller films. It's nice to see your range. I've seen clips from Layer Cake and Mother and you are likable even when it's obvious your character is a two timing douchebag. LOL. You have created a terrific body of work.

I dream of a day when I can meet and work with all of my heroes. But your work has made a meteor sized crater and left quite the imprint on my creative process. Maybe if you read my work you'd think it was crap. I won't lie, something like that would devastate me. However, I'm proud of who I am and what I've become.

Mentoring my cousin Rebekah through the minefields of an initial diagnosis and helping her build a readership through a really good blog helps me take my mind of my struggle some.

So when I finish the edits and Bella Morte: Beginnings is released onto the unsuspecting public, please know that next Missy's name, yours will be included in the dedication. Because sleepless nights like this remind of how important your work is to me and my creative survival. I respect you and your work. And as much as I love you as James Bond. I'm more than aware you are not him. And that like me, you would like the freedom to make your creative choices as you see fit. And not as the world at large would demand it.

Sincerely,
Amy McCorkle

Dear Daniel,

I got to sleep last night. 8-10 hours of it. I straightened up my room. Was going to do laundry but mom has a load in the wash. Promoted Hekate Press. Promoted my backlist. Read 2 chapters. More reading than I've done in years. Promoted my position in a contest with three books, Gemini's War, Letters to Daniel, and Gunpowder & Lead. Now I'm sitting down to blog.

What I want to talk about is what a nasty piece of work I can be when I'm healing from an episode. It becomes a rollercoaster of emotion as opposed to the occasional bad day where I need to just *take it easy*. Where the 'by your bootstraps' approach is bullshit. And sometimes bipolar disorder has you in its vise-like grip and yanks you up, tears you down, and whips you violently from side to side and you are left to desperately hang on for your sanity has you sleep deprivation, among everything else your chemically imbalanced body can throw at you.

At these times you are forced to other people for support. Maybe people who have as many issues as you do, just tucked away in other places. Sometimes they just aren't in a place to give you anything. My mother and father are at the top of this list. My sisters take their cash, their time, and play on their love and concern for their grandchildren. They are selfish and take and demand anything and everything.

My parents give me a roof over my head and food to supplement my meager SNAP benefits. That's all they have left to give. At times like this that is a most wonderful thing. But I need comfort emotionally. I need to be tended to. Not in the clean my mess, make my meals kind of way, although, that is especially nice when you feel as fragile as I've felt since this last Friday when the bottom dropped out.

There are people who have really seen me through this last week and I want to thank them now. And before I launch into this, I have been having a shitty time of it. And when people say *I can't make it, this is too hard.* I understand that feeling from personal experience. But I've always made a choice to survive the earthquake. And hang onto the tsunami of a shit storm of feelings that bombard me. Making that singular choice is not a panacea, but goes a long way as you feel your way along the dark passageways searching for a just a pinpoint of light to give you relief that a way out is possible. While some people joke about the train I *choose* freedom. Friendship. Good, healthy, supportive friendships are the life blood of hope. In this world I feel secure in stating I have three that have come through for me in this instance.

First up, the usual suspect. Missy Goodman. Though she had her own shit, and I mean serious shit, to deal with this holiday season, and I felt betrayed by her abandonment, it is always with the clarity of walking *out* of the darkness that we know just how much our friendship means to the other. We have been through hell and lived to talk about. And though this crash came at a rather inopportune time, we are proof, that if you use the tools the therapist and psychiatrist give you, what once was a tsunami can be seen as a simple ripple in hindsight compared to the war you once fought for your sanity. And recovery becomes a matter of riding the wave until you have finally sighted the safety of shore. I am not at one hundred percent. But thanks to Missy I have managed to accomplish tasks even as I recovered. Thank you Missy for this last week and everything you do for me.

Next up, the ever stalwart, ever faithful friend, Pamela Turner. Full time writer, author, screenwriter, and blogger and wife and mother she always finds time for me, her friend. Her touch is not the gentlest, but on Christmas Day, she came over and I made breakfast for us. I kept dozing even as she was here. My mother kept scolding me awake. But Pam never complained. We talked shop, we talked about how dealing with this time of year was especially hard. She can be direct, but for this last week she has been a shoulder anyone should be proud to call friend. Being alone during times like these is hard. She is brilliant, she is the kind of friend who goes the mile and then some. She has not always been treated the best. And over the years she has entered into mine and Missy's inner circle. She is simply fabulous. And if there was a trophy for friendship I would surely award it to her.

Finally there is Delilah Stephans. Direct without being cruel she endures my constant questions and has become a valued friend to lean on via Facebook. I trust her implicitly to keep my confidences, and I can trust her integrity in working for her at Hekate Press as Marketing Director. She took Bella Morte on the pitch of an idea. But there are countless other stories I pitched that did not grab her and she did not hesitate to say so. I took one of them to Muse. She doesn't mind me taking books to other houses. Not that the other houses that I'm at do either. She learned a lot working for Lea at Muse, it's where we met. I have an out clause as Marketing Director should my film/tv dreams come to fruition and I just don't have the time for the lifting there. She understood I was feeling the burn out and depression and she had no problem with me taking a breather from the computer for awhile. She talks to me in the evening when the anxiety hits and I need to write, online.

And an honorable mentions go to Rebekah, my cousin, and Nicole. Their joy and persistence at beating this rollercoaster we're on and plowing ahead on their books makes me feel like on the whole, that there is always hope, no matter what stage one is at in the journey.

Sincerely,

Amy McCorkle

Dear Daniel,

Feeling stronger today. Still not one hundred percent but the light is oh so much brighter. I want to talk about something today that is close to my heart. Stigma and stereotype.

I often talk about my journey and my recovery as beacon of hope for those still struggling in the depths of despair. I rarely talk about the experiences of those who are the friends and family of those persons with bipolar disorder except in the terms of how they function in relation to my recovery.

The truth and whole truth is, when someone has been diagnosed with bipolar disorder the whole family has it. And both sides of the coin will, at least in the beginning of the journey, at times, fail to see and comprehend what it is truly like to be the other person in the equation.

Bipolar disorder exists on a spectrum. Bipolar I, bipolar II, and unofficially bipolar III. They can exist autonomously or with traits of other illnesses. My diagnosis is bipolar I with mixed episodes. What is a mixed episode exactly? It's when you are cycling so fast you feel as if you are physically being torn in two different directions at once. One minute you are fine, the next you're sobbing, the next you are so hateful you can't stand yourself.

I'm fortunate. I'm much more likely to harm myself than ever hurt someone else. I've never had an issue with too many violent outbursts, but I have felt the rage and I have been in its grip before. And let me state now, that it is no joke to be at its mercy. In this state I have thrown things, I have cut my own hair short, and I have said and done other things I am far from proud of.

There is a stereotype that everyone is paranoid and violent. And while those symptoms DO indeed exist and believe me I have been paranoid, but reaching out for help is something I have never rejected. I've never stopped taking my meds because I was 'feeling better' either. And that really is a struggle for some.

There is this idea that somehow one is weak because they need this medicine and that is simply not the case. It's like you wouldn't stop taking your metformin or insulin if you were a diabetic would you?

The difference is the whole family must be treated. There is a stigma in that if people knew about the sick person in their family there would be shame to cope with. When in fact they are already feeling shame. As is the person tormented by the illness. Sometimes an improperly treated mentally ill individual has the end result of being a tormentor as well as being tormented. The guilt one feels as a result of their actions is horrendous. Paralyzing and so strong you can taste it. And making amends for it is hard because sometimes what we do is so out of character for us that it shocks everyone around us. And it becomes 'oh no, what will they do if I look at them sideways' which sucks for pretty much everyone involved.

The stigma and stereotype that follow those of us living with mental illness is no fun whatsoever. A perfect example of this is when Maurice Benard gave a s/o to everyone with bipolar disorder stating if he could do it so could they when accepting an acting award, there was laughter in the crowd. Not applause for his courage an bravery which there should have been.

So this goes for everyone living with mental illness either as the person struggling with the diagnosis, or the family and friends grasping at as to how to survive it and learn to live with it without self-destructing themselves.

You are all, courageous, you are all brave, you should all be commended for being at whatever stage you're at in the journey. And not ever at any moment laughed unless you are using humor to survive and live through the situation and through life itself.

Sincerely
Amy McCorkle

Dear Daniel,

I was going to talk about stigma and how people sometimes think you can just 'think' your way out of it, but I think I'm going to save that for another day, maybe for the group blog. I want to talk about the kind of year 2013, on the whole has been. And on the whole it has really been one magical year.

I have been blessed with the best of friends. Missy the best friend who is more like a sister to me and Pam, who resides in the inner circle. Can't say that about everyone, but it's true. These two are my rocks of Gibraltar and Missy is also my woobie LOL.

Creatively speaking I have accomplished more in this one year than I have ever before. City of the Damned (novel and screenplay), Gemini's Legacy (book 2 in the Gemini Rising trilogy), When Doves Cry (novel and soon to be treatment and pilot), You're the Reason (screenplay), Cornbread (novel), Bella Morte:Beginnings (novel, treatment, and pilot) and Bella Morte:Devil's Backbone (book 2 in the epic 8 book Bella Morte series). That alone would have thrilled me.

Professionally the accolades have been overwhelming. 2013 Moondance International Film Festival Semi-Finalist for Gemini's War. Count 'em, not one, not two, but three, Amazon Bestsellers. Bounty Hunter which hit #9, Gemini's War which hit #24, and Letters to Daniel, the memoir based on this blog hit #2. And finally Missy and I won the 2013 Fright Night Film Festival Best SciFi Screenplay Award at Fandom Fest. Not only that, I sold 34 books at Fandom Fest.

A definite high point has been meeting and working with the likes of Tom Sawyer and Rich Ridings as my mentors along the way. And a special treat has been meeting Grant Wilson, an uber-talented guy in his own right, he is a genuine and open guy and he took the time to really listen to me at Fandom Fest, and some really neat things could come of that meeting. But nothing as they say in Hollywood is done until it's done.

I took some leaps of faith this year by entering screenwriting contests, some small, like That Book Place's Author Fair Writing Competition, and will know by the end of January if Missy and I are finalists. A giant competition, Scriptpipline's First Look Project which I will know if I won or not by mid-February. The Nashville Film Festival Screenwriting Competition. It is attached to a prestigious festival but I've never seen anything quite like it. Advancing to semi-final round I find out in February. I find out if I'm a finalist in March. Then there's Indie Gathering, winners are announced in July. And I plan on entering Imaginarium Film competition and literary competition later this year.

The most awesome thing is that I started three new blogs this year, this one included, and they have all garnered me success in some tangible and intangible ways. I'm mentoring two young women. One of which is my cousin. They make my day just by writing 150 words a day. I hope whoever reads this finds hope in my story as the last few entries have been dark and about I wrestle with my mental illness.

Reflecting back on what has been a fantastic 2013 I can only hope, as my best friend Missy says, that the golden horseshoe doesn't drop out of my behind anytime too soon. Hope your year was as grand as mine and here's to hope 2014 is even better for you Daniel, and everyone else who actually reads this blog,

Sincerely,
Amy McCorkle

Dear Daniel,

On dreary days like these I do the things I think will clean house internally as well externally. I made my bed. I took the trash out of the room. Or what my mother lovingly refers to as my 'dead soldiers. Empty cans of whatever caffeinated diet soda I'm drinking (whatever happens to be on sale that week) and empty coffee cups are spirited away and of course I do the backed up laundry and scoop the litter pan. I only have one little kitty. She is an orange tabby named Chyna, for the WWE wrestler. Mostly because Missy and I couldn't agree on anything else. My room still isn't great shakes but it's way better than it was and I always stay on top of it. At least better than I did at the last place I did because I didn't want my cat to crawl up somewhere and end up like the hoarders show where they find 72 cats 40 some odd of them dead. And of course a shower.

Then setting down to write becomes something of a chore, especially after all that. You want to do nothing other than pig out and watch a movie. Which I think I'm going to do a Bond marathon. Casino Royale, Quantum of Solace, and Skyfall. But even as I write that I know I'm only going to make it through one at most if any at all. I have a treatment for a television show to write for a joint venture for me a Missy. Yeah, another one of those. This story has had many incarnations. From novels to screenplays, to a book we co-wrote and I took the lead on to this television series where I may be writing the treatment but Missy is driving the bus. She's working on the pilot. I simply do the sizzle and sell on this and act as a sounding board.

When Doves Cry has been our Star Wars, our Godfather, our Clerks, as it were. A family of characters that we never seem to be able to say completely goodbye to. As the years went by, and yes, this was our initial story together, the story, of course, has morphed over time. The book will look somewhat like the television series and vice versa. The elevator pitch is the Sopranos meets

Dallas.

Often times Missy and will have arguments about things. Creative differences. And I know those rows, should the series get picked up are coming with producers and the money people, I'd rather there be no in fighting going on. To survive Hollywood we will need each other's backs. Someone who'll have the guts to say what's what. Say no to the other when or if their head gets to swollen. Fortunately I have more than one person in my corner willing to be direct without being cruel. Without using it as an excuse just to be an asshole about it.

They say what you do on January 1st you'll be doing the rest of the year, so even though I didn't want to particularly blog or clean (the room, the litter box, or even myself) I figured it was a momentum thing.

The truth is when you recover from an episode like I'm doing it too comes in waves and stages. And just as I went on a cleaning blitz shortly before my crash, in the recovery process I had to clean up the mess the illness had left behind, emotionally, physically, psychologically, and spiritually.

Do I still feel a little wobbly, a tad fragile even though I'm on the other side of it? Yes. My mother and father left out of town to visit my aunt who is really unable to travel. And I had all kinds of anxiety. Like irrational anxiety. I told my mom I felt like the kid who had prepared for one thing and then they flipped the script on me. Then Missy flipped the script on me today. Nothing major. But it was enough to make me feel abandoned and like she was going back on her word.

She hadn't abandoned me. She just *changed* things on me. And it triggered the lost little kid feeling. Nothing major. Nothing I couldn't get my shit together on. Because the overreaction was on my part. Not hers. Now, the roles have been reversed and sometimes she handles it well, others well…she's been known overreact too. But we've been through much tougher shit than this. Stuff that would break the strongest of men.

So as I heal up from my mixed episode, I know today is a day that is a slight bump. That because I got stuff done, I'm going to chalk up in the good column.

Sincerely,
Amy McCorkle

Dear Daniel,

Ever daydream about the simple things in life? I mean, I've never been one to get to caught up in delusions of grandeur, but at 38 I've never owned a car. It would be nice to own a car. Nothing fancy. Just one that I owned straight out. And a house. One that I own with a finished basement incase of tornadoes. Sump pump in case of floods. Built to withstand earthquakes and tsunamis. Can you tell I have serious issues when it comes to weather?

Enough money to pay off my debt, keep myself fed, stay out of debt, and just do what I want for a living for the rest of my life and get paid for it. To keep my hard one and fought victory over bipolar disorder. To have the strength to ride the wave when the bottom falls out and I need to be given a little TLC as opposed to screaming and yelling.

To be taken seriously. To be respected. To be understood. To be loved. And maybe not necessarily in that order. To have people with me who can be happy for me and for me to be happy for them. And when people I respect and admire succeed I feel like, hey, I can do that too.

But here's the fact. I don't need the insanity of stardom. I like being able to write about what I want when I want and even though I dream of awards for my work and being well compensated for it and meeting my heroes. I want to have the core group of people around me who will know when to call me on my bullshit.

Even if it makes me mad. Even if it hurts my pride. As long as it's coming from someone who knows me to the core and will keep me from running off into the abyss, I'm willing to take it in the chin. Because everyone needs that one person in your life that will tell what's what. To keep you humble. Mind you NOT to put you down or demoralize you and chip away at your self-confidence. Honestly, I have too many of those in my life now as we speak.

Right now I am not making it rain dollars and cents. The largest royalty check I have ever received is 36 dollars. But I am content in the publishing world to do things a certain way. My career for the last three years has been this crazy ride upward. And I know creatively I am at my peak behind a computer after reading something inspiring or watching a movie.

Now for Christmas I got six books. It has been nine years since I read any book, and before that five years before. So I decided to ask for books for Christmas. I write paranormal and urban fastasy and dystopian so I asked for the right stuff. Sherrilyn Kenyon. Veronica Roth. And JR

Ward.

My spirit animal is Kevin Smith and his gift of storytelling. Funny, sweet, and sour at times, he is self-deprecating and cheers everyone on to pursue their passion their bliss while proudly pursuing his brand of his.

In many respects people look at me and I'm living the dream. Published author. Bestselling author. Award winning author. Award winning screenwriter. Award winning blogger. Mentoring writers. A sliver of a chance at a television series. Based on a series I'm loving to write.

But here's the underlying reality. I got a late start writing. Perhaps even later than I wanted. Living in a house as an adult with parents who dismiss you and your feelings out of hand is hard. You find yourself on that nasty rollercoaster. Sometimes things are good. But more times than not they are rocky and so I hide in my room and I write.

Missy has it good at her mom's. But here's the deal. I don't know how much longer I can hold out in this situation. I'm banking a lot on the Nashville Film Festival and their screenwriting competition. And possibly meeting some people there who can help us take our career to the next level. And to do that I have to stay in this house another 7 months. Which honestly seems like it could be disastrous. They break my heart every day.

I wish this wasn't the case. But they do. Of course, they're my parents. What am I going to do? When I let something blow over mom always manages to needle me with it hours later. As if I'm the bad guy. So for now I put my head down, put my blinders on and write my fucking way out this one Joan Wilder.

Sincerely,
Amy McCorkle

Dear Daniel,

You do something long enough, it becomes a habit. Addictive. Well, food is my addiction, but so is writing. And I got away from writing the way I wanted to on this blog mostly because I was spreading myself so thin doing so many things. I find when I want to those things I wake up in the morning and get so much done that my evenings are empty and free to do with as I like.

Things have been so gloomy as of late on this blog. I'm hopeful that someone has read it that needed it. Has seen even when things are bad that there is always light. I haven't felt suicidal in quite some time, so I've been blessed. But today I wanted to talk about the angels who have descended into my life. And thank them for what they have done for me.

The first on the list is Vicki Lynn Thompson. I really do believe she was angel, because I saw her at the beginning of the year, she connected me with Tom Sawyer and then she just vanished off the face of Facebook. I mean Facebook is where I connect with others and network. Twitter too. I know, you're a private man, that much comes across in your interviews. I get that. I just tend to bleed like someone's tapped a vein on this and other blogs I write for. I mean within the first twenty minutes you will know that I have bipolar disorder, had a dicey childhood, and that I'm a writer. I can't control it. It's just who I am.

I know people will hurt me because of this fact. That's why I hesitate to call too many people my friends. And why even though I use this blog in a way that you're like this silent witness to my story I know Daniel Craig, actor, is nowhere near this blog. But like I said in a sense you can be. I don't pretend to know you. This blog is essentially about me and how I've survived and conquered many obstacles in life.

But here is the thing, I have angels all around me. You, in a way Daniel, and your work, and how you carry yourself professionally has been an angelic presence in my life. If you didn't have the chops that you do acting wise it occurs to me I might have never had a breakthrough novel with a hero everyone absolutely went crazy for. Now, I wrote it and the hero is my creation but Another Way to Die garnered me several royalty checks and a couple of awards. Eventually GLADIATOR became a bestseller and an award winner. Your work fueled my imagination. And Bounty Hunter has been the book that became the screenplay that broke me through at film festivals. Truly, if I could thank you for inspiring me to my best work I would. Not in that, show up out of nowhere weird way. But perhaps one day my work ends up in front of you and you decide to work on the film.

Or maybe 'your people' tell you about the blog. And I never know if you know how appreciative I am of your work and how it's inspired me, but you do. That would be enough for me. Gratitude is what I express. You have been an angel in my life, well, at least your work has and I want to thank you for that.

Tom Sawyer on the other hand mentored me in the way a television treatment should look like. Grant Wilson, who I met at Fandom Fest, has become a champion of mine and Missy's based on the 8 book series, BELLA MORTE, that I'm close to 30K into on the 2nd book in the series.

And finally, to my publishers who all gave me a break of sorts. Lea, Frank, and Dave. And now, Delilah.

Let me take a moment to talk about Delilah and Hekate Press. First off, Delilah is a brilliant cover artist and a fabulous artist period. If you hear otherwise, it's just a lie or sour grapes talking. Delilah's brand isn't for everyone. Meaning, she's a direct person. She's not cruel. She admits she can be bitchy but she gives a heads up about it. She is only human after all. But, if you're willing to help yourself, and to reach out when needed she is the kind of person who will go to the mat for you. So when she came to me and asked me to be the Marketing Director for her new venture, one she had been thinking about for years, I was touched. I am proud to say I am employed by Hekate Press. And that my beloved series, BELLA MORTE was accepted there. I probably could have taken it any one of my houses that I write for. But I wanted print books at the same time as my ebooks. And I wanted the best cover artist around, hands down, to be working on the cover concept. And when she told what she had planned I got super excited.

Not only that, she is a good friend. And good friends are hard to find. I look forward to the day I get to meet her in person. She is an angel along with several other unsung heroes not mentioned today, you know who you are.

Sincerely,
Amy McCorkle

Dear Daniel,

Today's blog is simple. I am showing off my new and shiny official cover of Bella Morte: Beginnings. Check it out to your right. The tagline: *A young woman bent on revenge. A destiny that keeps getting in her way.*

To say the least I am over the moon about this cover. It has received a huge response on FB and I will inevitably place it on pinterest and tumblr and perhaps even on Bubblews. But here it is for my hero to see me taking another huge step forward. Swordsmanship, elemental powers, light versus dark.

Justice Xavier's journey starts out hard and only gets harder. In book 1 she has been brutally violated and enslaved for most of her life. She must cope with the overwhelming power within her and learn to master it lest it consume her and everything around her. Fueled initially by her rage, her long lost father and legendary gladiator father Duncan must mentor her. With the steady guidance and patience of her conduit warrior, Matthew they travel across what remains of the former United States, now know as Ke'lan in a desperate search for her mother.

I'm including my cousin Rebekah's mock-up cover for the book she is currently writing, Gears of Golgotha. A tale of Mages and Chemists and Gears that run and protect the earth. With a girl whose power blossoms into the world's last hope. A tale of prejudice and acceptance an allegory of our time. Rebekah is all of 19 and the pitch she wrote and the excerpts she's read to me are impressive.

I think wow, it took me years to develop those skills and maturity as a novelist and author. I'm proud of her and the steps she's taking. She's hoping to have a finished novel by April to pitch Hekate. She's already bowled over by Delilah and her artwork.

I have to admit, as we lunched at Panera she bowled me over with how good her writing on a FIRST DRAFT was. She has her own issues and the fact she can do math in her head (I can't), already has a successful blog, her learning curve is off the charts.

Right now she's scared to go back to school. I know where she is. But I don't want her to take the long way around like I did. She's worried about things that aren't in her control. If I have a message to her it is this:

You are bright and beautiful. Having a bipolar diagnosis doesn't have to define you. You are not your diagnosis. You are talented. You are lovable. You are enough. I want her to her understand that more than anything. Having an education is important, but remember write with passion. Write with abandon. Color outside the lines. And remember, when things are hard take a deep breath, count to ten, and reach out for help. Seven Counties of Kentucky saved my life. To Rebekah and all those like us out there find your Seven Counties and write your own happy ending.

Sincerely,

Amy McCorkle

Dear Daniel,

It is freezing here today. In my room it is nice and toasty to the point it is almost hot. The rest of the house it is need a blanket kind of cold. So I turned on the fan in my bedroom for a little while. I know I know, windchills in the negatives and I'm hot. My internal thermostat is definitely broken lol.

But that's not why I write. I'm writing today about how one chooses to live one's life. Growing up was hard for me, but then, here's the reality, it's hard for a lot of people. There is now, more than ever, a culture of victimization. The horrors of human trafficking, domestic violence, and child abuse make it very easy for one to slip through the cracks of the world's justice systems and foster system that make for those who live through these nightmares hard to recover properly.

I look at me. And I look what I've been through. And I *know* I should be a statistic. I have friends who should be statistics too. But for the grace of someone. At least *one* someone intervening they are not and neither am I.

I know people will look at this blog and see something that it is not. A delusion fan trying desperately to get the attention of someone who inspires them. But that's not the point of this blog. It never has been. It never will be.

It's to show that you can live through hell and choose not to be a victim. That you can reach out for help and do the work it takes to heal yourself and pass that lesson on. You can become a survivor. And once you've earned that badge of honor to can choose to move forward and choose to live.

There are those out there who are stuck in the victimized mode. And they find it difficult to take responsibility for their lives and actions. I too, was once there. It made for bad relationships and hollow meaning from friends. It conjured pity, not empathy, from others. I found as I continued my journey to healing that I didn't want that life. That it wasn't enough for me. People's pity was a pale shadow of the love I needed to cultivate for myself.

Finally I became a survivor. That was the journeyman part of the healing path. It's one thing to make the decision to be a survivor, it's quite another to go through the process of doing it.

There's a lot of two steps forward three steps back kind of action going on.

The one thing I always knew though was that all I had to be was myself. I didn't have to compromise on who I was or make apologies for it. I just had to get my ass out of the house to my therapy appointments, my psychiatry appointments, and my nurses appointments. I was not 'crazy' or 'delusional'. I may love passionately. Feel fiercely. And may love writing more than anything else on this planet, but I also learned during this time if I needed help, I could reach out for it. And that by not reaching out for it I was doing myself and everyone else around me a huge disservice. What is the saying? Pride goeth before the fall?

In 2010 a terrible thing happened. My best friend lost her father to a botched liver transplant surgery. And as her father lay dying slowly in the hospital I realized my life and writing career wasn't just going to fall into my lap by magic. I had best get down to the business of living and I started submitting *Another Way To Die* to different presses. It was there I went from surviving to choosing to live. (Thank you Harold Goodman, Missy Goodman, & Pamela Turner) And when the first contract came I cried. Thank you, Lea. And now with Bella Morte, and Delilah K. Stephans I feel like I'm at another threshold. Thanks to everyone who helped me go from victim to survivor to living. You may not be named but you know who you are.

Sincerely,
Amy McCorkle

Dear Daniel,

Normally I wouldn't use this blog as this sort of platform but here I am. Having accomplished something through the help and support and belief of so many people in my professional life that even twenty-four hours after I still am on cloud nine.

Earlier in the year I was asked to be the Marketing Director of Hekate Press. This only after I pitched Bella Morte: Beginnings and the idea of it as it an 8 book epic series and was told yes, send it in. I was touched. I knew I could market, but an entire company. Managing my backlist was hard enough, did I really have what it took to market an entire company and see to Delilah's vision that each author had a real marketing plan as well as market the house?

Well, having been trained in marketing my own work by one of the best, Lea Schizas. And taking cues from someone who could sell ice water to Eskimos in Tony Acree. And shown the undivided attention by the likes of Frank Hall and Dave Mattingly. Each of MuseItUp, Hydra, and Blackwyrm respectively. They all believed and still do believe in me and for that I must and am very glad to tip my hat to all of them.

Last night I felt very much like the Queen of the World and it was due in no small part to all of them. A special nod to G.L. Giles, fellow Blackwyrm author who hooked me up with Target Audience Magazine three years ago initially as a book reviewer. Without you G.L. this most definitely would have never happened.

That being said, Ellen Eldridge is the owner and editor-in-chief of Target Audience Magazine. A premiere indie online magazine which will be making the transition to being an online as well as print. I have had the distinct privilege of gracing the cover as featured author and had several articles run in the magazine. Ellen is also a big fan of this very blog. So perhaps, this progression was just the next step in our professional relationship.

In March a full page black and white ad of my cover for Bella Morte: Beginnings will run with a call to action to head to my article in the online version of the magazine. And the online version of the ad will link to the Hekate Press website.

So big whoop, right? Here's where the exciting part comes in. ALL HEKATE AUTHORS who write a blogpost about the promotion or marketing side of their new release and/or what inspired them to write their newest book out will be run in the online version of Target Audience Magazine. No money exchanges hands. The authors have the option of a discounted ad but ONLY if they want it.

Win/win. So on truly the coldest day of the year I wanted to announce on my blog where sometimes I struggle to find the happy I have found some of the biggest happy I could have possibly found and it is some of the HOTTEST news I could possibly share.

I know this sounds goofy and corny, but I hope my silent witnesses are proud of me. Because three years ago this would have never seemed possible to me.

Sincerely,
Amy McCorkle

Dear Daniel,

This is my view. Purely my view. And when it comes to marketing and promotion I consider myself *very* good at what I do. But while I have been working very hard to set up things to make things good for the Hekate Press authors I've been informed some people may take offense to my personal style.

Before I really launch into this I want to tell my trusted and valued friend who I lost my cool with last night over this I am apologetic in the way I presented my views on this to her. However I am *not* apologetic in how I run my position as Marketing Director for Hekate Press.

I made an announcement last night that Hekate Press authors should go to a local Con. I mentioned scifi cons because they're affordable and are open to all genres of fiction. They generally affordable and dealer tables aren't that bad either. *That being said,* there is a wide variety of cons ranging from highly affordable to HOLY CRAP THEY COST HOW MUCH?

Here are some answers to that problem (even if they are highly affordable).

Share a table. That's right. You heard me. Share a table. If the Con allows for it share the table. That includes being a representative of your publishing house.

Double up in your hotel room. Maybe triple up. Or quadruple up. Hotels even when they are negotiated down by the event can still be an expense too daunting for some to face on their own. I understand. I've been in this place myself. So when in the red or narrowly in the black cash fund wise find a way to share expenses.

You only have ebooks. Do what some houses do and get cd-rom versions of your book or vouchers like others. I know it's a hard sell but nothing ventured nothing gained. (I'm pretty hard core on this particular one because that's how I built my audience).

Travel issues. Car pool. Share gas expenses. And find a Con close to home.

Food and spending money, save for it. Most people only have one book a year come out. Plan in advance and pick one con to go to.

For mystery and romance authors you may hesitate hitting a scifi con. And you want to hit one of the more expensive cons in your genre. While that may be ideal it just may not be plausible or possible in the beginning. Take your snob hat off (yes, I wore it at one time too) and think outside the box.

The cost of books you say is too much to do this. Again find your release date and start saving.

I can come off as harsh and hardcore at times but that's only because I've been willing to do these same things at times. I've watched my career grow with the connections made at such cons and festivals.

Does this mean you *have* to do it? No, absolutely not. But I know there is something to be said for taking a chance and I have the record to prove it. So please, take this message in the spirit in which it is intended and be inspired to take control of your careers. Not just Hekate authors, but all authors as well.

Sincerely,

Amy McCorkle

Dear Daniel,

I had written about half a blog before this came to me. One minute my mother is fine. The next she is completely and utterly delusional. She is under the mistaken impression they get me anywhere these days. And when I mentioned I might be moving out she requested it be near where she lived. Halfway between Shepherdville and Mount Washington because they provide so much of my transportation.

This is the hard part about being a small press author. There are few who are the bestsellers where large sums of cash come rolling in. Sure there's more creative control and I am more proud than anything to call myself an indie who worships at the feet of the Indie King Kevin Smith who does it all. Writes books, does podcasts, has a television show, and makes movies the way he wants to. And he's self-sufficient and helps his friends. Meets his heroes. *That's* the indie life I want. And who the hell wouldn't?

Until then I struggle in some respects. My mother is angry at Roy, my nephew's father and she's taking it out on me. I have been perfectly content to stay in my room, write, and leave her be. Yet she had to come to my room and command me to live somewhere nearby since I depend on them so much for transportation.

Which is such a crock of shit. My friends Missy and Pam are the ones who take me just about freaking *everywhere*. Understand that? E-V-E-R-Y-W-H-E-R-E.

Friends, thank god for them. I think I'd go insane without them. And my publishers. Who seem like good people. And my writing. My writing is my sanctuary, but when she gets like this it's hard to hide in it. So I come here. Vent to my silent witnesses.

I knew I had to get out of this house. So last night I called and made a reservation at a hotel nearby. Me, Missy, and Pam are going to watch the pre-show of the Golden Globes and me catty then watch and handicap the awards. And cheer our favorites on.

I know from the few interviews I've read of yours that you're not big on the red carpet stuff. And I'll be honest as much as I want to dress up and be recognized for my work the throngs of camera and microphones and hot lights doesn't appeal to me at all. It triggers all kinds of anxiety in me that I wouldn't wish upon my greatest enemy.

And while I might complain about my anonymity in the small press, I must admit, I enjoy it when I get the rare fan letter, but I like being able to walk the streets unnoticed. I like people I just don't like being suffocated by them.

Which made Fandom Fest such a rarity for me. The honest truth is with award show season in Hollywood upon us I've created a little award show season for myself and Missy with scripts that runs through April. The finalist and award winners announced from January-April.

The contests are That Book Place's Authors Fair writing contest, Scriptpipline's First Look Entry Project, and Nashville Film Festival's 1st Screenwriting Competition.

I must admit I haven't been dwelling on these because I have been consumed with the books I have been writing and the job as Marketing Director for Hekate Press I've been doing.

I'm actually, after a brief sabbatical back to myself. I got away from what is my true passion and that is the writing. I've just got to learn to stay balanced. Which is, honestly the key with anything. So now, as my anger and anguish is extinguished over my mom's meltdown and me going down the path with her on that particular nasty ride, I can get back to writing on Bella Morte: Devil's Backbone, and later Order of the Dragon. A series ala the Dark Hunters series in the idea that these characters live in the same world and sometimes cross paths. It's about dragon shifters and their riders. No pun needed please.

As it is I feel better. Thanks for listening.

Sincerely,

Amy McCorkle

Dear Daniel,

There are people out there that I know and love that are struggling I won't them to know they are not alone. That there are those of us out there struggling just the same. And then there is what I want to talk about today.

A path diverging. My small press career is booming. A job as Marketing Director. Juggling series I never thought possible. Screenplays and a teleplay in competition. It seems like I should be content. But I googled film schools in Kentucky. And one pulled up in Louisville. And it was affordable, if I can just get someone to co-sign on a loan.

I've been seeking everyone's advice. My father's (John's) and really I know no one who can co-sign for me. And my brand of seeking out people at conventions and conferences and FB and twitter seems to be doing quite well for me.

The night of the Golden Globes Missy read a large chunk of Kevin Smith's Tough Shit to me. And in it he recounts how he and his friend/producer Scott Mosier witnessed and I quote, "That's when Eisener released the kraken". That's a funny as shit story because Kevin lived it and he has talent for painting a picture with words and telling stories like few others can.

I sought counsel from my editor at Target Audience Magazine and she pointed out I have carved out a nice career for myself by writing in the small press, attending conventions, and signings and networking that way.

And if anyone besides my cousin is reading this then they know this is true. 28 contracts, by the end of this year 14 books will be out. 4 Amazon bestsellers, 3 successful blogs. 1 Screenplay win 2013 Fright Night Film Fest Best SciFi. 7 Preditor & Editors Top Ten Awards over 3 years 2011-2013. 2 Moondance International Film Festival Semi-Finalist Awards 2012 & 2013. Recently named Marketing Director of Hekate Press. Mentoring young writers struggling with mental health issues.

Mentored by the likes of Julie Butcher, Christine Bell, Tom Sawyer, Rich Ridings, and Grant Wilson.

No one has ever handed me a ten grand check for anything to make things easy on me. So perhaps the film school opportunity is not for me. My family is being uncooperative in even saying they would provide me with transportation.

At this point I must thank my friends Pamela Turner and Melissa Goodman. They keep me going when perhaps my illness would seek to keep me down. They are the special ingredients to my success.

My publishers, Muse, Hydra, and Blackwyrm and all my friends there.

Bertena Varney, for blessing me with the grain of an idea for a character that seems to be my breakthrough story to the mainstream.

And especially my friend and boss, Delilah K Stephans, who believed in my capabilities and strength to bless with the position of Marketing Director. Next to Missy and Pam she really has been great.

Actually there are too many people to thank. But perhaps the film school opportunity will pass me by and Nashville will be some luck my way. Or even the First Look Project. Or even the Author's Fair Competition.

Anyway, may your life continued to blessed, and may I get off this merry-go-round of emotion.

Sincerely,
Amy McCorkle

Dear Daniel,

You know I wasn't going write one of these things for awhile. But two things have sent me back to this memoir. One a good, no possibly GREAT thing has happened. And second has really PISSED me off. So let's start with the good, no possibly great thing that has happened.

I pitched mine and Missy's many drafted screenplay, currently in competition at Nashville and Indie Gathering, *You're the Reason*, to Gina Deeming, an Executive Producer on the independent film, Mark of the Veil, now touring film festivals she told me to give it to their director.

Of course that just means it's going to be read and may be going nowhere fast. But let me explain something. That screenplay is extremely special to Missy and me. I won't downplay that fact. I mean it was the first screenplay to get any heat at all. First from Zide/Perry, then from Lee Daniels, both ultimately passing on it.

The versions it has been through. A close but not quite there deal with Lee Hardin (a local indie), and bungled attempt at working with a producer who didn't want to work with a couple of divas (arrogant youth, I'll cop to it). But here, it seems the universe has offered us another opportunity.

I thought Grant Wilson was the real deal, (and believe me when I saw that he is all that and a bag of chips professionally and genuine to boot), but Gina Deeming seems to have seen fit to sprinkle her fairy dust on me and Missy and perhaps give us a chance to see that script that we first penned in January of 1999 on the screen at least in Film Festivals and possibly distributed in some fashion or another.

But until that grain of a possibility blossoms to its full potential I turn to what has me TOTALLY ticked off.

I don't know what it is that makes assholes come out of the woodwork when they see a vulnerable young adult struggling to come to terms with a mental illness that is plaguing them in a public way but I WORDS for that person who decided to strike out against my cousin who is rocking the writing world with her Ravings of a Coffee Crazed Writer blog and her heartfelt addition to the By the Seat of Your Pants blog.

She was attacked for DARING to share the fact she has been diagnosed with bipolar disorder. What she has done and accomplished in the wake of the newness of the illness is nothing short of brave, courageous and spectacular.

And some nameless JACK ASS has dared to call her out and say 'quit wearing your mental health like a fashion statement' to which I say fuck off and go fuck yourself. The way Rebekah is rocking the bipolar diagnosis is nothing short of stellar. Open and vulnerable and direct she is facing misunderstanding in places no human should have to and to have you, nameless stranger attack her for her seeking out a way to cope and conquer this illness without any shame or fear of retribution? You're the one waving your arrogant ignorance and a modicum of ability to string a put down together, you are the picture people see in Webster's when they look up the word coward.

Whereas when they look up the picture of my cousin, Rebekah McAuliffe, college student, aspiring author, liberal idealist not afraid to speak her mind in family full of loving if not conservative idealists not afraid to let their daughter be who she is.

Bipolar disorder is a lifelong struggle. Even those of us who have come from a dark place to a triumphant one have support, medicine, and the encouragement and acknowledgment of the disease and truly how hard it is in the beginning and how it can come back and bite you in the ass later in life if you mistakenly believe it just 'goes away'.

So Rebekah, rock your author's aspirations. Rock seeking treatment from your counselor and NAMI. Rock your education. And most importantly when cowards like these attack you? Don't take the bait. Because right behind you here I am, and that pencil necked jerk, whether they be male or female is gonna know they bit off way more than they can possibly chew.

Daniel, if you're reading this I hope you know how much your work inspires me in times such as these, when I can't possibly do enough to protect cousin from the ugliness of cowards such as the one who chose to attack her.

Sincerely,
Amy McCorkle

Dear Daniel,

I think sometimes people forget this. I doubt you do. Given you did a PSA going so far as to dress up like a woman for effect to show the inequality that exists still between the sexes.

I've been struggling today. Not with bipolar disorder. But with issues like trust, boundaries, and sex and how sometimes a guy will say it was 'just a misunderstanding' after stepping passed those boundaries and shoving you back down into a cesspool where your past that you've worked so hard to pull yourself out of still seems to swim around, waiting for your next boegyman to push under.

Not this time. This time I'm not going to be quiet. This time I'm going to shout this offenders actions from the rooftops.

You're the Reason, is a screenplay that I wrote with Missy Goodman. It has been through countless drafts. It has gotten heat from three different producers including the likes of Lee Daniels and Zide/Perry, and god me help a producer's name I cannot remember, but do remember he produced a film with Steven Segal. I met him at B. Dalton's where *You're the Reason* was born.

So why am I telling you any of that? To shout this one essential truth Missy and I wanted to get out with our fictional tale. Boegyman can be anywhere. Look normal. Wear a charismatic mask. Be an old friend. Be someone you once took under your wing. Sometimes on the news you go oh he looks like a predator. But beware they hide in the most insidious, banal of places.

So today I was writing and talking to an 'old friend' on Facebook. I had indeed once taken them under my wing when we were in high school. Today, as I was emerging on the other side of my multitude of flying high manias and crashing to low lows I was happy to be getting my writing mojo back, as I had been fighting for it since late last month and for the most of this one.

Mind you, this person is married. And has a child.

Now, what a person does on their own time one thing. I don't begrudge them that right. I said as much. But I also said I have hang ups and am not into a friends with benefits kind of relationship to 'take the edge off'. I figured that was the end of that part of the conversation. While I was offended he seemed to get the message that I wasn't interested.

So ladies, gentleman, young, old, liberal, and conservative, republican and democrat. Here is a lesson I want you to lean in and listen to closely. NO MEANS FUCKING NO!

He started to skype me. I told him I didn't have a webcam or a microphone. He begged me to open. I said if it's profane I want no part of it. This computer, like most of my life, is on freaking loan. He said it was just a video hello. The connection failed. But later on it came through. And yes little boys and girls perhaps I should have known better, but here is the morale of that bullshit tale, I TRUST people. Yes, even though I had the kind of childhood that I did with my biological father, his brother and his friends I somehow retained that sense of trust. So I opened it and got the shock of my life of grown ass man dancing around with his dick in his hands. I instantly cut the feed.

I told him I was offended. I told him I'd been abused growing up and just how bad it had been. I unfriended him and blocked him.

I'm going to give him the courtesy he did not give me and I won't share his identity. While I have nothing against those working in the porn industry, I have no desire to be subjected to it.

So what happened to me? I didn't want to come out of my room. I crawled into bed. I cried. Didn't have the energy to write. Felt shame like I had done something wrong. And I FUCKING

DARE some ASSHOLE to post to MY blog that I should have known better. I've known this guy since I was 17 and he was 15. I'm 38 now. I was so depressed I couldn't write. Not even a simple email to one of my closest friends to say what had happened. I didn't want to leave my room. Understand, my room is not that big.

This jerk came into my life and really pushed my back against the wall and made me pull upon resources I shouldn't have had to but as I was drowning and felt I'd had my voice robbed from me I went to McDonald's ate 3 burgers, 2 McChickens, 2 chocolate chip cookies, and a large coffee with three splendas and 6 creamers. I reached out to a good friend and he said he wouldn't name the name but that I had done nothing wrong. That the guy had. Missy took my every call. She listened to my every tear and came over to the house and had chili and stayed until 9PM. And Pam answered a tear message left on her voicemail.

So in case anyone was listening to today's lesson:

1. NO MEANS FUCKING NO!

2. Predators come in every shape and size. Be careful who you trust.

3. And no matter what, don't let them steal your fucking sunshine. They haven't earned the right, and certainly don't deserve it.

Daniel, I know I make you my silent witness. But I get to use your physicality as characters. And the one I'm writing on now is wrestling with his darker side. And it's very cathartic for a day like today.

And tomorrow I will write like I'm on fire. I only have a hundred or so words to go tonight but I will be ready to write up a storm tomorrow.

Sincerely,

Amy McCorkle

Dear Daniel,

What's life without a little whimsy on wheels? Throughout my twenties and early thirties I, quite accidentally fell into a life of screenwriting and independent filmmaking. We're talking seriously, micro budget, guerilla filmmaking. Long hours, little if any pay for people involved, nothing ideal involved. Along the way we met some great actors (Donavon Shain, Paul Reynolds, Vicki Jones, James Tackett, Stacey Gillespie, Jennifer Boeringer, & Joyce Casey). Met great friends, Pamela Turner, (yes, *the* Pam Turner of my many posts). She came in for an audition as Grace Donovan in a screenplay that is in its umpteenth incarnation. Missy and I thought it was a simple romantic drama and in competition at Nashville. But, as Kevin Smith once put about certain works of his, *You're the Reason,* is as indie fuck as it gets. It weaves tale incorporation addiction, mental illness, abuse in all its forms.

But that film didn't get made, we reconnected with Pam when she became the DP on *Too Far From Texas.* Mine and Missy's first foray into indie as fuck filmmaking. Solid script. With four fantastic actors, and two complete unprofessional. Working in the hottest and humid temps that year *without a/c* because interfered with budget level sound equipment. We dealt with prima donnas who were constantly changing their lines making it ultimately impossible to edit the film. We were green and at times the inmates were running the asylum.

Our second foray into film, the hero (our lead) showed up hung over and proceeded to drop his lines making a short film shoot into an agonizing affair where the competent actor caught it like a dread disease. However, the competent actor was also a graphic designer and created a fabulous movie poster for us. We were able to edit the film (also an indie as fuck affair) and were able to screen it for a small cast and crew. We entered it in a multitude of film festivals, but again solid script, solid cast, cheap equipment. You do with what you have and what you can afford.

The third film we shot and cast, we had a superb script, a fantastic cast, and we we're thwarted by a hurricane. By the time we finished shooting I was exhausted. And indie as fuck filmmaking is hard as hell. I was burnt out and I'd decided I didn't want to write screenplays or make movies anymore.

I just wasn't built for the grind. I was still getting better. I wasn't at a place where I could handle that much stress. Where I was responsible for dealing with the different personalities when I could hardly handle my own.

So I turned to novel writing. In 2009 I saw this movie, you may have heard of it, Casino Royale. In May of 2010 I wrote a novel, *Another Way to Die.* It sat on my hard drive until November of the same year. When Missy's dad was in the hospital dying from the botched liver transplant surgery he'd received. I had a few scripts on my hard drive as well. I submitted them to a film festival. And the book to Lyrical Press. I never heard back from the festival. Lyrical

Press asked for an R&R (a revise and resubmit). Under the mentorship of Julie Butcher I burned it to ground saving what I wanted and rewriting from start to finish. In February of 2011 I attended digicon. I submitted the book to six publishers. 4 of them offered me a contract. I went with MuseItUp. And well, 28 contracts, 4 Amazon Bestsellers, 4 publishers, a new job as marketing director for a small press, 7 preditor and editor awards, 2 Moondance International Film Festival Awards, and the 2013 Fright Night Film Fest Award for Best SciFi Screenplay I stand ready to do something I thought I would never do again.

Make an indie as fuck movie. Only, this time it will be a documentary based loosely on this blog, and the bestselling memoir it inspired.

People need to know things.

Like there is a light at the end of some pitch black tunnels if you are suffering from mental illness, and no, it's not a train.

People with mental illnesses are NOT freaks, lazy, or any other derogatory term that comes to mind. We are simply sick and in need of treatment and with treatment, recovery and great things are possible.

I am also a survivor of extreme childhood sex abuse. As the previous post talked about, I brook very little argument about this subject. This documentary is meant to take away the taboo that puts the blame ERRONEOUSLY on any victim of abuse whether its rape, physical, emotional, or psychological violence. To talk about subjects that when hidden do their most damage and lets the abuser off the hook.

This is a passion project for me. And I'm going set up a fund me, indigogo, or kickstarter campaign. I don't know if I'll raise the full amount or 3-5K I need. But that's my next project. After I write the last few thousand words of Devil's Backbone I will be faced with many things to do. Getting a script/shot list prepared. Getting funding.

Edits on Bella Morte:Beginnings. Reading Gunpowder and Lead: Outlaw for my partner on that project. Lining up publicity for Beginnings. Lining up marketing for Hekate Press.

And of course next month I hear back on something I thought I'd never do again. Write screenplays and enter them in competition. This one Nashville Film Festival's Screenwriting Competition.

So, now you've inspired me to write this blog. To publish a memoir. And a documentary. Along with all these other good things. Whoever is reading this, you are *all* my silent witnesses.

But Daniel, or whoever is reading on his behalf, thank you for making Casino Royale. It changed my life. 2011 I turned a corner in my treatment. But you work changed my career, it *gave* me one. It helped me make my own dreams come true. And for that I could never thank you enough.

Sincerely,
Amy McCorkle

Dear Daniel,

This month feels different from last month. Just like last month felt different from the last week of December. Last month was about getting stable again. Finding a way to finish Bella Morte:Devil's Backbone. And figuring what was next on my creative horizons.

Of course, it's been a while since I sat down to write one of these letters and copping to the fact last month was more like bare knuckling it through a roller coaster ride as one minute I was fine, the next I was flying on a hypomanic high, and the next it was as if the bottom had dropped out is no joy.

It was an unpleasant reminder that relapse is part of the disease and that one must be kind to oneself in the face of it and take care of yourself. Because often it will not only tax you, but those around you who do not understand at all what you're going through.

But the nice thing is I can feel the steadiness returning. Even after some unpleasantness with my best friend. Of course once I realized that was more about her than it was me it made it easier to build towards my pattern of feeling better this time around.

I got in to see Anita, my therapist and got some perspective. We talked about the nature of my illness and how I usually struggle off and on from October to December and how by January I'm usually back in the swing of things.

But 2013 saw me break that particular pattern. I *rocked* the fall of 2013. I wrote 2 books and a good chunk of a 3rd one. I wrote a pilot. I wrote the treatment for the pilot. I mentored to young women struggling with mental illnesses. I started two new blogs one of which without posting this last week. I was rocking the marketing of both my career and that of Hekate Press.

However, something went on with one of the young girls I was mentoring and it upset me a great deal as I feared for her well being and safety. Her family was shaming her. They didn't want to acknowledge her diagnosis of bipolar disorder. She felt isolated and alone and as if she had no one where she was to deal with this. She is an innocent and sheltered girl and their approach with her, telling her she would grow out of it by the end of college really pissed me off.

I remembered being her in college. Only I was 900 miles away from home. Only she's a few hours drive from home. She's heavily involved in campus life. And by her starting her blog her SAI Provincial Officer saw it and loved it and eventually, where I could not help her, she could.

Rebekah is a strong young woman. Resourceful and talented. And it was a relief to know she was reaching out to others for help and not isolating herself.

But in December I had reached my taxed out point and the bottom dropped out. And as I said, January was a month spent getting back on track. Somehow I finished Bella Morte:Devil's Backbone. And began the hunt for the next project.

There is a project that is cooking called Order of the Dragon. It's not ready yet. I can feel it when I'm working on it that it's not ready. I don't want to force it so I let it be.

There's an awful sense of not quite ready madness that overtakes me when I hunting for that next project. As I do things needed for the documentary I also need to feed the writing beast. And finally I've found it. Nation of Blue.

The madness of waiting for competition results hasn't set in yet. I'm sure when it does it will make it difficult to concentrate.

But until then I can say I feel like I'm stronger today than I have been in a while. Maybe not like I'm conquering the world, but like I can finish my work. So here's to the work it takes to getting Letters to Daniel documentary done and Nation of Blue book done.

Sincerely,
Amy McCorkle

Dear Daniel,

The results of the First Look Project are to be announced this Saturday. I know it seems like such silliness. Such whimsy, but I hope I win. It means a chance at my Bella Morte becoming a television series. That would be special. That would make the journey so worth it.

By now everyone who reads this knows my journey. But the reality is I still live at home with my parents. In August of 2012 I made the conscious decision to do so. So that I could travel to conventions, sit on panels, and sell my books as well.

In September of 2012 I decided to turn back to screenwriting after a four year hiatus from it.

Not anything serious, just for the whimsy of it. Because I hadn't ever adapted anything. But one

month from the print book debut of Bounty Hunter Missy and I were writing the screenplay that would serve as our breakthrough win at the 2013 Fright Night Film Festival.

The only real crappy thing was there was no real recognition except for the mention of it on their FB page. Of course I cried anyway. It's not every day one's work is picked as the best of anything and everyone who entered the festival contest is no doubt wishing they had been selected as the best.

But last year it was as if I was writing as if on fire. Hearing Kevin Smith's Burn In Hell's message loud and clear—*why not,* I took the message to heart. And when Missy came to me to rewrite *You're the Reason,* although I did so with reservations I moved forward on it anyway.

2013 was the year that I worked so hard I did not come up for air. In February I wrote the first in a four part novella, City of the Damned. From March to May I co-wrote two screenplays, You're the Reason and adapted City of the Damned, and 2 books Gemini's Legacy and co-wrote When Doves Cry. In May I wrote the first draft of Bella Morte.

From June to July I prepared for Fandom Fest. Made a splash there, had fun there, won there. And in July began writing CORNBREAD. In September finished Cornbread and discovered the Nashville Film Festival Screenwriting Competition thanks to Missy. And entered You're the Reason, Bounty Hunter, and City of the Damned.

And decided to write a pilot for their teleplay competition, whimsy at its best seeing I had never written one and wanted to desperately. So I decided to base one off of Bella Morte.

I wrote pilot that kicked ass. I didn't know if it would win. So many factors go into winning. Who reads it, what their personal tastes are, but I knew it was a great script I could just feel it in my bones. So then I wrote television series treatment with the help of three men. Each of them giving me invaluable advice.

The treatment now sings like a operatic ingénue. So on huge amount of whimsy I entered it in the first look competition. A competition that could see mine and Missy's dreams of having a show on television come true. So yeah, I'm a little excited.

I also encouraged my friend Pamela Turner to enter. If I can't win, I hope she does. But it's whimsy, as Kevin Smith would say. And right now I'm on book 3 of the Bella Morte series as I re-wrote the first draft and wrote Bella Morte:Beginnings, my first 70K novel.

So, I'm hoping on the treatment I believe in. For the First Look Project announcement on Saturday.

Sincerely,
Amy McCorkle

Dear Daniel,

I want to address something that perhaps every star, whether it's in the acting community, or any other part of life that attracts gossips, sycophants, naysayers, or well, stalkers. I wanted to say if this blog makes you feel like I'm any of those things, then perhaps, this blog has missed its objective.

I think because of certain stories girls are fed as children it is expected of us to sit around and wait to be rescued. What I realized really early on was that in this culture something about made me 'unlovable' or at least 'tainted'. I was no princess and no man was going to come rescue me. And that I had best figure out how to crack the fucking code and rescue my own damn self or I was going to die in the situation I was in.

Not to say that in my books that there wasn't hero for my heroine. Yeah, I'll admit it. I dreamt of a knight in his shining armor to come rescue me.

Mind you, I wasn't delusional. I didn't actually believe any of the actors I dreamt of coming to my aid in my books were going to realize that OMG there is the woman of my dreams living in the middle of BFE Kentucky whom I didn't know even existed until right this very minute. Let me drop everything I'm doing right now and go save her.

The very notion is absolutely ludicrous. Insanity. And yet there are people who are going to read this blog and think that is the point of this blog. And there will be little I can do, if anything, to control that response.

It makes me sad to some degree. But more than that it kind of really pisses me off. But then, if I respond to them does that give them the right to attack me? Well, no. Trolls are just that. And if you don't feed them they eventually starve themselves.

Here are the facts. Three years ago this month I signed my first publication contract for Another Way to Die. It went on to win 2 awards. I now have 5 books with MuseItUp Publishing. 6 with Hydra Publications. 4 with Blackwyrm. 15 with Hekate Press.

I have 9 books out. 4 of those are Amazon Bestsellers. I have garnered 7 Preditor & Editor Awards. 2 Moondance International Film Festival Awards. And 2 screenplay awards.

I have three successful blogs.

And I am producing an independent documentary. I am the hero of my own story as I have survived some tough shit. But everyone has tough shit they've gone through. I'm willing to guess that you as well as my other heroes have their own stories to tell. And that because I'm so open with my story there are going to be those who hate me for it.

It is inexplicable to me as to why. It doesn't sting any less. But here is the reality to that. My life now, for all its ups and downs and fantastic and horribleness co-existing, is far better than any haters could be.

People who want to drag me down better have something better than some bullshit, idyll gossip and bitterness to try and do it with, because far bigger boegyman, and far uglier demons than them have gone that path and failed.

So in closing, thank you Lea for giving me my first big break as an author. And have a piece of United States cheesecake with me to celebrate that fact.

And whoever is reading this, no that no one, should you really want it, stand in your way when it comes to achieving your dream. Thanks again silent witnesses, as I do the countdown to this Saturday the 15th to whether or not Missy and I won with our television series treatment of Bella Morte. (And good luck to Pamela Turner in the same category!)

Sincerely,
Amy McCorkle

Dear Daniel,

You may notice some changes happening to my blog. What started out as a simple gratitude blog and grew into a memoir, and ultimately as an outlet for my frustrations as I coped with my bipolar disorder, has grown into something of an outreach campaign.

You may notice two new tabs at the top. So far the pages are empty. The team of Healing Hands Entertainment is coming together nicely. But I don't have the pictures and bios of everyone just yet, so I don't want to unveil it until I am ready. And the documentary won't show until it is completed. So far it will be carried by HULU and will be available for viewing online at NAMI of Louisville for free. There's also a possibility of That Book Place and Karen's Book Barn carrying a few copies a piece. I will be selling the dvds at Film Festivals and Conventions.

I want people to know there's a light at the end of the tunnel. That finding support in friends and family is a needed component, but when all else fails treatment with psychiatrists, therapists, support groups with other people who are traveling the same path is key to recovery. My lifeline was lithium in the beginning. But not everyone reacts to the medications in the same way. I want people to know that the road may be dark and rocky in the beginning, but that there is hope to be had and that as they feel their way in the dark to that pinpoint of light.

It takes work to recover. But hope is there. And sometimes you find it in the strangest of places. I found it in books, music, television, and film. I found it in your work.

In September of 2009 I saw Casino Royale on dvd and changed my career. I found a hero prototype. Here was an a hero who was strong, with something of a death wish, not caring whether he lived or died and only answered to M. James Bond has always been a bad ass. But your James Bond is the baddest ass of them all. Yet, he is not invulnerable. He falls in love. He is always driven by duty, but also by how he feels for a woman. He does everything he can to save her, even when it's been revealed it is she who betrayed him. What a character, what performance.

I wanted to write something that would leave me as exhilarated as the Casino had. It took me awhile to summon that character and story. But in May of 2010 I wrote *Another Way to Die.* It became the first of 28 publication contracts I would sign between February of 2011 and this year. The next one was *No Ordinary Love,* a scifi romance, signed in April of 2011 and the third contract was for *GLADIATOR:The Gladiator Chronicles*, signed in December of 2011. All of them went on to become award winners, and GLADIATOR went on to become an Amazon bestseller.

In 2012 I wrote *Bounty Hunter,* which would become my first print book, it hit #9 on the Amazon Bestsellers chart, and a screenplay Missy and I adapted from it went on to win Best SciFi Screenplay at the 2013 Fright Night Film Festival. I also wrote *ORACLE:The Gladiator Chronicles, Set Fire To The Rain, Gunpowder and Lead, and Gemini's War:Gemini Rising.* The latter winning two awards and going on to be an Amazon Bestseller.

2013 was even more insane. In February I wrote *City of the Damned*, March through April I penned *Gemini's Legacy:Gemini Rising,* and co-wrote with Missy *When Doves Cry,* and screenplay adaptation of *City of the Damned.* And the original screenplay *You're the Reason.*

After Fandom Fest/Fright Night I wrote *CORNBREAD,* October Missy and I penned the pilot *Bella Morte,* adapted from the contracted series for publication of the same name. That fall I also penned *Bella Morte:Beginnings* and *Bella Morte:Devil's Backbone.*

And in May of 2013 I started this blog. In September it ran as book that went on to become a #2 bestseller on Amazon. And in May of 2013 I graduated the therapy portion of my treatment of the bipolar disorder and have been asked to participate in the Moth style story slam by Seven Counties and to be a part of their Night of Celebration and Recovery.

2009 marked a real turning point in my recovery and my life. And I have your work to thank for that in a way. So I know if I've said it once, I'll say it again at some point. Thank you, Daniel Craig. My professional life wouldn't be what it is if today if I had never seen Casino Royale.

Sincerely

Amy McCorkle

Dear Daniel,

This blog is late. Very late. And maybe on a day like today that's a good thing. Because I've had a moment or two to cool off and think twice about what I was going to write. But let it just be said, DON'T SHIT WHERE YOU EAT MY FRIEND, because once you burn a bridge you can never go back.

Let's just say today was the best of times it was the worst of times. Let's just get something off of my chest. Don't ever tell me how to do something and do it in a patronizing, condescending tone. Don't call my dream 'not real' and imply that my vision is not good enough in your opinion to do the job that I want it to. I know 5 or 6K is probably enough to get it down.

Don't assume I'm stupid because I'm not following your plan.

People have told me this 'person' who's rubbed me the wrong way was a jerk, an asshat, and myriad of other words. But I always said, I will wait and see how he or she continues to treat me.

In this person's defense, I think they were trying to 'help' me. Instead they left a bad taste in my mouth. They asked if they could ask me a question but I was away from my computer. Honestly I don't want to know what their question is.

I don't think my vision for my work (Letters to Daniel) fits their con. I do believe their heart is in the right place however.

Their con, in the past has been very good to me. My first panels. Two publishers found. A breakthrough screenwriting award. A valuable connection in one of their goh's.

I try to stay positive about them, because you never know about the don't shit where you eat my friend clause. The bridge you burn today is the one you may need to walk back across tomorrow.

But I'll be honest there are other cons I want to attend more so. Cons that would treat me better. And treat my work with more respect.

So here is the tentative schedule:

March: Author Fair
April: Nashville Film Festival
Conglomeration
Documentary Shoot
May: Various Bookstores for signings
Documentary Edit
June: Various Bookstores for signings
August: Indie Gathering
September: Imaginarium
October: Austin Film Festival (maybe)

November: Author Fair

Perhaps I will sell well, and win some awards. And the documentary will take flight.

Sincerely,
Amy McCorkle

Dear Daniel Craig,

Holy. Fucking. Shit. Letters to Daniel the documentary is going to premiere at Imaginarium a Film Festival and writers con. *Un-freaking-believable.*

How does that happen? I mean I work to make something like this happen. I dream to make something like this happen. With Missy busting her ass alongside me the entire time.

I *wanted* something like this to happen. They're going to highlight *Letters…* and I'm going to get to see my film on a movie screen. I'm going to get the word out about mental illness, getting help, and stamping out stigma to even more people than originally thought.

For the asshat I dealt with the other day, I had an angel open a door and make a dream come true for me last night.

I was so excited last night I could barely sleep. Here I was touching the fringes of something I had always dreamed of doing.

So how did I get from there to here?

How did I go from broken down and barely hanging on to my dreams and my sanity by my fingernails to this? A thriving author, blogger, and screenwriter. A skilled marketing director. I still live with the diagnosis but I have it these days it doesn't have me.

How I wish I could tell you just how much your work and how you handle yourself professionally has inspired me to do my best and how to carry myself in the hardest of situations.

The lesson I carry closest to me is it about the work. It is always about bringing my best, most authentic self to what I do. To be open, honest, and direct.

There may be setbacks. There may be people who rub you the wrong way. There may be obstacles that seem too big to climb.

But that is all bullshit in the end. Look inside yourself and hack your way to where it is to where you want to be.

When I was 21 I wanted to be a published author. I had no idea what a blog was. And I dreamed of making movies that would be seen by many. I also dreamed of seeing a film of mine on the silver screen. Of doing a Q&A. Of writing award winning screenplays.

When I was 23 I was diagnosed with bipolar disorder and all of that seemed a million miles away. I'm 38 now. And to everyone whoever said I wasn't legit. Or couldn't do it. Or perhaps was reaching beyond my grasp. I have a big, resounding F*** Y**.

And to those who stood by side in the hardest of times and believed in me when it was not easy to do so. I want to thank you. Because there is nothing sweeter than premiering your film at a festival and showing the naysayers than nothing and no one can stand in your way.

And if you have a dream. An impossibly large dream. There are the three words I say hang onto because you never know what can happen.

Never. Say. Die.

Sincerely,
Amy McCorkle

Dear Daniel,

I live in a house of contradictions. On the one hand my parents offer me a roof over my head, supplement my groceries, don't ask me to pay room and board for it. This allows me to travel to cons, festivals, and signings. Enter in contests. Pursue my dream how I see fit.

But in the next breath the side swipe me and bloody my nose and knock the wind out of my gut with a one-two emotional sucker punch that leaves the most skilled fighter wobbling in the wind. The worst part of it? I know I'm stuck. Until next January I am official stuck in this weird halfway hellhole, where one day it's all we go together like peas and carrots and the next it's like they're the tornado and I'm the house in their path. And now, all quiet on fucking western front.

I know, I know. I chose this. I chose to move into this house, with this dysfunctional lot. Today I made sure I took my meds on time. I didn't drink copious amounts of caffeine. I got a chapter done. And I guess I should thank their fucking asses because now I have something to write about.

I know it's lame to dream about a Prince Charming or a bad ass ready to whisk me away from all of this. I guess there's this part of me that dreams of finding someone to share my life with. Someone who will come to my awards ceremonies (should I be invited) with me. Someone to celebrate *how hard* all of this really is in the face of emotional turmoil.

But here is what I have to come to terms with. I am enough. I am tough enough. And when my enemies who sometimes hide behind the masks of family and friends wound me as deeply as they do I have to know this Prince Charming thing is a frickin' fairytale because my taste in men is absolutely horrible.

I pick intellectual and emotionally unavailable men.

So when my match comes, and even in times like these, when I doubt he will ever come, I've got to know to hold out for the best one. Someone who makes me their #1. Who will hold me when my parents let me down for the millionth time and let me cry.

My parents suffer from mental illness too. But this is what I've learned. Ultimately you are responsible for your own behavior.

They wounded me horribly last night. So I was horrible to them right back. This morning I owned up to it and apologized to both of my parents. Today they have been the tornado and me the house in their path. I didn't want to up the ante, as my therapist would say, so I walked away and put myself in my bedroom.

Now I'm here. Talking to my silent witnesses to get this awful feeling out of me so I can feel better. I have finished a chapter on the Odd Ones. A thriller I'm having edited before I submit to a NewYork agent. Yes, that's right I'm pushing myself to the next level. And when I get to the bookstore I plan on finishing this blog post and promoting it. And finishing the chapter I was working on last night of BELLA MORTE:VENGEANCE.

As for the documentary. Shoot date might be in March. And perhaps the editing will start in March and finish in April as well. Things are going good with a contact I've made that might be a grass roots fundraiser which will help with marketing and distribution.

So as tornadic as my family is. I succeed in spite of the chaos they often rain down upon me without much as a second thought as to how that might affect me creatively. Last night it made what I wanted to do impossible.

But with a good night's rest, and a schedule to go by I'm getting plenty done. So to you Daniel, and my other silent witnesses, I thank you all.

Sincerely,
Amy McCorkle

Dear Daniel,

Today was an astoundingly great day. The results were announced on the 4th Annual That Book Place Author Fair Story Contest. And guess what?! Missy and I scored a win in the screenplay category with our adaptation of my novella of the same name, City of the Damned.

How many days do you get to wake up and say I have two award winning screenplays? With the acceptance of Letters to Daniel to premiere at Imaginarium and the possibility of it screening at Cinema Touching Disability in Austin, TX I am over the moon. I wanted to go out to celebrate all of this. As it is we had chicken in a pot (a truly delicious simple dish to make) and my parents bought Dairy Queen blizzards for everyone. (Meaning me, Missy, my seven year old nephew Jonathan, and them.)

I am so on cloud nine. It's not every day I win a contest. Or even final. It has been an auspicious start to 2014.

Words seem to fail me how hard I've worked, and the people who've helped me or believed in me along the way. Sometimes you make your heroes and in effect you were a shining light in many ways. I know I never expected this blog to take me where ultimately it has.

The gratitude I have for those who go unmentioned cannot be measured in simple words or gestures. Because the people who've inspired me have been many. But everyone needs a big break.

Along the way there have been those who have taken the time and the patience it takes to show a not so young writer the way in how to write a treatment. How to write a pilot. How to craft a story so that people will keep turning the pages until they reach the end.

I think in some ways I was fortunate that I was left to play in the creative sandbox without too much instruction as to what was the right way to write. My voice developed naturally and uninhibited.

But at some point I'll be honest it seemed the screenplay success was never going to happen. So I stopped writing them. And focused solely on my books and my dreams of becoming a published author. I tried self-publishing back then and it just didn't work.

However, it was three years ago in February that MuseItUp gave me my first big break. The editing was arduous. But I developed as an author there and found the small press a welcoming place for me.

Then last year Missy was watching Kevin Smith's 'Burn in Hell' tour on youtube and we started watching it together. She wanted to revisit '*You're the Reason*'. Which, if I were totally honest I wasn't sure I wanted to do. But the more I watched Kevin the more I realized that the screenwriting and filmmaking dream wasn't dead yet.

It may have been buried beneath an avalanche of fear of implosion between me and Missy, two Chiefs, not enough Indians. I don't like to bend. And if she feels strongly enough neither does she.

But here's the reality I have much to be grateful for. I am living proof, if you just work hard enough, long enough, good things will happen for you. *Don't be afraid to ask for a little help. Because a little help, plus a lot of hard work can and will take you far.

Sincerely,

Amy McCorkle

Dear Daniel,

Into one's life, a little rain must fall. And for me it's been a lesson in patience and disappointments. First let me explain, quality books take time. So my first disappointment is about the two hundred dollars I shelled out for a themed costume for a launch of my series Bella Morte which won't be able to be utilized until August, after book one has been out for four months. I know, what's 200 dollars and a wait on a release date? 200 dollars out of 766 dollar a month disability check is huge. I had planned a themed release party at Conglomeration. More money spent. Arranging for a room party at Conglomeration. Almost burning a contact in my one of my publishers and had to scramble to see what I could piecemeal together. Fortunately I never had a chance to launch Letters to Daniel, and have two releases from said publisher to highlight at launch party, When Doves Cry, a co-written effort with Missy, and Gemini's Legacy, book 2 in Gemini Rising.

Second, at NaFF Missy and I neither made it to the second round or semi-finals with any of our scripts. Which means we only have the finals to hope for. And as down as I feel I can't help but believe in these scripts as they are *really* good. But we won't know anything until Monday when the finalists are announced.

And third, shortly before my meeting with a therapist this morning to interview about possible inclusion in the Letters to Daniel film my parents, who had been on a good streak decided to shit all over me and make me feel like a loser and crappola on a shingle. I had to go in there and act like nothing was wrong and that yes I would love to interview her.

Fortunately like most shitstorms mine passed as I had breakfast and interviewed Shelly for the film. She agreed to be interviewed and had the kind of personality that I could really dig. Nice and calm while I was spinning like a top talking about the film and what it meant to me.

She was impressed with me and given my family is never impressed with me it was a nice change of pace.

However, good news, in the 4th Annual That Book Place Author Fair Story Contest, Missy and I won the screenwriting category with City of the Damned. So, even though the last few days the shit has seemed to have rolled downhill, not all things have been bad.

Bella Morte: Beginnings will not be held up indefinitely. It has a late April drop date so I should have the books in time for the book signing tour I have set up here locally.

And I plan on stepping away from the Marketing Director Position at the end of the year for Hekate as I have too much of my own stuff to concentrate on and while I can do it short term I think I would definitely do Hekate a disservice if I tried to push it long term.

I'm hopeful Delilah understands as I value her professionalism, talent, and friendship. As I value all my publishers I will continue to push all of my works with them and will tour the cons and make the move to self-publishing with my future works.

So maybe the rain and the shitstorm was to get me to make a move I've been needing to make.

Sincerely,

Amy McCorkle

Dear Daniel,

On being taken seriously. I often wonder, in the grand scheme of things when things are going so well that if God likes to throw in a hiccup of two. I have the feeling I will be launching Bella Morte:Beginnings at Fandom Fest. Or even Imaginarium. Patience has never really been a strong suit of mine. I mean, I work hard. I want to see results, yesterday. So when I found out Bella Morte:Beginnings wasn't going to make its original publication date I didn't handle the best in the world.

I mean I had lined up a great tour, publicity, even a costume to where at the Cons I planned on attending this year. With the late announcement I had to cancel said tour, which made me look REALLY unprofessional. And I now have a 200+ dollar I created that has to wait until much later this year to debut. But in the end the argument goes, I'll have a better book. Which in turn will sell better. I just hope I haven't burned my bridges at the bookstores for good.

I was depressed, angry, and let down. Struggling with feelings of inadequacies, I felt like my editor didn't believe in me. While the feelings are very real I know my editor just wants to put the best product out there that she possibly can. She wants the book to make money. That's how she makes her money. On sales. And while as an author I can work with a pushed back publication date it makes my life as a marketing director slightly more complicated.

Setbacks happen. Whether the book isn't ready, the author is throwing a fit, or the editor isn't going to rush their work it's normal a house just opening its doors to encounter some wrinkles. That being said, I love all my editors, including Tir, my editor on the Bella Morte series. And I love working at Hekate under Delilah Stephans, I just had to get passed my disappointment and get back on the horse and get back to work on Bella Morte: Vengeance (book 3).

Of course, I'm working on BLACK OUT: An Aurora Black Novel. A self-publishing venture that I hope to grow into a self-sufficient continuing series. Delilah was the one who told me she felt I had the ability to write two books at the same time. Not that I hadn't already done it. WHEN DOVES CRY(w/Missy) and GEMINI'S LEGACY I wrote at the same time while penning two scripts, YOU'RE THE REASON(w/Missy) and CITY OF THE DAMNED.

And of course I'm co-producing, writing, and starring in and co-directing the documentary inspired by this blog. It bears the name of this blog too. It's opening the film festival portion of Imaginarium and that gives me great joy.

And City of the Damned picked up an award for Best Screenplay in the Author Fair Story Contest. Another reason for rejoicing.

The icing on the cake is that I belong to a group known as Adrian's Angels. Yes, yes, I know a fan club of Adrian Paul television's Highlander. They're a great group of ladies, and sometimes being in their company yields great benefits. Adrian voiced a character in the animated scifi action flick War of the Worlds: Goliath. It yielded me a contact that could give me the breakthrough Another Way to Die was for me as an author. So fingers crossed for one of the the three scripts I sent their way will catch their fancy.

I don't even mind that me and Missy got shutout at Nashville.

But I want to take a moment to thank two people. One is obvious, Missy. Without her standing by me when I was really sick I may not have made it out alive. Bipolar disorder is a wicked mean machine and if untreated it destroys the one who has it and everyone and everything it touches. Missy could have left me in Texas to face the illness alone. She is a whip smart woman and a great writing talent in her own right. Often I think she gets stuck in my shadow because I am such an in-your-face-like-me-or-not-here-I-am personality. She doesn't want her claim to fame to be Amy's Best Friend. She wants to be known as an author, a screenwriter, and a filmmaker in her own right.

Second, I have a friend, one of my best friends, personally and professionally. She works hard, and frankly, she was the one who blazed the trail for me to follow. A brilliant author, a talented screenwriter (she made the 2nd round at Nashville this year) and a generous blogger. Her work ethic blows mine out of the water and she taught me if you want a writing career you have to go after it with gusto. And that even then it may take awhile for it to come around to what you really want it to be. Pamela Turner is the author of Death Sword, Rayne Hall's Ten Tales Anthologies, and her first print book, the Ripper's Daughter. Take a moment and check it out.

And you too Daniel, without you there's no blog. Without you there's no memoir. Without you I'm not opening Imaginarium. Thank you so much to all three of you.

Sincerely,

Amy McCorkle

Dear Daniel,

Have you ever stood out on the edge of cliff of opportunity and looked out onto the horizon and there was all the opportunity you could ever want or desire? And in that moment you had found a certain level of success that some people aspired to but never made it to but still wanted more?

I never feel more alive or more like myself than when I am creating. Right now I am juggling four projects. Letters to Daniel the documentary, the third book in my Bella Morte series (Vengeance), BLACK OUT: An Aurora Black Novel. And more recently The Gladiator Chronicles, a screenplay adaptation of my series for MuseItUp Publishing.

I feel good when I'm writing and editing. It's like I'm doing what I was born to do. Promoting things I'm passionate about like Hekate Press not a hard thing to do. Promoting three books at once? Gemini's Legacy: Gemini Rising Book 2, When Doves Cry, and Gunpowder and Lead: Outlaw a little more difficult.

But the one thing I don't have a problem with is giving a shoutout for is Imaginarium and the man behind the magic, Stephen Zimmer. Check it out here: http://entertheimaginarium.com

Imaginarium is a writing convention, gaming festival, literary costume contest, and film festival all rolled into one and it's happening here in Louisville, KY. I'm proud to say Hekate Press is one of the sponsors on board with it and I am really excited about it.

I know I must be getting on Stephen's nerves but I hope he realizes just how much I believe in his vision. I wouldn't choose to make Hekate's big splash there if I didn't. Or launch my beloved Bella Morte series there. Or co-launch a second book there with my young cousin and her first novel there.

Most exciting to me is their agreement for me to premiere my documentary Letters to Daniel there. That's huge. Enormous to me. Stephen teased me about Imaginarium becoming McCorklefest.

They are also holding two other contests, a literary awards festival and possibly an unproduced screenplay competition. I plan on entering them all.

I don't know if I'm a fireball, but when something as great and as special as Imaginarium falls in your lap you want to wring every last drop of greatness out of it. And I highly recommend everyone looking to sit on panels or learning something about every genre of writing from romance to screenwriting and playwriting to attend this very special convention and film festival.

When I say I believe in Stephen and his vision I make no bones about it. I tweet Monster Energy to sponsor them. I tweet @thatkevinsmith to attend. I tell @MauriceBenardMB that he and his crew should enter their film The Ghost and the Whale into the film festival.

I think Imaginarium could one day be as huge as the Austin Film Festival, Sundance, or even SXSW with its unique blend of scifi fun and accent on writing I am proud to say I'm one of the first to stand with Imaginarium. And I hope to see you there too.

Sincerely,
Amy McCorkle

Dear Daniel,

The question isn't how many times can you get knocked down, but how many more times it takes for you to get back up. Of course, I've been knocked down countless times. Had the wind knocked out of me by different people I thought I could trust. Been open and honest to a fault and let people in without thinking twice about what I shared. This blog has been an open letter to anyone who'll listen to explain that pain is a very real part of the journey. That dark hearted and mean spirited and manipulative people can be just as real now in the damage they seek to do as they ever were in the past.

My film inspired by this blog and memoir was a very personal and important thing to me. Almost sacred in nature. To have someone actively sabotage it and come after me as a person and as a writer well, I don't pretend to understand or like it. I guess I should know better. This person has done damage in the past before. They're manipulative and controlling and nothing but a gossip.

This Con community that has welcomed me into its family has been nothing but kind and supportive. Yet this person has been nothing but catty and negative when it comes to people who've done nothing but do kind things for me and help me up the career ladder.

From Fandom Fest to Imaginarium this person has nothing but nasty things to say about people they've worked with or been so called colleagues with.

It's not as if they haven't tried to control me or drive a wedge between me and people who are real friends before. As Missy's father used to say. If you aren't going to listen you're going to have to feel.

This time 'this debacle' as their former employer supposedly called my film will not look like the same film that left their editing suite. Pamela Turner and Missy Goodman once again have proven why they are the very definition of what good people and true friends are.

Stephen Zimmer has proven to me why everyone, including myself adores him so on the Con circuit. Dave Mattingly proves to me why people gravitate towards him as a publisher. They are genuinely good people. They have your back and don't listen to the ranting and ravings of a disgruntled party.

In the end I know I have to put the negativity behind me. I've never had an experience where the person literally set out to destroy me and my dream in a scorch the earth manner. As if to say 'you'll never eat lunch' in this town again.

But the reality of all of this was I was letting this person get over on me. Letting their negativity get the best of me. Well no more of that. I remembered this blog and what its intent was. To provide me with a soft place to fall when chaos around me reigned.

So let me state here. I'm going have oatmeal for breakfast. Then I'm going to pack my lunch to take to Pam's where I'm going to re-edit the film. I'm willing to bet it's going to be a hundred times better without the negative about it.

It's really good to have the people who count stand by you while the people who don't just kind of drift away into the background. Whether their screaming or silently murmuring it's nice to know I can feel good about moving forward without their influence on me anymore.

Sincerely,
Amy McCorkle

Dear Daniel,

I just saw a fellow author sharing his struggles with being diagnosed with bipolar disorder. Of how he didn't mind the label but perhaps feared being 'fixed' or 'medicated'. It's been awhile since I've address this issue directly if I ever have.

When I was placed on medication my life was in such chaos that I craved a solution. My mind was such I couldn't write. I was sleeping one hour a night. I heard my name being called and what sounded like fingertips tapping on glass.

My thoughts raced like on a race track. I could practically see them like streaks of neon light on an oval course. I couldn't take care of myself. I may not have been quite bat crap crazy at the time but I sure as hell could see the road signs from there.

I was horrible, just wretched to my best friend and partner in crime Missy Goodman. I threw things, I threatened her. And yet, I begged her not to hospitalize me. I was a whore to her. A bitch. The worst of the worst. And yet when I reached out for help she didn't reject me she helped me find the support I so desperately needed.

Texas wasn't ideal for this breakdown but there was some help to be had and she drove me there, in the kind of neighborhood that perhaps you shouldn't be in that kind of night all to help me.

They placed me on Lithium at first and while ultimately they took me off of it the medicine literally saved my life and my sanity. Over the course of the next year there were bumps along the way that would test both of these things.

I had to move back to Kentucky where, honestly I would get better mental health treatment. A better drug cocktail that would lead to my breakthrough in treatment. In the course of 15 years I've gone from someone who has not been to care for herself to a woman who tours the Con circuit with 12 books 28 publishing contracts, will be premiering a documentary based upon the memoir this blog inspired and is moving into self-publishing with friends.

So to the person nervously waiting in the doctor's office, you aren't alone. You are brave. You are courageous. This can be done.

Sincerely,

Amy McCorkle

Dear Daniel,

The theatrical premiere of Letters to Daniel: From Breakdown to Bestseller will be IMAGINARIUM at the CROWN PLAZA HOTEL in LOUSIVILLE, KY in SEPTEMBER. A major league writer's convention that will combine all the fun of a scifi and gaming con and film festival with that of a writer's conference. Me and the team behind LETTERS TO DANIEL have the distinct honor of being the premiere event at Imaginarium.

Me, Missy Goodman, and Pamela Turner will be watching the film that without a great team effort would have never come into being. There are others who are just as responsible for its inception. My parents, Faye and John Keough, (who have, let's face it, haven't always been at their best in this blog), my aunt and uncle, Debbie and Frank Gray, who due to some technical errors on my part won't get to see their contribution shine as much as I would have liked. Then there is Tim Druck and Missy's beautiful letters which were really touching and added to the film. Again, technical difficulties. And the goddess that is Pamela Turner. She is an artist extraordinaire and deserves to be treated as such.

Letters to Daniel as anyone who reads this blog knows is my attempt to grapple with my bipolar diagnosis and move forward, conquering the world as I go. Hopefully helping those dealing with similar issues, and letting them know that even though the world can be a very dark and foreboding place that there is hope. And that there is a way out. There is light at the end of a very dark tunnel, and no, it's not an oncoming train.

There can indeed even be triumph over an illness in which relapse can be a a very real part of a yearly cycle. But that therapy and medicine management can teach you how to cope and live and thrive with the disease.

That these tools can teach you that you can not only survive but move out of the pain and get joy out of life once again. That's what the point of the documentary is for.

It is my grandest hope that everyone who watches it is moved and becomes away that those with mental illness are just the same as anyone else. That the stigma, so often unfairly attached to those who are diagnosed with any kind of mental illness, are seen as those struggling just like anyone else just to make it day to day. Only their issue is depression or bipolar disorder as opposed to diabetes or having lots of kids under foot.

I was once given great encouragement by the likes of Victoria Lamb and Michele Val Jean. People who may or may not know just how much their kind words meant to me. I also received words privately from those struggling with bipolar disorder about how much this blog meant to them.

While the documentary found on this blog will not premiere theatrically until September I'm of the strong belief it can help people today. Please, if you know or someone suffering from bipolar disorder seek help from NAMI, the National Alliance for the Mentally Ill or a local mental health facility and know that there truly is hope.

Sincerely,
Amy McCorkle

Dear Daniel,

We're coming up on the year anniversary of the start date of this blog and there's a lot to reflect upon. This blog has literally saved my life, saved my sanity, and at the same time become so much more than I ever imagined that it would be. I think it has become bigger than me in some respects.

When I first created Letters to Daniel it was done with the notion to thank you and to tell you how much your work has affected my life (all for the better). But it quickly morphed into my memoirs. A place where I could tell my life story in an honest, open, and frank and direct manner.

You, in effect, became my silent witness. I mean, I knew you weren't there. That perhaps no one was listening at all. But Letters became my voice when I felt like no one understood or that no one could understand the turmoil I had gone through or was going through. All the while I knew better things lay ahead. Better things had to lay ahead lol in some cases they couldn't get much worse.

What I quickly saw was that there were others going through what I was going through. That I wasn't alone and that there were lots of silent witnesses out there who were listening and understanding and going through pain of their own. They were finding solace in my words and that meant a great deal to me. It helped with my daily recovery and helped keep me on an even keel.

My blog quickly became more than that. I had a selection of the letters formatted as well as adding introductions by friends and a publisher to give it context. I self-published it as a memoir and it became an Amazon Bestseller hitting #2 on their list. It was a thrilling accomplishment and made for what at the time my third bestselling book.

I continued to write on the blog there was need in me to keep writing on it. It morphed again when I read that Imaginarium was having a film festival along with its writing convention. When I told Stephen Zimmer what I planned on doing things started to move very fast.

And while there were some unfortunate losses, and brutal attacks the documentary inspired by this blog got made. It was bigger, stronger, better for the re-edit and I feel like people are going to receive it well. I even got up the nerve to enter it in the prestigious Austin Film Festival and the Rendezvous w/Madness Film Festivals.

I worry that my dreams often exceed my grasp but I believe on some level for anything to work the dream has to be huge. When I was in my early twenties I was a shell, shattered, unable to even care for myself. The idea of creating this blog, of writing books, of seeing anything clearly was so far beyond anything I could've done at the time it isn't even funny. Not even in the ironic sense.

But you see there were quotes that I lived by. And a quality I had in spades. *Never, never, never quit- Winston Churchill.* And *If you are living on the downside of advantage, and are relying purely on courage, it can be done—Russell Crowe 2000 Oscar Speech.* Perseverance, medication, and a hell of support network. My psychiatrist, my group therapy ladies, and therapist, and of course the usual suspects Missy Goodman and Pam Turner each, not only responsible in their own way for my healing, but each responsible for seeing to it that my film, Letters to Daniel: From Breakdown to Bestseller got made.

At this point special shoutouts to my Aunt Debbie and Uncle Frank and my mom and dad, without them, no film either. I know mom and dad take a beating from time to time on this blog but they, even as they run hot and cold I know always that they love me and that is essential in anyone's healing process.

And of course your work and unbending ear as I talk to you, or at least how I imagine you as a silent witness would be.

I am forever grateful to you all and if I've missed a name please forgive me, as I'm very tired.

Sincerely,
Amy McCorkle

Dear Daniel,

Respect. I've seen people lamenting about the state of their careers and the seeming lack of it. I used to be quoted in my therapy sessions, group and solo times as saying 'no one wants to be the imposter, yet everyone's greatest fear is that they are the imposter'.

Honestly it used to be my greatest lesson I couldn't learn, well maybe second only to I wasn't my diagnosis, but that I had bipolar diagnosis not that I was bipolar diagnosis.

And in a way I believe the two were insidiously linked. Depression has a way of messing with your self-confidence level. Whispering in your ear that no one respects you and that you're a joke for believing a career in the arts was within your grasp.

Now, while my career seems to be doing well, (and while I can't complain I remain hungry for more mainstream success as I think many of us do) I want to take a moment here to say something. I recently saw a FB post that argued that without a mainstream blessing you aren't legit.

For those with small presses or are braving a more independent road I believe you are just as legit as say you're more traditional counterpart. Each path has their pros and cons and a simple, rash decision either way could damage your future just as easily as say believing NY is a panacea and that the independent world is a shortcut to success.

That being said getting to where I am now professionally has been a long and hard road, but the last three years have been sort of insane. And the success I've had professionally seems to have dovetailed with my recovery.

I no longer struggle with the issue of am I the imposter, or the I am bipolar. I am not an imposter as a writer, and in spite of what some people out there might believe even if you are holding down day job while you pursue your dream job either you are a writer or your not.

Now there are those who use their day job as an excuse as to why they *can't devote as much time* as they'd prefer or have three million as excuses as to why they can't do it at all. Now that group I have no patience for.

That doesn't mean those who struggle with legitimate issues such as depression yet *still find a way* don't have my full and utmost respect. Mysti Parker, Pamela Turner, Missy Goodman I'm talking to you all.

But everyone has that setback that threatens to undo them entirely. That breaks their hearts and threatens to break their spirit right before the long road back starts. For me that moment was September 2000. It very nearly broke my spirit and derailed my dream for awhile.

I worked at a place called Children's World for a time. I worked with pre-schoolers aged 3-5. I did especially well with the special needs children. The very type this place were horrible with. The 'teachers' there were a joke. Their 'director and assistant director' even more so. I suspected a young girl there was being abused. I took my concerns to the director and was fired for the 'fact I was not fit to work there'. I had been diagnosed with bipolar disorder and they used that fact to get me out of there.

Myra Hutton was a joke of a director as was her assistant, Natalie. It very nearly destroyed me. It triggered a second breakdown. I could barely function. I was forced to move back to Kentucky.

It's funny how things work out though. The road to recovery really took hold there. My mom and dad(John), Missy, (even Missy's family), were there in the beginning as I took those first very difficult steps to wholeness.

I struggled a great deal with the imposter feelings and seeing myself as something more than my diagnosis. Still I took my medicine, I attended my appointments with my therapist and psychiatrist and clawed my way back with my support network. Carla Bell Deal was crucial in the mix, but my greatest strength I drew upon was from my best friend Missy and my half evil friend Pam Turner. (And of course my mom, dad, aunt Debbie and uncle Frank). All of these people along with the parade of nurses and my girls from group helped put me back together.

I did not allow my heartbreaking moment to destroy me. For those struggling I too had a moment of truth. But I'll blog about that another time.

So for those who wonder if their moment will ever come know that if you stay hungry, and you define for yourself what success should mean good things will come.

Mysti, you are not working in a vacuum. Pam, I still want to be you when I grow up. And Missy, one day we'll be the female Matt Damon and Ben Affleck.

And Daniel, it did my heart good to see you front and center on the PSA for the campus sexual assault awareness campaign. Another reason why you're my hero.

Sincerely,
Amy McCorkle

Dear Daniel,

It's funny how life is. This blog inspired by my publisher Lea Schizas suggestion three years ago that I should create bipolar writers blog. I decided to do a spin on that. A gratitude blog that quickly spun into something altogether which morphed several times in under a year and produced a memoir and documentary.

You'll notice that today I placed the 1 is 2 Many PSA in my sidebar. As a sexual abuse and rape survivor I feel that it is imperative that I do my part to show my solidarity with my fellow victims, survivors, and thrivers. That fact you're in it all the better. It makes it relevant to this blog as I envisioned it.

But onto exciting news. A few months ago I submitted the Letters to Daniel documentary blog to http://Film-Com.com to be held in Nashville. It's a business market that brings industry professionals from LA, NY, and Nashville and perhaps elsewhere to Nashville for 4 day and three night networking and new project expo.

I sent my sixty dollars in and put Letters… name in the hat never dreaming in a million years that it would get picked. Because, I can count on two fingers over the last fifteen years that Missy and I have gotten picked for any screenwriting/film award. Yes, I've won awards at Moondance but that was for a short story (first ten pages of a novel both times).

And while that was totally awesome, and helped get us to this point imagine my total shock when I opened my email this past Saturday night when this came in the mail:

Greetings, Film-Com Content Creators -

This is a brief note to indicate that if you are receiving this message, your project is an Official Selection of Film-Com 2014. This means:you will receive all-access laminates for you and up to three other team members for:

—the VIP Reception on Tuesday June 17

—the Packaging, Financing & Distribution Summit on June 18

—the How to Pitch & How Not to Pitch Evening Session on June 18

—have a free booth for two days at the New Project Expo at Titans Stadium June 19 & 20

—access to three Networking Breakfasts with industry executives at the Hilton Nashville Downtown June 18, 19 & 20

—attend the annual Film-Com Industry Gala at the Governor's Mansion

—are now a Finalist for the Direct Pitch Sessions to industry execs

—have discounted rates at three hotels in downtown Nashville

—discounted rates at the finale event at the Schermerhorn Symphony Center under the Film-Com Block Rate.

I ran thru the house screaming for mom. She had already gone to bed so I woke her and dad up from a dead sleep. They didn't exactly appreciate that. But I was so giddy with joy that they quickly forgave me the faux paus.

Then the bottom dropped out. I couldn't get Missy to take 4 days off. I couldn't get the rest of the money together. The depression that I was going to miss out on this golden opportunity so close to home hit me hard. I was angry at the world. Why would god give me this opportunity only to snatch it away.

Then I started listening to those around me. I'd prefer to do both New Project Expo days, but as it turns out I can only do one. So we drive down do one networking breakfast and the booth one day and drive back. Not ideal. But to paraphrase Oprah do what you can. And to follow in the great footsteps of Nia Vardalos who only had enough money for an ad in Variety one day for her one woman show one day may be all that Missy and me need to get all our work in front of the right people.

So it looks like Letters to Daniel the documentary is our little movie that could. And the PSA by the way it touched me in a big way. It's good to know our president as well as so many people I admire find women worth the time of day to speak out against a serious problem.

Sincerely,
Amy McCorkle

Dear Daniel,

This blog, if you take nothing away from it, should be those with mental health issues, are members of society deserving of equal respect and the kind dignity one would give anyone who might be considered 'normal'. Nothing will bring the claws out in me faster than the bullying of and maltreatment of anyone with a mental health issue or those who are their supporters, friends, families, husbands or wives.

Those with illness deserve to be treated kindly with tenderness and care. And most of all they want to be treated with respect. Very few of them play their situation for pity, and their pride often keeps them from getting the help they so desperately need. But when one has a mental illness be it PTSD, Depression, Bipolar Disorder, ADHD, or those wrestling with Autism, they aren't to be mocked or feared or bullied by those who refuse to understand and treat them as an 'other'. They, we, deserve to be treated with kindness and compassion. And our family and friends who stand by us day by day deserve to be praised for their patience and love, no matter what form it comes in.

And I feel when one of us are attacked out of simple ignorance, the simple fact of not knowing better is one thing. But when you willingly spread venom against someone because they are different and can't begin to fathom the damage you are inflicting upon the person with a mental illness and their support network. And of course then there are the liars.

People who hone in on someone's weakness and exploit it for their own gain. I know people good people. Honest people. Who have worked hard to get where they are. And are being attacked for no good reason. As you know I've been attacked and lied about and my bipolar diagnosis was at the heart of the attacks. People lying about me threatening that I'd never eat lunch in this town again so to speak.

All I can say is the issue was resolved and I've already caught the interest a distributor at Film-Com and I can't wait to go.

Other people's victories are smaller but no less important. Some survive the war, only to need the help of friends and family to find new solid ground. And a new 'normal'. They are to be praised and commended.

I have my support network. My first line of defense has always been Missy Goodman. I often think of Beaches when I think of our friendship. No, we did not bust up over a man. And no neither one of us is dying from cancer. But she is my rock and even though we may disagree she would cut a bitch for me. Then there's my Mom and Dad. They have not always fared well on this blog. But you know parents and children are going to disagree. And I have to admit where it comes to the Letters to Daniel film they and Aunt Debbie and Uncle Frank have been superheroes in helping getting it done.

Then there's my half-evil, 333, friend who next to Missy is someone who doesn't judge me for who or what I am. She's helped make Letters to Daniel the film a possibility too. She's my angelic friend with horns, a tail, and a pitchfork. Her weapons of choice are a rocket launcher and a flamethrower.

Then there is my biggest professional friend. Delilah K. Stephans. She is, in a word, AWESOME. A loyal wife. A solid sounding board. A talented writer. And a woman with a vision for publishing success and talent for cover art that transcends it's form. She's constantly learning and the way she describes her husband and the way he treats her is one those things from a fairytale.

Mental illness is a thing not to be held up and mocked and blamed for someone else's discomfort. For the person who feels uncomfortable around the mentally is the one with the true problem, not the other way around.

I graduated therapy and have been mocked for this blog and the form I chose to put it in. I had people say things like I was obsessed with you and thought I was going to marry you. *GIVE ME A FUCKING BREAK! YOU HAVE NO IDEA I EXIST, AND YOU'RE MARRIED FOR GOD'S SAKES TO ONE OF THE MOST BEAUTIFUL WOMEN ACTING TODAY.*

These same people called me crazy. Delusional. And it hurt me because I thought these hypocrites were sweet loving people who called me their friends. I had learned my lesson. They didn't understand me and they certainly didn't understand the purpose of this blog. Now they're going after a friend of mine, I won't say who. They're much too private to spill their pain and anguish out in public. They've chosen to take the high road. To that I say bravo, as I had to take the high road not that long ago myself. I won't spread that story either.

The lesson I learned there was the truth will out. And hopefully for my friend karma does for her as it does for me.

Sincerely,
Amy McCorkle

Dear Daniel,

I come to this blog today with burnt skin, a bruised heart, and the gratefulness that comes with having great friends in the writing community as well as friends and family on the inner circle who have rallied to my cause.

I always write with an open heart. Sometimes I'm mad, sometimes I'm happy, sometimes I'm defending others. At five o'clock this morning I found myself in desperate need of defending and a shoulder to cry on after receiving one review from a troll that I was too inexperienced to fight off on my own. I often tell people to take the high road and not feed them.

But this attack seemed to be personal and have nothing to do with the book. It called me 'A Woman too Fat to Walk' 'Ever Self-Promoting' "Writing unpublishable romances' 'On Disability and using my ever Trendy Label of Bipolar Disorder'. That's all I'm going to share here because really their words don't bear that much repeating. It seemed like they were out to hurt me.

And some things at five o'clock in the morning are easier to handle than others. People have rallied around me, my parents, Missy, Pam, Mysti, Leona, Stephen Zimmer, my cousin Rebekah and other anonymous helpers who I am forever grateful to.

All I really have to fight off the coming depression is to stand back and damn it, look at how far I've come in bipolar struggles.

There were times when something like this would have destroyed me and knocked me way off the path. The road back would have been long, hard, and fraught with peril. I would be sleeping close to fifteen hours a day. I would isolate myself and perhaps turn away from the project completely, never to look at it again.

THAT WAS THEN. THIS IS NOW!

Am I blue and depressed? Yes. Am I allowing it to stop me? FUCK NO!

As I step back look at what might have happened to me 15 years ago—fail at hygiene. Fail to keep my home clean. Unable to crawl out of bed. Let this rat bastard define who I am and what I've become and what this blog turned memoir turned film about possibly.

But this rat bastard is looking at a much different human being with the tools to fight off an asshat like him or her and I refuse to let them define my life for any reason. I worked too hard. Earned too much. Fought too hard to get back on the road to wellness and balance to let them have a say in what I'm about, let alone this blog/book/film is about and is intended to be.

What I've learned is when you are feeling alone and devastated is to allow yourself the sadness and to cry. Reach out immediately to your friends and colleagues. Lean on them for emotional support and cull them for professional advice.

The reality is I make myself vulnerable on this blog. I talk about my life, and my work along with my relationships professional and personal are fair game for me to use. I understand there are consequences to this.

There are going to be people who twist this blog's content to mean things other than the intended meanings. I can't stop them. All I can say is this is my emotional truth. This is how I survive day to day.

I AM A PUBLISHED AUTHOR WITH THESE HOUSES: MUSEITUP, HYDRA, BLACKWYRM, & HEKATE. And I recently ventured out into the world of self-publishing under the banner of HEALING HANDS ENTERTAINMENT.

Yes my work has romance, but there are other genres represented. SciFi, Fantasy, Dystopian, and Thrillers. I also co-write screenplays, television treatments, and pilots.

I've won awards, been a bestseller many times over. IF YOU ARE GOING TO BE STUPID ENOUGH TO ATTACK ME GET YOUR FACTS STRAIGHT.

The thing I'm most proud of, Letters to Daniel, and what it's grown into, now a documentary being featured at Imaginarium and Film-Com which me, and the two other producers on it, will be attending.

When I was drowning in Texas and a shitty mental health system, it was Missy who saw fit to stand by me through the worst of it down there. When I got back to Kentucky Pam joined the team. I owe so much to them.

So, anonymous troll and hater, you wanna take me on? Think the fuck again. Because you aren't fit to lick the bottom of my shoes.

Sincerely,
Amy McCorkle

Dear Daniel,

The last few days I've run the gamut from angry to hurt to sad and depressed. And earlier this month I was absolutely joyful at being selected for Film-Com. But today I want to talk about someone who talked me down off the see-saw of should I go or shouldn't I go to Nashville for Film-Com while dealing with a terrible kind of grief she and her family wasn't ready for.

You see if you haven't figured it out by now by following this blog, I'm a bit of a bull in a china shop. If I want something I tend to put my head down and go for it and I don't look up until I get it done.

Barbara Ehrentreu recently lost her husband. I sat virtual shiva with her online not that long ago. I was going back and forth on Film-Com. Whether to go. Whether to go for a few days. Or not at all.

At the point I was talking to her to offer her comfort she offered some advice to me. She said I needed to find a way to go. That opportunities like these didn't come along all the time and as an official selection I got a laminate that not only got me in but paid for my booth.

I had been at a point where I had decided not to go and was angry and depressed, not just with me but with Missy whom I felt like was sandbagging my efforts to go. (Which honestly we just move at different speeds on some things sometimes. She can cherry pick. I'm more of an all or nothing girl.)

Barbara encouraged me to do what I could do. Go for a day at least. So I started gathering up a head of steam and what went from one day went to two went to three and now is the full four day and three night experience.

Her, in the throes of grief had been kind and compassionate enough to set me on this path. It is easy to see now that Missy wasn't sandbagging anything, but simply stating what she was and wasn't willing to do in order to go. Which in all fairness was what I needed to respect.

But Barbara has always been a kind and generous soul. She's had me on her blogtalk radio show more than once when I was launching a book. And while everyone is always eager to unburden themselves on someone else, myself included, Barbara was commended by several in the shiva for the kindness, guidance, and compassion she has often shown others.

She is a shining example of what a good and decent human being is. And what good they can do even when they are despairing.

Another person I'd like to talk about today is Pamela Turner, trouble shooter, and Letters to Daniel savior extraordinaire.

We couldn't figure out why the movie would not burn correctly. Somehow she figured it out and the film is awesome! I am excited and can't wait for the movie to screen at Imaginarium but Film-Com has me nervous. But in a good way. Thanks to Barbara and Pam I'm heading to Film-Com with my film.

Of course lest we forget Missy, who's been the Rock of Gibraltar the whole time holding me firmly by the ankles so that I don't float off into the clouds of mania. Spin like a top right of the table.

But my prayers and many thanks go out to Barbara who deserves the kind of joy and peace that come from being loved and lifted up in a such a time of need. If you can keep checking in on Barbara. The grief doesn't just 'go away' once the funeral is over and the crowds go home. Often times that's when it's the hardest.

Sincerely,
Amy McCorkle

Dear Daniel,

Often I come here to sing the praises of others, and on rare occasions I have asked others for money, most recently for funds for the documentary based on this blog and memoir. Today I want to talk about who makes us writers look as good as we do. Our editors.

My first editor was Lea Schizas. Having her edit me was like marine bootcamp. It felt like my skin was being ripped off. It was not a pleasant experience. BUT that being said she tore me down and built me back up. I was a better writer for it when it was all said and done.

My line editor Greta Gunselman who has gone on to do freelance work and content editing has been with me since the beginning. She has done two books for me away from MuseItUp Publishing one which has already been self-published and a second which will become self-published at the beginning of next year. She rounded off the rough edges, has sharpened my grammar skills and has graciously come aboard with my self-publishing venture. She deserves all the accolades that come her way.

Then there is Tanja Cilia, content editor extraordinaire who's worked with me at Muse and Hydra she has helped whip me into the writer that I am. And I can never thank her enough for what's she's done. For without her guidance I may have never become the writer I am and I can't thank her enough.

And finally I want to tell you about Ana Jobrail aka Annie Rodriguez. She is my editor over at Blackwyrm. She has done the work on the Gemini Rising series and When Doves Cry. She is a gentle soul and works hard to see that your dreams come true.

Well recently she was robbed, well recently she was robbed and assaulted in Egypt while on vacation. Everything was taken from her. Her cash. Her purse. Her credit cards and passport. She has been placed on bed rest for six months. She is currently in Romania with her son. Her home, however, could be sold as the back payment of the sewage bill was not paid by her son and his wife. And her car payment is three weeks late as they have not paid that either.

I know this sounds like a scam, but it's not. I've known Ana for quite some time and have never come on any blog to beg for cash for anyone other than my own particular goals. Ana is looking for donations or editing work. She is a fantastic editor and does wonderful work. I point to Gemini's War and Gemini's Legacy as evidence of the kind of work she can do.

Here is the gofundme link to give donations: http://www.gofundme.com/9f887w and you reach her under Ana Jobrail if interested in hiring her as an editor.

Sincerely,

Amy McCorkle

Dear Daniel,

I'm not sure what it is I did to deserve some of the success I've gotten. Nor do I pretend to know why it's this blog that seems to be what is breaking me through to what every writer and filmmaker dreams of, mainstream success.

It all started here with a simple thank you a little over a year ago with the knowledge you would most likely never know about this blog or anything I wrote about on it. It quickly became so much more than that. It became a place where I could share my story, my memoirs about who I'd been growing up and I'd survived a brutal upbringing on the one side of my family. But thanks to my mom, (who admittedly needs a little help herself) and a stepfather (who, in response to the creation of this blog said he was making one too, only to call it, *All the Lies Amy Tells* in jest) who, if not always stable, were always warm and loving.

Mental illness runs in my family like Cancer does in others. Bipolar Disorder especially. I won't name names because it's their story to tell and some can't even bring themselves to get the help they need. But maybe if they take a moment to read this blog they'll see that medicines I take for it aren't poison they actually give me direction, help me focus, make my dreams a reality instead of just grandiose daydream with my head in the clouds.

Ellen Eldridge suggested that I get in touch with the gentleman and driving force behind the You Rock Foundation. The You Rock Foundation's mission is to help those deal with depression through music. My film, Letters to Daniel fits into that mission even if it is bipolar disorder.

I feel like I've been hammering at this wall in the film industry and this emotional honesty is going to be what gets me in, when all I ever really wanted to do with this project was help people.

This is all icing on the cake. The trip to Film-Com for possible distribution? Never in a million years did I think that would happen. To be talking to a distributor already. Holy CRAP!

Now You Rock?

Un-freaking-believable.

I don't really know what to do with the feelings these things conjure up. Last night I was crying. Not sad tears but, the, I can't believe it's not butter tears. The I've worked a long time for this and I can't believe it's finally here.

What I think is sweetest is that I didn't get here alone. There are people who have always been there to support me or accept the path I was on even though they did not always understand it. And as sweet as this I know the climb isn't over yet, that big things are in store for me and those who helped me get here.

I have to thank the inner circle. #1 Missy Goodman. The picture of patience. She isn't a saint but she plays one on television. She is a talented author and blogger and screenwriter in her own right but she often follows what rabbit hole I go down to make sure I don't get lost or meet some unfortunate end. When things were roughest in Texas and those first few months back in Kentucky she could have chosen to turn and run. I think, perhaps, I might have. But she didn't. God only knows why she didn't, but she stuck by me through thick and thin.

Then there's team member #2 Pamela Turner. Also a talented author, blogger, and screenwriter/filmmaker in her own right. She is 333, only half evil, but if you cross her look out. But if you gain her friendship she is the kind of friend that you should be so lucky to have. When Missy has been unable to take me to the doctor's it is Pam who has taken me. She's paid for medicine I couldn't afford, and along with Missy has made the documentary based upon this blog happen.

There are so many to thank, like mom and dad, Aunt Debbie and Uncle Frank, Danny Jones for the beautiful song that plays at the end of the film, all of my publishers, and Stephen Zimmer for his unending patience with me, or as he put it Amy on 11. Really everyone should be commended for that.

The You Rock Foundation is perfect for something like Letters... and the vision I have for it. So a special thank you to Ellen and You Rock because you too, are making my dreams come true.

Sincerely,

Amy McCorkle

Dear Daniel,

All of what I have accomplished as been without an agent or an assistant or any of the crap they tell you that you *have* to have in order to be viewed as successful. But my life is beginning to feel as if it is on a race track. And while I'm not even viewed on the Z list I know that I have things that agents or publishers would find desirable. Namely I get out there, I get seen, and I work hard every day either writing, promoting madly or both.

Now, I have to admit, there's a certain level of comfort that comes with promoting online. There's a level of perceived anonymity that comes from sitting behind a monitor, you're only link to society a keyboard and wherever your thoughts may take you.

Some people think this blog is nothing but an exercise in self-promotion. But the reality is this is where I come to lay my thoughts bare. To confess my soul's torment, happiness, triumphs and defeats. It's my safe place so to speak where I can say what I want, how I want, when I want. It's a place to heal and learn from. It's my true north when it comes to writing.

But the conventions are harder. Because even though I yearn to take part in all of them the closer I get to them the more anxious I get. I have to gear myself up for all the people and selling of the books I have to do. Smile, be personable, be happy. Make sure I don't run myself into the ground before the 3 days are over.

Not that I don't have a great time. Not that I don't make fantastic connections. Make friends. Sell my pants off. It's just the anxiety will press on me. And by the end of the weekend I am drained and crabby and just want to be left the hell alone.

Not because the people bother me personally. Honestly, it's the readers and the impulse buyers who make going to these things such a joy. Seeing familiar faces, having something new to offer them is always fun.

It's just my energy runs low and I need someone taking care of me. Which is why I finally decided to breakdown and query agents. I've sent the first batch out. Ten to be exact. I wish to be a hybrid author. Although at the rate New York is going I wonder if it's a dinosaur going the way of the bricks and mortar bookstores.

I think it's a smart step though. I write screenplays and teleplays and as you know (not really you, but the people who are reading this blog know) this blog has become something of a beast I need help containing.

An agent is needed to help me organize. Today has been productive but not in the sense I want it to be. I want to be writing on the second book in the AURORA BLACK series. I have fun writing those kinds of books. And on this one I get to write a little romance in it.

But the agent for my book series I'm looking at now is the Bella Morte series. I'm not sure I pitched it right to everyone. But then it was four or five o'clock in the morning. It was good that I did it when I needed to do what I considered the boring stuff. Because honestly I think my career, if I really want it to step up into the next level, I need a little bit of help.

Sincerely,
Amy McCorkle

Dear Daniel,

I talk about Missy and how awesome she is a lot on this blog. That's because we have truly been through the fire and then some. When I experienced my breakdown in San Antonio fifteen years ago it was just us down there. Mom and dad sent care packages. Jerry sent nothing. He disapproved of us moving down there to begin with. Why? I don't know, the man is a chronic alcoholic who is a real asshat at times and I was so hungry at times and I called him once and he denied me any help. He simply told me to move back home.

Here's the truth of it, Missy calls Texas our grand adventure. It was absolutely nuts the way we packed up everything we owned, shoved it into her Ford Escort and drove from Bullitt County, KY to Bexar, TX all in an effort to make it in the film industry.

Yep. You heard me. Because we couldn't afford LA or NY we opted for an area rich in independent film country. We were going to make it in the film industry. We attended the 6th Annual Austin Film Festival on producer's badges. That's right. We quit our jobs and moved clear halfway across the United States when I was already exhibiting signs that I was not a well girl.

Once at the Festival we thought we were the shit. Good Lord we were dangerous. We happened to encounter a man by the name of Jim Vaughn. I only wish we could find him now. He was the best thing about that Festival for us. We commuted two hours each way during the course of the Festival. Once, leaving the headlights on, forcing us to walk back to the Omni hotel where the clerk refused to let us use the desk phone and pointed us in the direction of the pay phone. (Russell Crowe, we feel your pain) and call a tow truck. I asked anyone if they had jumper cables and heard someone actually utter the bullshit phrase, we jetted in.

We had no furniture. Only air mattresses to sit and sleep on. A tiny 13 inch, yes, you heard me right, a thirteen inch television on which for a good deal of the time we were down there we had no cable or internet. Yes boys and girls you can survive without either. And meals consisted of spaghetti five days a week and hot dogs the other two.

My condition, fragile to begin with, quickly deteriorated. Common sense would have sent us home much earlier than when we finally broke and returned.

I heard my name being called from a distance. It sounded like fingertips tapping on glass. I saw shadows out of the corners of my eyes. A lot. Sleep deprivation was my enemy. Each night sleeping less and less. Until only getting an hour, only to be awakened by Missy opening the refrigerator.

The breaking point came when I became so enraged I wanted to destroy everything in the apartment, (and we didn't have a hell of a whole lot). I walked in circles, pulling at my hair, crying, raging through clenched teeth. I needed to get help. I needed it badly. So Missy called my Aunt Rosie (a Roman Catholic Nun who is the coolest bitch you'll ever meet) and she and her fellow Ursaline Sister Norma, who didn't speak a lick of English came and picked us up and took us to the University Hospital.

So I waited and after an eternity I went numb, just absolutely the opposite of what I had been feeling. I was taken back to be seen. I have an extensive family history of bipolar disorder. I talked about how I had felt earlier. I talked about how I felt then. I talked about my family history of it.

The younger psychiatrist said yes, you have bipolar disorder. Her boss said no, it's all in your head. I shit you not, that's what the lady said. Only they didn't call it bipolar disorder then they called it manic depression. Honestly I didn't care what the fuck they called it as long as I got the treatment I needed. But I didn't and by midnight I was crying and depressed and on the other end of the spectrum

Rosie took me and Missy home. But it was Missy who, at midnight, in a city she barely knew, in an area of the city that could be a little scary for the most brave of souls took me to the mental health clinic where they diagnosed me as dystemically depressed and put me on Zoloft. Folks, do you have any idea what an anti-depressant does to a rapid cycling bipolar chick. Let's just say it doesn't help.

After three days of torture my sister Sara instructed me to go back and ask to be evaluated for depression and manic depression. It took all day, but I got the diagnosis I needed. I got the medicine I needed and thanks to Patrick, an angel whom Missy and I worked with at Northwoods Cinema we had a wonderful Thanksgiving after going to bed hungry and waking up that way for a good chunk of time.

There are many other stories of how Missy was the kind of friend anyone should be so lucky to have stand by them. But sometimes I get so busy helping everyone else with their work, listening to everyone else about their stories, that I forget to help the one person who has been with me through thick and thin.

Today is Memorial Day here in the United States. I honor those who have served and sacrificed so that I can have the life I live today. But I also honor Missy, because without her perhaps, there would be no career, no festivals, no films, no books, and no Cons. You should know she is a brilliant author, screenwriter, and filmmaker in her own right. She is an award winning screenwriter and short story writer. The success with the documentary is due in no small part to hers and Pamela Turner's hard work alongside me. So as much as the blog and book are mine. The documentary is truly ours. And I hope you tune in tomorrow when I talk more about Pam.

Sincerely,
Amy McCorkle

Dear Daniel,

I talked about Missy yesterday. Today I want to tell you about Pam. Her full name is Pamela Turner. Just so you know. Her books, Death Sword and Exterminating Angel are freaking brilliant. I don't even read that genre as a rule and I love her stuff. Death Sword is a Chanticleer Review Finalist!

She also writes terrific short fiction and has been included in several of Rayne Hall's anthologies. Her stand-alone piece, Family Tradition was an EPIC Finalist for short fiction (the Oscars of the ebooks).

She is also an award winning screenplay writer for her short screenplay Cemetery. See what talented company I keep? Between her and Missy I am seriously blessed.

But that's not why I'm writing about her today. I'm writing about her because I want her to know just how grateful I am to have her as a friend. That I appreciate having her in my life. And that I couldn't do half the things I do without her there.

When I am broke there have been times she has provided me with the cash for the medicines I so desperately need in order to stay sane. When everyone else bails or simply 'cannot help me' she's the one who takes me to the doctor be it the psychiatrist, the emergency room, or the clinic.

Missy and I met her when she came in to audition for a film yet to get off the ground. She didn't get the part, but when our DP bailed on us to work with a big Hollywood guy (in retrospect I can't really blame the guy, who were we to Cameron Crowe?) but at the time we were desperate and it was Pam who stepped up to the plate.

And the irony of ironies, of ALL the people we worked with on the set for that disaster of a film she is friend who stuck. Not because she's not a good person deserving of every success she gets or will get in the future. But because she may be rough around the edges and I think people forget she has a very soft heart.

She is wounded by things that others may easily brush off as nothing. Even I'm guilty of it sometimes. But that being said she all kinds of AWESOMESAUCE.

When I first met her I wanted to be her when I grew up. When I needed direction she kindly showed me the way. She introduced me to Savvy Authors and digicon where I found my first publisher. She introduced me to the comic con scene and Stephen Zimmer and Fandom Fest. Where it seemed each year brought me more success than the last.

She seems to be my Golden Buddha. I rub her belly and good things happen. When I thought all hope was lost with the Letters to Daniel documentary it was she and Missy who rode to the rescue and in effect gave me a more powerful and a more moving documentary to premiere at Imaginarium to pitch at Film-Com and to talk to the You Rock Foundation with.

Pam is the kind of friend who, if you show her loyalty she will have your back in ways you never dreamed possible. She often suffers the idiots around her in silence. She's much too professional to ever gossip or talk trash about colleagues, *even if they couldn't be more deserving of it.* She takes the high road and this can be hard on her.

She came into my life in 2001 as a colleague and quickly became so much more. She has been a great friend, and if anyone deserves good things, no, great things, it's her. She recently had her first print book come out via Blackwyrm Publishing, The Ripper's Daughter. If you get the chance buy it, it's on Amazon. I was a beta reader on it and it's a terrific tale.

If anyone is privy to a friendship like the one I have with Pam you should consider yourself so lucky. They don't come around often. So when they do, cherish it. Don't fritter it away.

Sincerely,
Amy McCorkle

Dear Daniel,

I often talk about you and how you gave me a publishing and film career. And I credit your work being my inspiration. And all of it is true. But in some ways this blog could have just as easily been called Letters to Maurice. As his impact has been just as big.

Fifteen years ago I was an aspiring writer and wannabe screenwriter and filmmaker. And for my film I wanted the one and only Maurice Benard to star in it. For those of you living under a rock, or perhaps don't know, Maurice Benard stars in General Hospital as Sonny Corinthos and in the forthcoming film The Ghost and the Whale. He also happens to have bipolar disorder and is a tireless advocate for those suffering with the illness in hopes that they (we) will seek out help.

At the time I suspected that I had it. But you know Maurice and his lovely wife Paula had the guts and the courage to talk about their journey when it wasn't in the mainstream or very trendy to talk about. Although, that being said, mental illness isn't trendy, it's something that is still, to some degree talked about in whispers and shadows. The only place where I see it being used as 'trendy' is when the media outlets mislabel a misogynistic a-hole who shoots up a college campus.

Maurice had the courage to fight for the storyline on General Hospital. The courage to be open with his struggles. And honestly it gave me the courage to seek help sooner rather than later. His courage gave me the courage to keep going back to the doctor when there was a misdiagnosis in order to get the right diagnosis.

To keep taking the meds even when things weren't perfect. He gave me hope that one day I would be well and that success in the creative industry was possible for someone like me the night he accepted his Soap Opera Digest Award for Favorite Lead Actor and said 'for anyone out there with bipolar disorder if I can do it so can you'.

I remember crying that night. Not because I was sad, but because it struck at the very heart of me. I hadn't written anything in months and I didn't know if I would ever write anything again as I struggled to get to a stable place where I could do my best work. But those words, *his* words re-lit the candle of hope that had seemingly been snuffed out.

Recently I read his account of the audience's reaction to his speech. That there had been some laughter in the crowd at his words. It angered me. That was his moment to shine up there. He had overcome so much and yet they would laugh in the face of it. I didn't understand it then and I certainly don't understand it now.

If that speech were given today it would be met with applause, not laughter. But fourteen years ago people were barely talking about mental illness. His work as advocate has saved many lives, including mine. So, even though I can't afford to fly out to LA and see The Ghost and the Whale, *his* film about a man struggling with bipolar disorder, I support it one and ten percent from KY. And today he tweeted I deserved the success this blog/book/ and documentary was bringing me. Well he certainly deserves all of the joy, success, and stability he has fought so hard for.

I used to not understand what he meant by his words he couldn't do it without his wife Paula. And while Missy and I are not a romantic pair I understand perfectly what he means by that now.

Sincerely,
Amy McCorkle

Dear Daniel,

I took a chance today. Actually two chances. I want to release a second volume of letters. I plan setting the first volume of letters on permanent FREE on Amazon. What started out as place to initially thank you and everyone else who has every helped me. Or to let off steam whenever I needed a place to be emotionally honest with myself. Or even just get something off of my chest so that I could get in the frame of mind to work. Became something bigger. I started getting comments from people saying that I really helped them understand what they were going through. That I was giving them hope that they too could crawl out of a tunnel that seemed to be pitch black and it was all they could do to feel along the walls to find their way out. In the sense that your work and Maurice's advocacy and been my way out of the darkness I was acting as theirs.

I didn't really know what to do with that. But I was touched just the same. I had been where those people had been. I had been struggling to just get out of bed, get in the shower, keep from having a hair trigger temper. I had needed heroes who understood me. And while I laude you and Maurice there have been so many nameless people on this blog. Those who have fed me when there was no money. Gave me a place to stay when there was too much friction at home.

Then the army of one named Missy who, along with the doctors and therapists put me back together. And Pam who has unfailingly been steadfast in her support (even if she is half evil). And of course the parental units who run hot and cold on me in their support. I am ever grateful to them for what they do take part in, even if they don't really understand what it is I do.

No, the two chances I took today were calling Maurice Benard's management and your publicist to see if I could get introductions to my second volume of letters.

Maurice because he too has bipolar disorder and copes with it on a daily basis and his advocacy got me into treatment, and you because, well, your work got me a career I have always wanted. And as I sit here writing this I'm well aware that the chances of either of you actually saying yes to this is slim to none I had to take the chance that you might. If I didn't I would have lived with the kind of regret that nags at anyone who dreams big then fails to capture any part of that dream.

The documentary is something that has really just blossomed into something I could have never dreamed of. But it all has to start somewhere. And for me it starts with you and Maurice Benard.

I hope you can understand this isn't me just fangirling and hoping that you will pluck me from obscurity. Letters to Daniel has NEVER been about that. It just hasn't. And what may have started out as something as intensely personal has kind of taken off like a rocket.

I have secured bestseller status with the first book, so I'm not looking for that kind of thing. Even the blog was never about that either. The film? I thought I might get into 1 festival, Imaginarium. And that was a huge IF. But then they said yes and that they wanted to make it a premiere event of the Con. And then Film-Com accepted us. And then The You Rock Foundation came and along and showed interest.

This second volume is my way of keeping the blog alive in it's grown purpose. To help people. To make people see that even in the darkest of circumstances that they too can break through their obstacles, whatever they might be and make their dreams come true.

Sincerely,
Amy McCorkle

Dear Daniel Craig,

I have often talked about my mom and (step)dad and just referred to my stepdad as just dad. Because really, for better or worse, even when I feel like they don't get me, they don't support me, and they don't cheer in an ideal fashion they do their best and at the end of the day I know they do indeed love me, allow me to live in their home as I pursue my dream and supplement my grocery bill that's far more than others I see getting. So while at times they do forget about me and put others accomplishments above mine I figure, they're coming in September to Imaginarium and dad is coming to the PREMIERE event along with my Aunt Debbie and Uncle Frank. I have support. But as I've taken this journey I've learned who deserves to have an emotional relationship with me and who doesn't.

And the one that doesn't received a lot of coverage early on in this blog. My biological father. I won't say his name because he's not the target of my ire tonight. It's his former ex-wife current girlfriend, old lady, caretaker, whatever you want to call her. And I will say her first name because clearly as co-dependent personality she thinks her mostly spent cache as my former stepmother who talked shit about me behind my back as a child earns her the right to say anything to me about how I live my life. Her name is Doris. And right now if I could beat the living crap out of punching bag it still wouldn't cool the coals of fire she has stirred up in me.

A few years ago I wrote my biological father a letter telling him how I felt about what he did to me and others, how his behavior basically got us to the point where we were. And it was as if a hot poker had been cooled in my chest and weight had been lifted from my spirit. I mailed him the letter and well he just took it to mean I blamed him for my life turning out so shitty.

As anyone reading this blog knows, my life may be difficult at times but it is not shitty. Or terrible. If anything it turned out great in spite of him. He doesn't acknowledge mental illness as a real illness and sees me as a mooch because I'm on disability and food stamps. The goal through all this work is to get OFF of those things. But I use them to survive and pursue my dreams and goals.

So when some dried up, bitter, angry, emotionally broke old woman thinks my biological father is something special it calls into question her basic ability to make sound decisions. Mind you I used babysit my baby sister for her while she worked and went out on the town. She married a man who had held gun on her and my sister so she could have the big wedding only to divorce him two weeks later.

She expects me to let her lecture me on the fine art of emotional relationships. Every single time I put myself out there for either of them they make me uncomfortable, they make me feel like I'm in danger, and like I don't matter. One shouldn't be made to feel like trash for being different and I AM different.

I have bipolar disorder. I need help to get by for it. I've come a long way WITHOUT ANY HELP from them. People like Pamela Turner who is brilliant as a writer, a blogger, and filmmaker and screenwriter. With rough edges of her own she really allows me to be me when no one is can or will. People like Missy Goodman who has literally at times lifted me up and carried me and all of my emotional baggage and accepted me as I am. Also a brilliant writer, blogger, filmmaker and screenwriter. My mom, as moody and as tempermental as she can be loves me and as hard as it is to get her to come to any of my events she still supports it even though she doesn't get it. My dad by choice who called me his little iconoclast, who he took he walking as a kid. Turned me on to NPR, Moth Radio, and along with my aunt and uncle turned me on to all kinds of movies.

Of course, Jerry left his mark on me. Pain, addiction, his own struggle with mental illness. Doris, always close with Brandy and eventually when Sabrina was born making us feel like the other kids. I recall one Christmas, Sabrina's first where everything Brandy and I got fit into a single t-shirt box while Sabrina was showered in her young state with countless gifts.

However, in the end I think I'm the one who won out. She got Jerry and Doris for parents. I got Faye and John.

Daniel, I know you're not reading this, but in magazines I see you out with your daughter and can't help but hope she got a Johnny-Dadddy (our nickname for John when we were young) for a father as opposed to a Jerry. And I hope on this Father's Day that she's as grateful for you in her life as I am for John being in mine.

Sincerely,
Amy McCorkle

Dear Daniel,

I wanted to have something good to end this volume of letters with. Talking about people best left in the past wasn't something I wanted leave the audience or you with for that matter. The people discussed in the previous letter don't approve of how I live my life. Which for the record is none of their business but for all to know I don't drink (except for the occasional celebratory drink or New Year's Eve), I don't smoke, and the only drugs I take are those I need to in order to keep me balanced (my bipolar meds), my allergy medicine (off brand Claritin), and Prilosec for GERD. And of course the occasional Tylenol or Motrin. Hardly a hardcore drug users medicine chest.

That being said, I work hard every day. Though not everyone can appreciate what I do as hard work even my parents have time just how hard I'm busting my tail end off. But hard work reaps rewards. I've talked about Film-Com which a week and a half away. Godspeed to me and my time. I want to enjoy myself, but I don't want blow my opportunity either. It's not every day I get invited to one of these things.

I've talked about Imaginarium and how there will be book launches and a movie premiere of BLACKOUT: AN AURORA BLACK NOVEL and Letters to Daniel Vol 1&2 and the screening of the film.

I've told you of the busy schedule I'm keeping this summer and early fall. But I've also told you of the many contests I've entered. Nashville, Fright Night/Fandom Fest, Indie Gathering, soon Imaginarium. And I've been waiting to hear back on them. Probably the hardest thing for a writer to do is wait and given we all write on spec we spend a great deal of our time doing exactly that.

Nashville was a bust. But tonight I got word on Fright Night/Fandom Fest. Both of mine and Missy's screenplays finaled. That's City of the Damned and Bella Morte. I'm getting a table and selling my books there. If I could show you a really awkward happy dance that makes me really look stupid that's how happy I am tonight.

I would like to acknowledge some people here that really made this happen. First and foremost my sister from another mister, Missy Goodman. We have been writing together a really long time. Last year we broke through at this festival screenplaywise and we would like a chance to win again. We sold a lot of books there. I'd like to do that again. Missy and I met while working at a bookstore 18 years ago. We started writing together a year later. The road has been long and hard filled with obstacles for both of us. But it bonded us in the kind of friendship you don't find every day. Yes we argue. Yes we fight. Sometimes. But we are always there for each other. And the success we're tasting now is all the sweeter for it.

The second person I'd like to thank is Pamela Turner, a brilliant author, blogger, screenwriter, and filmmaker in her own right, we met her in 2001 and worked with her on a 2004 project that I just won't talk about as a professional. We had everything go wrong on that set, including having two people who didn't know their lines. We liked some of them we barely got along with others. And Pam became the friend who stuck by us like glue. She was disciplined, serious about her craft, and took no prisoners in her career. A little rough around the edges with a tender heart of gold she became a friend when no one else wanted to be. She showed me the ropes in ebook world and told me about free online writing conferences where I found my first taste of publishing success. She also pointed me in the direction of my first Con Fandom Fest and the literary track director, Stephen Zimmer.

Stephen Zimmer is a haus! He regularly champions up and coming writers and authors and helps them get started in their careers. He's helped me, Pam, and Missy every year at Fandom Fest and is the man behind the magic at Imaginarium. He has a big vision for Imaginarium and I believe in it what it could one day become. It's in its first year and I am incredibly honored that he picked Letters to Daniel the documentary to be the premiere event. Because I also have two book launches there and am entering other contests he wants me to get a t-shirt that says McCorklefest on it.

Now, other than the fact I hate my last name it tickles me that he says that. But my last name is what my readers know me by. It's my brand so even I were to get married I would always be Amy McCorkle or Kate Lynd on the front of my books or in my work.

But there you have it City of the Damned and Bella Morte are both finalists in Fandom Fest/Fright Night 2014 and the winners will be revealed August 2, 2014. And like I did last year, knowing like I did last year, I invite you and your family to come to the awards ceremony. But like I said snowball, hell. For now I'll just celebrate the moment and be happy. Because this is what I work for. For people to like and recognize my work. To enjoy my work. And by this blog and book and documentary to help people with my work.

Sincerely,
Amy McCorkle

Intro to Part 3 by Ellen Eldridge

In part one, Amy writes, "Sometimes, in the darkness, dreams are the only light you've got." She's right.

This collection of letters written to a muse shows the light in a lady who's found her way through some dark times. With humor and hope, she shares her horrors as well as her dreams.

Letters To Daniel, in all three parts, allows anyone who's ever struggled with a desire to do and be more to follow their passion forward. Let dreams light the way, Amy might advise. She's helped me. Her insight and fearless dedication to sharing her story may seem easy. It may look to the average reader that "anyone could do this," but I promise you it's not. I've never let my dusty diaries see the light of day. I've never published a memoir under my real name. Amy's strength is her gift and she shares it with us in this third and final part of her Letters to Daniel. He should be honored to get a chance to read these and know his art inspired hers.

My hope is that Amy's art inspires its readers.

Part III

Dear Daniel,

I often talk about Missy and what she does for me. She often compares herself to a pack mule and me as the thoroughbred. She does the hard grunt behind the scenes that often lifts me up from just another writer to someone who looks like a star. She is a Taurus in every sense of the word. Steady, calm, nurturing, and if she wants to give she will, and she will do it without question.

But there is a flipside to this Missy's bibliography reads like this: It's Your Love, co-authored efforts Gunpowder and Lead Series (2 more novellas to come), and the short novel When Doves Cry. Then there are our screenwriting efforts. They have been many and we are finally starting to see a payoff in that area. And again her helping me (a big nod for ALL the hard work both she *and* Pamela Turner have put into to this) bring my documentary based upon this blog to life.

However, here's the thing. She has never had a solo book launch. She has never had the day where as she put it last night where the mule was prettied and shined up to show and be made to feel like the star. Everything that is out with exception of It's Your Love has either been a shared effort or as she put it, my dreams coming to life.

So here I am doing for her what I should have been doing all along. Doing for her what she does for me. Letting her shine like the star that she is.

Her most current project is My Summer With the King, a coming of age tale about a twelve year old girl named named May and her friendship over the course of that summer with the King himself Elvis Presley. It covers her relationships with her single mother Rose, her sister Daisy, and her cousin Thelma. The rush of true love with Jack, and the confrontation with her mother's menacing boyfriend Nick.

It's currently undergoing revision but the first draft is fantastic. She plans on having it edited and will launch it at Imaginarium! Where I am already quite busy but it's simply not fair for me to expect her not to taste some of the solo joy I am tasting. Screenwriting has always been something we did together and while we've done some books together it's simply nice to be known for something you've created on your own.

Maybe it's a selfish thing, perhaps it about being in control. But everyone deserves their day in the sun. And Missy certainly has earned hers. Be on the lookout for her relaunched blog, FB page and her official author site.

I really believe in her the way she has believed in me. I hope everyone who reads this will join me in celebrating who Missy is and what she wishes to become over the next year. I really want her to feel like she can shine her brightest around me and not just to be a mirror who reflects my light.

Sincerely,
Amy McCorkle

Dear Daniel,

I spent my birthday quietly, thanks everyone for the birthday wishes! Promoted a few of my friends' work and had an interesting discussion with Stephen Zimmer. He asked me if I didn't want the success and the fame why was I working and going at it so hard. I told him I wanted to be protected. It made me think. From what? Success? Failure? Disappointment? Well I do want the success and I have always been ambitious.

The truth is, I have always been a driven person. Even as a kid. I wanted to be the best at what I did. But with the writing contests I could never unlock the mystery to winning the competition. Winning I've found to be two parts writing from the heart. One half part finding the right reader. And one half part dumb luck. And all of it born from busting your ass on a daily basis.

Still you can go your whole life and never win a damn thing and go without signing a single solitary contract.

I find I'm still as obsessed as ever where it comes to winning. But somewhere along the way I lost the mentality that I was an 'imposter'. I think it happened somewhere along the 13 books that are now out and the myriad of contracts I've signed and the self-publishing ventures I've made.

None of this came to me gift wrapped in a box with a box on it. It started when I was kid and the bibulous desire to write and create was stirred in me by the acts of reading, watching television, and going to the movies. I thought I want to do that. At five years of age. Now that would take a while to crystallize into any form of validation of my writing. But the desire was there. I was given wonderful teachers who introduced me to the Success program where we had a notebook and once a week we were given a prompt and we would write stories about them.

I wanted success. But I found only emotional truth brought any kind of success. I kind of stumbled onto this when I was 13 when I wrote a short story about the French Underground and the survival of people living in the woods. This was way before I ever knew about the Bielski Brothers and the movie Defiance. I'm 39 years old now it's been awhile since I wrote the story. But inside of it was the story of survival, and a love story. (I had a boyfriend at the time.) The name of the book was A Candle In the Darkness. I won my school's competition for it and received a medal at a county wide awards ceremony.

Validation. Emotional truth and people responded to it.

But it was a lesson I had to hear and learn again several times over. But this last time. When I started the blog, by the time I had graduated therapy I had learned the lesson. But talking to Stephen tonight made me think about why I was so nervous, so scared of going to Film-Com.

I'm just as afraid of success as I am of failure. I've gotten some blowback recently that I won't go into here from people that I love and adore and I don't want to lose them because I'm 'livin' above my raising'.

I forfeited a booklaunch. Stephen if you're reading this please attach book launch back to screening of Letters to Daniel. But please try to slide in the one thing we were talking about.

I do want the fame and the glory, but I always write because the stories in me drive me to write them. I don't control them. They most definitely control me LOL. I want to be financially set. I don't want to have to struggle anymore. I want the power to meet my heroes on equal footing.

I work really fucking hard at what I do. And for people to dismiss that or take it personally really bothers me. The list goes like this:

1. Writing
2. Chyna
3. Missy

4. Pam

5. Parents

6. Siblings

7. Debbie & Frank

Everything else is secondary. I'm starting to be known on the scene here locally. Now just to find a way to make that spread out. Feel the fear and do it anyway. Thank you Stephen for setting me straight tonight. Film-Com here I come!

Sincerely,

Amy McCorkle

Dear Daniel,

As I sit here pushing ten o'clock in the evening east coast time I am less than 48 hours away from the official start of Film-Com. I have been busy prepping packets to hand out. Doing laundry to get packed. Getting banners and business cards ready to go. I even cleaned my room finally to make way for some possible hardware this summer and fall. Who knows, right?

Choosing to go to Film-Com was hard. As ecstatic as I was at the invitation I was paralyzed by fear. So I went back and forth as to whether or not to go. It was a once in a lifetime kind of opportunity. People might want to buy or market my documentary.

Honestly when I decided to make the film in January I didn't think anything would come of it. I thought I would show it at a few small to medium sized cons and film festivals. Never in a million years did I dream it would blow up so fast.

I just wrote on this platform how I felt, what I was going through, how I was getting there. And people responded. The blog became hard work in that after the first two months of writing virtually every day I felt burned out. I was promoting Gemini's War, the first book in the Gemini Rising series. Getting ready for Fandom Fest last year.

Yet the blog was the one place I could go and be honest about how I felt about things. And as excited as I am to meet the executive and author at Film-Com I am scared that the whole thing could blow up in my face.

I have a completed film. A documentary. Where it was just me on this blog in the beginning I feel like the book and film were an exercise in different people in my life coming together to make a dream of mine come true.

Especially the film. My co-director, Missy Goodman also a producer and editor on the film Pamela Turner. A producer, editor, and all around Jill of All Trades on the production team. My Aunt Debbie and Uncle Frank for driving me to Lexington to record the sound files. My parents who provided their car for me to drive to the editing studio. To Mysti Parker, Tony Acree, and Ellen Elridge for all playing their role in getting me to Film-Com.

To think I would be entering the film world with a documentary? Not in a million years.

But now as I sit here less than 24 hours away from heading to Film-Com I have to thank those, at least anonymously who made my road infinitely more difficult than had it been something of an easier path.

Because of you I have a better movie. Because of you I am less dependent upon the past. Because of you I know sometimes people will let you down. But I also know that because of my therapist I don't have to let these things define me and that ultimately my success is my own and that those I celebrate with truly deserve all of the accolades I heap upon them.

So many go without praise on my blog, but it's not because they haven't done their part in this.

Still, there are teachers along the way. Mrs. Vickers, Ms. Pompeii, Mr. Lee, Mr. Birdwhistle. And so many others I can't possibly thank enough for being there when the world was eating me alive at that age. Then college. Richard, my debate coach for the first semester. I can't remember your last name but I remember going to Lawton, Oklahoma and going to the all you can eat steakhouse. I remember you being shocked that I could 'write'. Still I liked you. Making us sing on the trips we took.

I doubt you remember me, but I will always remember all of you. You all touched and saved my life in increments. If this film makes it I hope your memory is jogged and you come see it. Until then I hope you are content to know you saved this woman's life.

Sincerely,
Amy McCorkle

Dear Daniel,

Film-Com has come and gone and let's just say. IT. WAS. AWESOME. From the panels with industry professionals to the expo where I really shined to the pitch where my anxiety got the best of me. It was all incredible. Except for the really shitty Nashville traffic. But even then the drivers were accommodating.

Unfortunately Missy couldn't make the trip with me but Pam as usual was a great partner in crime who managed to work a little magic herself, for herself as well. And let's not down play the adventures we had on the roadways through Garmin.

The panels were fantastic. Meeting Joel Eisenberg in person at 6:40 in the morning was fanfreakingtastic. The man had a low bullshit threshold and it was wonderful. He took the packet. Which included the documentary Letters to Daniel, a data disc with books, scripts, and treatments on it. A one sheet with the synopsis of each book. And two one sheets for Pam's work and data disc with her work on it. He also took the memoir on which the documentary is based.

He was frank, fresh, and open and wanted to know about us. He let us talk as long as we wanted which honestly was nice because after coffee in the morning I can get a little chatty. Which led to the conversation about Bella Morte and he wanted me to talk to his editor at the time. Which was really awesome. And after I have some time to digest just what this last week really means to my career I'll get on emailing all the people who gave me their business card. Which was A LOT.

Documentary distributors en masse it seemed came to my booth at expo and took a packet after pitched them Letters… Even people standing close by would somehow take a packet. TV people took my packet. I won't name drop because well, it's tacky. People liked my story of coming back from bipolar disorder and abuse. At the booth I was totally in my element.

Going up to Gary Badderley after the panel was intimidating but I knew I had to do it. My nerves were horrible. But then standing in front of someone who can get your message out in a much bigger way than you can be intimidating for anyone. Most everyone who said they were going to come by the table came by the table.

The actual 'pitch' was a disaster. CRICKETS. With the exception of one person asking questions. And asking if I had a booth. I know if she came it was after lunch break and after they went back in to hear pitches again.

I had to leave and breakdown at 2:30PM. Because honestly. I had worked it out with my psychiatrist that I pushed all of meds forward so that I would stay awake during the day. So I could do basically Wed 5-4 Thursday 6-4 Friday 9-2 and I pushed it out until 2:30. I still had 4 packets left. I took a gamble took the banners down, made sure the number 47 was still up. Left business cards and the packets.

I really wanted to stay, but the all out panic attack I had standing on the stage in front of the queen and king makers made the pitch total crap. The guy in charge I think pitied me and shook my hand and said, 'it was a very nice pitch'. Who knows. Joel came in and said some very nice things about me. Which I really appreciated. But I felt like I had just blown my big chance. I mean everyone else was coming out saying we rocked it. We kicked ass. I wish I could say the same about the official pitch.

BUT. In just meeting people and encouraging them to come to my booth that's where my real comfort zone was and that was where I really shined. I felt like I was on top of the world there. Of course that could be the bipolar talking but, when the one executive who had responded in the pitch session to me had not come by 2:30 I had to go I could really feel the effects of my meds being pushed forward for that length of time. Erica Wester, wherever you are, thank you so much for taking on our table and looking for the executive with the hat and sundress on.

The anxiety was really strong and what I hope comes of this visit to FILM-COM are lots of things. Distribution first and foremost because it makes my second point all the more salient, I want people to get help. To not be afraid of the psychiatric community. To educate them and erase the stigma for those of us who have bipolar disorder and other mental illnesses. And let those like me out there know that there is indeed hope, that you don't have to live in darkness. And that help is indeed out there and joy and happiness can be had.

Sincerely,

Amy McCorkle

Dear Daniel,

I've always wanted to be mentored. To make contacts. To move up the ladder. That's not why I started this blog. I started this blog as a way to heal. It was an incredibly personal thing, that just sort of took off like a shot. I know when executives are looking at numbers that maybe 9K sound like a whole lot. For someone in my shoes it is.

I wasn't looking for followers. I wasn't looking to sell books. Not with this blog. It just sort of grew in that direction. What started out as a place for me to come and connect with my emotional truth. Or to vent. Or basically just show what a day in the life of someone with bipolar disorder is like has suddenly become something much bigger than me.

I wanted you to know that your work was like this light at the end of a very dark tunnel. And coupled with psychiatric treatment and therapy it became a way for me to feel along the dark walls and move forward even when I didn't feel like moving forward.

As the light became brighter I had to trust that it was better world than the sickness had to offer and that it wasn't a train of more of the same heading towards me. Things began turn around for me in 2011. When my first book Another Way to Die was contracted by MuseItUp Publishing it was inspired in part by Casino Royale and in part by the book The Girl With the Dragon Tattoo. With a hero which at least physically looked like you. The character itself was completely of my imagining and not the least bit like you given I don't know you and only know your work.

I went on to write and contract for 25 books. 13 are of them are out. 1 is due out this summer. All since 2010. I have been fortunate to win awards. 8 Preditor and Editor awards over the span of three years. A Moondance International Film Festival Semi-Finalist for 2012 and 2013. 2013 Fright Night Film Festival Best SciFi Screenplay Award Winner for Bounty Hunter. A double finalist for 2014 Fright Night Film Festival Screenplay Competition in both SciFi and Fantasy categories. (Will find out the weekend of Fandom Fest about whether or not I am a winner in either category.)

7x Amazon Bestseller with 5 different books, including the memoir based on this blog which hit #2 twice. And was the inspiration for the documentary I hope to find distribution for. The books are Bounty Hunter #9. Gemini's War(Gemini Rising) first time #24, second time #9. GLADIATOR (The Gladiator Chronicles) #43. BLACKOUT (An Aurora Black Novel) #15.

And now I find myself with lots of hooks in the water for distribution and a mentor after Film-Com. Life is pretty damn sweet. Next Monday I find out if one of those distribution leads plays out. And that Tuesday I find out if any of mine and Missy Goodman's scripts win or our

Letters to Daniel is selected to screen or win at Indie Gathering.

FILM-COM is only in its fifth year and is growing by leaps and bounds every year. I got in near the ground floor. I would love to go again if I have a project. And save up enough so I can stay in the Hilton. (AS IF!) When you're living on a $766 dollar a month budget and pull off a film and a trip to a big deal thing like this is something of a small miracle and is due in no small part to donations from friends, and family. The trip and packets and banners were all done on a $512 budget. And I have to say it was well worth it.

The people I met, Erica Wester you are so going places, people who were drawn to my documentary thank you so much. All this from a blog where I used you as my silent witness. To make it okay to open up and share my journey with bipolar disorder and abuse.

And Joel, thank you for everything. You made Film-Com worth the headache of Nashville traffic as Pam and I commuted from a hotel in Franklin to Nashville everyday and got lost except for the very last day lol.

I wish one day that I get to meet you. Not as some googly-eyed goofy fan, but as someone who has a cause. To show where your work has inspired me in my work. And has inspired me in how to unlock the creativity within, to heal the scars of mental illness through use of books, movies, television, psychiatry and clinical psychology.

These things all served a part in saving my life. As your work provided the key to finally unlock all of my dreams.

Sincerely,
Amy McCorkle

Dear Daniel,

I think a writer spends most of their life in two stations, waiting to hear good or bad news, or creating. Often the only way I can handle the waiting is by creating something else. Moving on to the next project. Letters to Daniel was different in that it kind of took off without much effort on my part. I think I've said this before, I expected to *maybe* play a few small festivals and then self-distribute at scifi cons.

I say this next part not to brag, but to give some context. I've been writing since I was five years old. Looking for publication and representation since I was 18 and finally, through the small press found myself on the path I am now. I am thirty-nine. Given the hard work and the trial by fire I've been through I'd say through the power of this blog Letters to Daniel has given back to me more than I have ever given to it.

People have responded to these letters offline. People in business, those who suffer from bipolar disorder, and those who know or have loved ones who battle this disease every day. To say some have a harder road than others is not an understatement and probably is an oversimplification of just how difficult it is to go through the healing process.

Because if you have bipolar disorder you're hit from all sides. First there's the illness itself. It hits each person who has it differently. It's almost as if you're on a spectrum. The symptoms, when left untreated slowly rob you of everything you have and are. Some can become addicted to the grandiose highs that are often associated with the illness. Some, in a psychotic state will believe they are God or some other religious entity.

It never got to the point with me, but here's my experience. Fifteen years ago people weren't talking about mental illness. Bipolar disorder was still called manic depression and my only sources of information were Maurice Benard interviews where he and his wife talked openly of their struggles and triumphs and the internet.

Well I just got my first rejection where the film is concerned. Well, I'll keep the business card of the entity involved. I never expected for this person to show any interest but she kept the door open for possible future projects. I'll save her business card. I sent her a thank you email. I'm nothing if not professional. And she got back to me quickly. And even if none of the other leads pan out I can still play festivals and self-distribute as first planned.

Am I disappointed? A little, but I never expected to have the opportunity to begin with. Fifteen years ago, as I struggled to just get out of bed, to take care of myself, to do little more than to go to bed hungry and wake up hungry and get proper sleep, I never dreamed of the day when I would have put together a blog, a bestselling memoir, or even willed a documentary about my journey with the help of some wonderful people wasn't even on my mind.

I am hopeful I will find an easier way for people to see my film. To get my message out. But as Marcel Cabrera told me, documentaries aren't really about making money. And if you're expecting to well, you're in the wrong business. Mitch Gain at FILM-COM echoed those sentiments.

Here I am, in a much better place than I've ever been emotionally and professionally. So one person said no. If that is the worst thing someone says to me about my documentary then I consider it a win.

For everyone who is struggling with Bipolar Disorder, or knows someone with it, know that with medication and therapy recovery can be had. And in the end that's the point of this film, for people to know that there is a light at the end of the tunnel. And it's not an oncoming train, it's hope for a stable future. And it can be had. I'm living proof.

Sincerely,
Amy McCorkle

Dear Daniel,

To be bipolar is no small fete. To be a functioning one in a society where you are dependent to some degree on others is a hard pill to swallow. Today and yesterday I went ring around the mental health insurance rosy to be told my mental health services were being cut because I was uninsured.

Let me lay it out for you. I have Medicare parts A and D. I do not currently have part B coverage which covers doctor's appointments. I was told that the government in its infinite wisdom had cut dollars to Seven Co. of Louisville. And the first people cut were people like me. That the best that they could do for me was write me out a prescription for all of my meds for the next 30 days while I wrestled with a health care system that said the AFA does not apply to you.

On the other side is a group of politicians, that instead of working to fix the problems with AFA are just trying to deny me and others like me coverage. I faced the terrifying very real, and paralyzing prospect of being denied treatment, of being robbed my medication and being thrown back down a dark hole, only this time there would be no reprieve. No light to guide me out. Everything I've worked for would be for not.

But then this is part of the journey. Nothing is a smooth ride. There are always trials and tribulations. So yesterday I spent all day on the phone. Then I went to Seven Co. Then to the

Cabinet for Women and Children. They gave me a wrong number. I called Social Security, *again* today. I was told enroll in Medicare part B in January. They sock it to me for 104 dollars and it's not even active until next July.

Well uninsured I can see my psychiatrist for 15 minutes for 90 freaking dollars every three months and they'll prescribe a three month supply of my medicine. Which Medicare part D pays for.

Grrr. Clock punching government workers who could give a shit about my mental health or others in my position. That's why I do this blog even though I have 'recovered' and even though I have a book with a second volume on the way and have documentary based on it.

Okay rant over. Now on to sensational news! The news from Indie Gathering is in and it's ALL FANFREAKINGTASTIC!

Let's start with the main event itself. Short Documentary category. Letters to Daniel received an Honorable Mention Award! I couldn't be more thrilled. This makes it its first award. And I can't wait to collect in August.

I also entered 3 feature screenplays. Bounty Hunter finished second in the SciFi category. And City of the Damned and You're the Reason received Honorable Mention Awards.

To top it off Bella Morte finished second in the TV Pilot category. Wow August 15-17th will be one heck of a weekend to remember.

Again, as with other awards ceremonies I have been blessed with I invite you and your lovely family to attend. But I also know you're not aware of me, my blog, my books, or my film. But, your work and how you compose yourself professionally have had a huge impact on my life and career. Thank you even if you never see this or know it.

Sincerely,
Amy McCorkle

Dear Daniel,

Having a mentor focus you and send you in the right direction is absolutely wonderful. Someone who cares to take the time to help you find your way. Someone who can see the situation objectively and who isn't invested even though they're in the industry. Someone who sees talent and value in what you do. He sees a future for Letters to Daniel the documentary.

He recommended that I join Toastmasters to get over my fear of speaking in front of large groups and start speaking about my experiences with bipolar disorder and in the process screen my documentary.

He said to put the other stuff aside for now but honestly I couldn't stop writing if I wanted to. It's just very much a part of who I am. I write like a faucet it's where I find my healing and safe place.

I'm working on two projects right now outside of Letters to Daniel. The second volume of Letters is due out in September as is the film at Imaginarium.

The others project are the book Land of Fire and Ash and the web soap pilot script Darius & Anastasia.

All the while I wait to hear back from Zharmae publishing and Gary Baddeley about distribution I push ahead with the writing.

I'd like to return to FILM-COM next year with the web soap series, perhaps with the pilot shot, a sharp trailer thrown together and 12 additional episodes penned looking for completion funds.

Big dreams. Of course with the dreams in place it's nice to have a plan in place. Writing a web episode has proven to be easy. All I have are nine more pages and the pilot is written. I know my audience. 18-34 year old women. Young people get their entertainment online. I even have the theme music selected for the web soap series.

An ambitious project I know but I've always dreamed of writing for a soap. Why not write for one I created. Especially in an atmosphere that is wide open for this kind of content!

Of course I'm driven to get Letters to Daniel out there as well. But Toastmasters has to wait until after the summer is over. But I think it would help immensely with my return to FILM-COM with Darius & Anastasia in tow.

But I'm focused and ready to take on the world. Sometimes a kind word or a suggestion by someone in the industry who cares can set you on the right path to getting your film seen and helping you get over the anxiety it takes to getting you the rest of the way there.

Thanks Joel, I can't thank you enough. And thank you Dave for the support. A shoutout to Pam Turner and Missy Goodman. And of course, a special thanks to you. All of the above have left their mark on me for the better.

Sincerely,
Amy McCorkle

Dear Daniel,

It's the middle of Con season. Three separate awards ceremonies. Three vendor halls I'll be seated at. Panels to be sat upon. Books to sell. A film to present. And waiting to hear back upon acceptance to five film festivals.

I'm waiting to hear back from my cover artist on the print version of Letters to Daniel print cover. Honestly I wanted them for Fandom Fest. Then do a huge launch at of Letters to Daniel Volume 2 at Imaginarium.

My plate is full to overflowing. I have 2 books coming out this summer. 2 novellas coming out this fall/winter. And I am writing on Land of Fire and Ash, an upmarket dystopian novel which I plan on submitting somewhere, and Life After Death: An Aurora Black Novel, the second in the continuing series after the bestselling BLACKOUT, the kickoff of the series, which continues to sell.

FILM-COM was mind blowing. But as great as all of this is until this morning I haven't felt like myself. I felt like there was a hitch in my giddy-up so to speak. Which meant I wasn't writing. Honestly, when I'm not writing I don't feel well. I feel cranky and just plain 'off' and it makes me a bear to deal with. To borrow a term from Maurice Broaddus I grind on everyone around me. I don't see it or feel it but they sure as hell do.

And let me just say sorry to everyone I came into contact with yesterday I was in a real FUCK YOU kind of mood. Irritable, the slightest thing setting me off. Today I've had plenty of sleep and woke-up at 5AM and have accomplished more like a normal schedule. One chapter each on two separate books. Now I'm working on the blog. And tonight I will be at Barnes & Noble working on the web soap series. Now that's a day that makes everything seem good and right.

I feel like I accomplished something. I only wish I had the dues to pay for Toastmasters and

I would start on getting over my fear of speaking in front of large groups. That way I could make money, distribute my film, and promote my memoir, all while advancing a cause that I care about very much, raising awareness of bipolar disorder and showing how you can come back from it.

Today I feel good, maybe I'm feeling a little bit up, a little hypomanic. I didn't feel ten feet tall and bullet proof which would be an indication my medicine was off. I just feel happy. Good. Even.

Being creatively productive is the only way I stay sane. What looks crazy to some, the impressive workload, the insane release dates, is my rock. It's what keeps me from going over the edge of mania. And when I'm depressed I know I can watch movies or television or hang with my friends.

Con season is great but it often messes in a big way with my writing routine. Right now I'm waiting to hear back from Zharmae Press and Mocha Memoirs on my Bella Morte books.

I'm waiting to hear back from money people, distribution people. It's insane in my professional world but for a long time I was sick and could not function properly. But in these last 3 to 4 years my career has blossomed in a way I could have never imagined happening. And the screenwriting world where me and Missy work together opening up as well I couldn't be more thrilled. Winning a contest is always a crapshoot anyway and to have our scripts and our film doing what they are is very sweet for us. After 17 years of friendship, battles, scrapes, and hard times our writing partnership bearing this kind of fruit is extra special.

Sincerely,
Amy McCorkle

Dear Daniel,

I heard back from Gary Baddeley and TDC. It's a no go on distribution through them. Which frankly to even be considered by them was incredible. But I have been given advice by two people now that I have tremendous respect for. Tour, speak of your experiences, screen your film that way. Sell your books Letters to Daniel Volumes 1 and 2.

All I'm waiting for now is the introduction from Tony Acree. I already have one from Susan H. Roddey. They were kind to do so. FILM-COM taught me a lot. Made me some invaluable connections. Garnered a mentor. Figured out how to distribute Letters to Daniel and to grow it organically.

Right now I'm having a hard time concentrating. My mom is in the hospital and has been for the last week. She has an abcess in her colon and has to have a bowel resection six weeks from now. It's been hard on this end. I want her well and home. I miss her. I don't know what I'd do without her. She isn't my main source of support but her and dad are right up there on the list.

Here's the irony, dad has to have knee replacement surgery *next week.* I believe in Western traditional medicine. But I also believe that surgeons are quick to cut. I know both of my parents need this surgery but it also terrifies me. I'll have no one to depend on with the exception of Missy and Pam if something happens to them.

I mean, I have sisters, but neither of them are dependable on a consistent basis. And my aunts and uncle who are wonderful will be swimming in the deep end too since my mom and dad help them on a regular basis too.

So my creative efforts are struggling. I feel like Land of Fire and Ash is slipping away and staying focused on my web series is hard. But I'm determined to do so.

That and Con season is in full swing! I'm anxiously awaiting the results of the Fright Night Film Festival Screenplay competition results in two categories and I have spread planned at Imaginarium. And to all the awards I'm going to be receiving at Indie Gathering all on top of my parents health issues seems to be conspiring to keep me from being able to write the way I want to.

Of course, sometimes blogging unstops me. Makes working on the other projects easier. Makes me raring to go on all the other things I'm juggling seem like butter to work on. Like since I've talked to my silent witness and confessed my fears and insecurities they up and vanished making me brave once more to charge headlong into the fray.

I've been called a force of nature by some individuals, just plain crazy by others, or even just a plain pain in the ass by some. Whatever you call me don't call me finished because in the creative world I'm not nearly done.

Sincerely,

Amy McCorkle

Dear Daniel,

Emotionally speaking it's been a bumpy time. Mom is sick and is due for major surgery. Dad is due for knee replacement surgery. And recently a friend of mine passed unexpectedly. I made friends with her via facebook and my one of my publishing houses. She was also an actress and had worked with you on Skyfall. She remarked that you were private and tended to keep to yourself and although this blog might suggest otherwise often when it's hardest for me I don't have any desire to come on here and blast my troubles. But I realize sometimes there's a bigger picture. That there are others out there who might take something away from my words forces me to write when I am sad.

It's easy to write when I'm angry or happy, the energy is there and the words often come fast and furious. But at times like these, when someone has passed, my loved ones are ill, or if events seem to conspire to rob me of a moment in the sun it's embarrassing to come on and talk about how I feel like no one understands where I'm coming from, because the reality is, someone, somewhere reading this *will* understand and it will help them. Just as writing this is cathartic to me.

Let's start with the seemingly petty. Large sums of cash, a lot of incredibly hard work went into the results I got at Indie Gathering. Suddenly people and things started either letting me down, going seriously wrong, or backing out of making the trip with me. I won't say their names. They know who they are, and although I'm working on forgiveness and resentment it's still hard if I allow myself to think about it too much. So I don't. However, things have worked out. Mom fronted the cash for a Greyhound Bus ticket, the hotel will allow me to ship books to them directly for sales at my vendor table, and Pam will be making the trip with me. Problem solved. Although the person who I expected to make such an auspicious journey with me picked another con and a family vacation over Indie Gathering. As is her right. And it still burns that she did that, for the second time. She doesn't understand why I feel this way. She doesn't get as excited as I do. Doesn't need the trophies, she's content with the win. She's more mature than me in this regard as I worked hard and I want to celebrate.

Moving on. Mom is sick. How sick? Her diverticultis flared. I believe the abcess was there in her colon in May and these much vaunted doctors she believes in without question fucking failed her and fucked up so that now she has to have major bowel resection surgery. Thanks for nothing Dr. Sasser. And with knife happy surgeon ready to slice and dice her I'm nervous and scared. And the surgery is scheduled for the third week of next month. Which collides with Indie Gathering. I pray that the surgery is at the beginning of the week. Since Mom has been home from the hospital Brandy and Sara have been scarce. Figures. During the day I take care of Mom. In the evening Dad does. But next week dad has knee replacement surgery. I wonder where the darling younger siblings will be then. Nowhere I suspect after the hospital stay.

Now to my most serious news. I mentioned a friend of mine had passed that you worked with on Skyfall. I knew her as Victoria Ley, author of the Darkseed Series. You may have known her as Victoria Shellie on the set of Skyfall. She was also in Les Mis.

She loved talking to me about her times on set and although she didn't understand why I admired you so much she didn't judge me for it. She didn't understand the point of this blog either. But even so, I loved talking to her on Facebook as neither of us really had the kind of money that would have supported transatlantic phone calls.

We talked frankly about our publishing careers and where they were at and where we wanted to see them go. She wasn't always happy with the status quo and although I love writing screenplays she found it to be a soulless experience, but she was really good at it. And there were people who wanted to turn her Dark Seed book into a film. How I hope her family pursues that in honor of her.

She let me talk about your movies to a point I think others would have thought I was a nut job, but really she understood what you meant as a source of inspiration to me and my success.

A bright star has truly gone out in the night sky. I for one, will always remember her and our long talks, which because of my career I had let wane regrettably. Her death came as a shock. And while she will no longer be a part of my life, my life is truly better for having known her.

Sincerely,

Amy McCorkle

Dear Daniel,

I come to the page tonight both scared and happy. Letters to Daniel has been accepted into its third festival, Louisville's International Festival of Film. To take place October 9th-11th in Louisville, KY.

I got the news at Moe's restaurant after leaving my mother's hospital room via the phone from Carol Hamilton. Normally I would have jumped up and down exhilarated that Letters to Daniel had just powered its way into another film festival. And don't get me wrong, I am over the moon thrilled that this unexpected success has come my way for a project that means so much to me.

But with Mom in the hospital I find myself in close quarters with people who tend to just rub me the wrong way. My sisters and cousin were all we're going to come clean the house and Amy you better clean your room. And Amy and Sara you need take care of everything on that end when your mother comes home.

I find it ironic that I did clean my room. Have all but one load of laundry done. And believe me, my room was a disaster! I'm not a hoarder, but believe me, you could see the road signs from there. It's just me and the kitty, Chyna who reside in this room and when it's a mess it's a claustrophobic feeling. With mom in the hospital it was especially so.

Seeing her so frail and small makes you take stock of your own mortality. I'm sure she was facing her own. But my sister Brandy who is the biggest follower on the planet there ever was, and my cousin Jill, who seems to think she's Lord God over everything was barking out orders left and right. Then she was preaching about the lord saving mine and everyone else's soul.

I cleaned my room. Guess who's cleaning my mom's house? Missy. That's right. All hot air and nothing of substance. They think they know fucking everything.

Brandy likes to be seen as the big dog on campus. She's sleeping up at the hospital with mom tonight. Dad usually does it but he needs knee surgery that he put off so mom could have emergency surgery. So what do I do? Go up early in the morning, stay till early in the afternoon. I clean my room, which I rarely do but I want mom to be comfortable when she comes home.

I feel like it's wrong to be so happy that my career is flourishing while mom is recovering. A little recognition would be nice but then, I'm thinking, I'm wrong to be doing anything to promote my career.

I feel like I'm in a black hole and it's hard to see my way out of it. But then, I haven't been writing either, not consistently. Not in a way that would say this passion fire and grit the way I usually do. This last month has really knocked me for a loop. I wish I could say to hell with familial obligations and bull head on into my work. But that's not reality.

It's not responsible either. Tomorrow I'll be up at the hospital until around lunchtime. And then I'll head on out back home. Missy is taking me to the grocery tomorrow. And helping me my clothes away.

And I have a screenplay I'm working on. And I just got the first image in my head for a novel. I think I'll go write on both of them. And I'll outline the idea for the season 1 finale of Darius & Anastasia, my web series. I'll write my way out of this funk if it kills me.

Sincerely,
Amy McCorkle

Dear Daniel,

I have returned from Fandom Fest. Was it as huge as last year was for me? Yes and no. Yes because I had double digit sales overall, 22 books. I sold out of two titles and almost a third. I sold one set of my Gemini Rising series books. And a copy of mine and Missy's When Doves Cry.

Nice.

We lost the screenwriting competition. Not so nice.

The panels went well. Nice.

Sucky sales Friday and Saturday. Awesome sales Sunday. A man from Bayou Con committee took my card for possible inclusion as a guest at their show. Very nice.

Being out of shape and being forced to walk all over freaking creation and having my leg cramp up on me? Not so nice.

But all in all the show ran smoother. It was nice and cold in the vendor hall. The set up was better and at least there was an awards ceremony this year even if Missy and me didn't win.

Also in the nice category, Pam sold out of her The Ripper's Daughter paranormal, historical, mystery with horror elements novel. And Missy and I managed to move one copy of When Doves Cry.

I came to the conclusion Saturday night that perhaps Fandom was getting to expensive for me. Which puts me on the line about attending as a participant next year. I wonder if I go next year it will be as a spectator. What with the film taking off to some degree it makes me think that festivals are more of a fit. But then, Fandom Fest is home. It's where I got my start, these last two years have been breakthrough on the sales front. To abandon it would be ridiculous. To stay without some need being met is no better.

I'm used to traveling with Pam and Missy. Having one chair means I have no back up crew where it comes to setting up. I know that sounds selfish but it keeps the event from becoming too much. Being crammed in at a six foot table doesn't sound all that fantastic but if I could finagle an extra chair next year I would have at least Missy to help me.

Which makes me feel bad about Pam because we've become something of a traveling trio. Seeing two of us without the third is odd.

But coming up is Indie Gathering. I am forced onto a Greyhound because no one really wants or can make the trip. But that's okay. That's life. Missy was disappointed at Fandom. She wanted to hear her name called. She wondered what I was going to say. I figured out how to work the camcorder on the phone so I will record the awards ceremony, or at least the portions where our names are going to be called. And that night I will put it up on the internet so that Missy can wake up to five awards being awarded to her.

I think for me, the Fright Night loss put Indie Gathering into a whole new light as to just how e special our accomplishment at IG is. 5 out 5 awards. 4 screenplays and 1 film, the documentary all scored a win of some sort. Two second places and three honorable mentions. Awesome. Two trophies. Three medals. Even better. Say a prayer Missy gets Sunday off so that she can ride up to Hudson and accept the awards with me and hear her name called for herself.

Anyway, Fandom is ground zero where this stuff is concerned and I guess I will always have a soft spot for it.

Sincerely,

Amy McCorkle

Dear Daniel,

I come to you bursting at the seams with joy and pride, first of all, the proof of my triumph at The International Indie Gathering. A film festival and convention that for me, at least lived up to all the hype and made the desperate struggle to get there completely worth it in the end.

I have worked hard for a moment like what IG offered me. The only drawback was Missy was not there to network and revel in the success like I was. Right down to the moment where I was interviewed by the Reel Network's Kristina Michelle and felt 'discovered' by independent producer Brian Boyd at my convention table where I was selling copies of Letters to Daniel Volumes 1 & 2 and the documentary.

I scored a scored a short film screenwriting gig out of it. The same producer is looking at all of my scripts. I found a pool of actors to possibly work with for my short film Rain Down On Me. Still another director there asked to see You're the Reason. An actress wants to work with me.

People wanted to talk to me after the awards ceremony. It was crazy. I even sold 13 copies of Letters to Daniel the book and several of the documentary.

Talk about a film festival that delivered on every level. I can only hope I can repeat the fete again next year. Being paid to write has always been a dream of mine and 500 dollars equals my monthly income, well almost monthly income.

And right before I jaunted off to Hudson, OH for my trip to Indie Gathering I sent your publicist my documentary and memoir. Those things scored me the screenwriting gig.

I wouldn't have had as much fun as I did if it weren't for my Aunt Sue. Aka Brenda Sue Duffey. She did the heavy lifting of that Missy and Pam usually do. She loaded the carts pushed them to the room and car. We sat up the table together.

While the convention itself leaves much to be desired the fact I moved as much as I did lets you know I really worked it to move the copies. I pitched to everyone who listened I had a guest of honor's guest turn his nose up at me and give me 30secs to pitch Letters to Daniel to him. He was a total ass. But I figure by pitching I just got practice in and it tortured him a little bit in the process. Win/win. LOL.

I met a really nice couple Rich and Jodi whose film Confidential won 1st place in their category. They even bought my books and documentary and my aunt's book.

I really wish perhaps people could have seen all that I did, experienced all that I did. Having never received hardware for my creative work it was nice receiving it and applause for the work I do with Missy away from anyone's attention.

Making connections was fantastic. The only thing better will be Imaginarium, when the film premieres. I have three free badges. I know it's corny and I know you have no clue I exist. Or even that this blog exists but those badges are going to waste. I'd like to invite you and your family to Imaginarium to see the film and be special guests at the Convention and Film Festival.

I know you have a million things going on in your career and life but I just wanted to put that out there. Because it seems your work has inspired me to breakthrough not just in my literary career, but to start busting through in my screenwriting and filmmaking career as well.

Sincerely,
Amy McCorkle

Dear Daniel,

I just want to take a moment and thank everyone who has helped me reach this stage of my career. I do this from time to time but this year has been especially huge. There are the usual suspects Missy and Pam. And while I mention them often it bears repeating that it wasn't just a miracle that I got here. It is due in no small part to Missy's never-ending source of compassion, steadying hand when I might fly off into the ether and creative collaboration that I survived the past, stayed with treatment and sat my butt down in the chair to write every day. Some it crap, some of it promising. All the while developing my voice away from the prying and unforgiving eyes of the world. To Pam who opened my eyes to the world of ebook publishing and introducing me into the world fandom and conventions. Plus always being there for me when I either needed this or that for my films. She's filled in the blanks when Missy was unable to. Both of them taking me to doctor appointments and paying for medication whenever I couldn't. Missy is the sister I never had and always wanted. And Pam the kind of friend I never expected and perhaps didn't deserve. But these equally talented writers and filmmakers have been the source of healing and though not every day with them is perfect it is that imperfection that I find the strength to sit down and write.

Then there are my publishers who have supported me and had my back from the beginning. Starting with Lea Schizas who gave me my big break with Another Way to Die and accepted my second and third stories in 2011. All of which went on to be award winners. And GLADIATOR going on to be my first Amazon Bestseller. Then Frank Hall, formerly of Hydra Publications ed who gave my first break in print, Bounty Hunter. It became my second bestseller and screenplay Missy and I have adapted on it has gone on to win two different awards so far. Dave Mattingly for publishing Gemini's War, my first 60K book. Which went on to become my third betseller. And back to Hydra and it's new publisher, Tony Acree, a brilliant writer and marketer, whose business acumen rewarded my faith in him when Bounty Hunter returned to print, and my three shorts two of which were co-written with Missy went on to become my 4th, 5th, and 6th bestsellers.

And finally to my long time editors and cover artist, Greta, Tanja, Ana and Delilah, you all made me look very good and helped my books become what they have while building me a small, but very loyal readership.

Stephen Zimmer, who made my dreams come true by making Letters to Daniel the documentary its premiere event at Imaginarium. Who allowed me a place at the Con Community table in 2011 at Sweatfest. A person who still amazes me with his energy and ability to write, promote, run a publishing house, help with literary tracks at other Cons to creating Imaginarium, a literary con with a film festival that honors its screenwriters. I thank you as a lot of these things come to me as a result from attending that first Con in 2011.

And finally to Ray and Kristina at Indie Gathering where biggest breakthrough in my film career yet has come. 4 screenwriting awards. 1 film award. A connection to Brian Boyd a talented actor producer who I hope to be able to afford one day which led me to John Iwasz and a paid screenwriting gig. Chance encounters with Nicholas Mackey the actor wearing the dude abides t-shirt and JoAnna Lloyd and Tim Hale actors that came by my convention table. All of whom are going to be in my short film Rain Down On Me. One of which has provided the budget for the film to get made.

I've got a TV Pilot and Web Series pilot written. I'm working on the Gladiator Chronicles adaptation feature screenplay. Plan to write a TV Pilot based on Gunpowder and Lead and a feature adaptation of Gemini's War.

My current novel is The Power of Goodbye. All good things come from a lot of hard work, helping hands and a pinch of luck, or as Missy puts it, the golden horseshoe shoved up my ass.

And of course your work inspires me to do my best work. I don't know if our paths will ever cross, but as you know I will be here at this blog telling my story in hopes that it will inspire others out of their darkness and yours did me. Oh and special s/o to Maurice Benard you inspired me to walk through that mental health care clinic and get evaluated. A move that in no small part saved my life and made this life possible.

Sincerely,
Amy McCorkle

Dear Daniel,

This is one of the saddest days of my life. I talk of unsung heroes a lot of the time sometimes naming them, sometimes choosing not to. But I'm a single gal without a partner and I've never wanted children. But for the last 13, almost 14 years I've been the proud and happy owner of Chyna. A neurotic and smart tabby who was the runt of her litter. I've always been a cat person as opposed to a dog person. And now, as I grieve tremendously for her, it's important for me to honor the animal that I actually reluctantly took into my home over a decade ago.

She was so tiny that she fit in the palm of one hand. We suspected wasn't fully weaned but she was, not in the entire time Missy and I had her a burden in any sense of the word. When she was little she would climb into bed with me and sleep on my chest. She passed away Saturday, August 30th, 2014.

She leaves behind an owner that owes her tremendously for being not just a pet, but as a friend and therapeutic animal she was a key component of my journey back from the bipolar breakdown.

Chyna came into my life in early July of 2001. As Missy and I left that month to see Maurice Benard and give him our screenplay You're the Reason, yes, the script that recently won an honorable mention award and Indie Gathering is that is an adult in age.

I was so fragile at the time struggling to heal mind, body, and soul. Attending group therapy, seeing a psychiatric nurse, and a psychiatrist. My dreams seemed so far out of reach. Yet every day I sat at the computer writing. Hoping one day to become a bestseller, an award winner, a filmmaker and everything else ever dreamed.

One nurse told me I was being grandiose in my aspirations. And while that is a symptom of my disease I was serious about becoming a writer and filmmaker. It destroyed me that someone who was supposed be helping me get better seemed to be circumventing the very thing that made me hang in there for so long.

Yet Chyna, as my pet and therapeutic companion was like my silent cheerleader. She loved me and I loved her. And animals don't judge. Chyna was neurotic as hell to the point being feral. But she always snuggled with me at night, especially in winter time when it would get cold in the apartment. And when she was little she curl up on my shoulder and keep me company. When I moved into my mother's and father's she stayed in the room with me and took to draping herself around my neck.

I should have something was wrong with my baby when she stopped coming to me at night, perching up high and her food seemed to never empty. I remarked to my now on vacation best friend that I felt Chyna wouldn't make it until she got home from Florida. Saying it is one thing. Having it happen the very next day was something altogether.

I was caught out in the middle of a severe thunderstorm, a treat I would have well passed up on just to have her here again. You always think you have time. But nothing is a guarantee.

She watched me go from a shattered human being to a thriving one under her watchful eye. She watched as I went from a very sick and fragile human being daydreaming about life, to one who is now watching the fruits of her labor come in.

She watched me graduate from therapy. It's been a rough few days. I said her name in place of one of the other cats and started crying again today.

It's hard at night because I'm so used to her coming to me for love and attention. And I just used to her presence in my life. I know it sounds weird that I miss her and have struggled more with the loss of her than my own grandmother, (I miss her too, but I got to say goodbye to her before she passed on.) With Chyna she couldn't wait for me. Perhaps she knew how devastated I would be and quietly went so that I would suffer less.

I hope she knows just how much she was loved and appreciated by me. And that she will always hold a special place in my heart.

Dad placed her in a box and waited for me to get home. I pet her one last time and cried. I cry even now as I am the classic cat lady and she was my mascot. Then dad buried her under the tree in the back yard. I wave to her every morning as I set up to work and drink coffee to start my day. I know it's a little wacky. But I still miss her and the loss of her in my life is still raw and fresh.

If you have pets shower them with insane amounts of love and affection. They deserve it because that's what they give to us and that's what Chyna gave to me. She will always be missed.

Sincerely,
Amy McCorkle

Dear Daniel,

All good things must come to an end. And I believe this blog in its current conception has served its purpose. I have shared my story of trial and triumph and this Friday night I will achieve something I have always dreamed of, a world premiere of a film with a Q&A moderated by a good friend named Tim Druck whom I have a great deal of respect for both as a human being and artistically speaking as a musician.

As I've shared with everyone who has bothered to stumble across this blog I am a survivor childhood sex abuse and have travelled a long road in healing and recovery from a bipolar disorder diagnosis.

I've not always been at my best on this blog. Sometimes venting, other times simply sharing what I did, what it took, to travel that long winding road to mental health wellness and to make my dreams come true. I huge nod to the head to the Daniel of Letters to Daniel, Daniel Craig, whom without perhaps I would have never had the courage to write the kind of books I write and bust the glass ceiling of publishing and eventually the courage within myself to self-pub.

This Friday marks a culmination of a lot hard work and serendipity of dreams coming true. Winning an award for your work is one thing. Getting to speak about my healing process through the medium of film is something I never thought I would be in a position to do. Let alone do it in depth before an audience of my peers.

To say I'm excited is an understatement. To say I'm scared to death about facing that audience is also true. Every artist sees themselves in their work to some degree. This blog is my life in all its good and bad glory. The same with the film. I feel like I'm baring my soul in an effort to keep my sanity.

Daniel Craig, a few words about you. I don't know you. You don't know me. Chances are we will never cross paths. But the memoir and documentary I sent to your publicist are meant simply as thank you tokens for what your work has inspired in my own creative life. This blog was born as initially an open letter to you and to give me some sort of framework to make it easier for me to tell my story. Of the interviews I've seen or read with you, you strike me as an extremely private person. And for that reason alone I highly doubt I'll ever meet you. This blog has misinterpreted on more than one occasion and its left me raw and angry at times. Essentially isn't really about you at all. It's about me and my journey. And it has been a long and arduous one.

I never expected the blog to take on the life that it has for me and for those it has touched or helped. And now with the biggest moment of my career before me I'm scared. Not in a bad way, but the film is so personal that I fear rejection of it will be a rejection of me. I simply have to let go and let what is meant to be happen.

So this week and Imaginarium Weekend is Letters to Daniel's current incarnation's swan song. I will be sure to post video of the Q&A and lots of pictures and possibly, if I'm blessed this way I will have video of maybe even an acceptance speech. But that's getting ahead of myself and really if I don't win that was never the point of this blog, memoir, or documentary. It has always been about sharing my story, getting better, and helping other people facing obstacles in their own lives.

And hence that is how Letters to Daniel will continue, with authors and readers and filmmakers all sharing their stories once a week to whomever they feel has helped them the most.

Thank you Daniel, Tony Acree, Lea Schizas, Frank Hall, Dave Mattingly, Delilah K Stephans, Stephen Zimmer, Mom, Dad, Aunt Debbie, Uncle Frank, Aunt Jan, Aunt Sue, and special shoutouts to my inner circle Pamela Turner and Missy Goodman. And therapists and nurses and psychiatrists I've had along the way. You all have, in your own ways saved my life and made my dreams come true.

Sincerely,

Amy McCorkle

Dear Daniel,

So here it is. My last hoorah of Letters… in its current form. The premiere of the documentary Letters to Daniel was a smash. Among the films all shorts and all features it boasted to highest attendance rate. It received a rousing ovation. I crushed it in the moderated Q & A. I sold copies of the book. I received hugs from my heroes and those who confessed to be travelling the same path.

And in a way your spirit, as well as those of my other heroes were represented and felt in the audience as the movie played. I was emotional during the film and when the applause started I almost cried. The only thing that would have made it perfect would have been to have you there. *As if that would ever happen.* Still I sent the book and documentary where they were promptly trashed I'm sure. But at Imaginarium, in that moment I was the belle of the ball. And all the hard work both in my personal and professional lives came together and I got to share my story and give hope to others.

A feather in my cap was the appearance of Imaginator Maurice Broaddus fellow writer and hero. Who when I made a trade for his book Knights of Bretton Court: King's Justice, personalized it with this: Thank you for being you. Bold. Brave. Honest. Here's a picture of him. He is simply the most awesome person and author. He made it to my premiere! And when the fantastic Q&A was over the first person to my table to buy my companion books to the movie was the original owner of Hydra Publications, Frank Hall. He gave me my big break into print with Bounty Hunter. He gave me a huge hug and told me how proud he was of me.

What followed was more sales and hugs even from other filmmakers in the competition. But as I've said all along this blog was initially about catharsis and giving hope and shining light into the darkness as others have done for me.

I sold 30 books. Blackout:An Aurora Black Novel, Letters to Daniel, Letters to Daniel Vol. 2, Bounty Hunter, and the Gladiator Chronicles. I am now out of Letters to Daniel and copies of the documentary.

The triple booklaunch for me, Missy, and Rebekah (my cousin who also struggles with bipolar disorder, who sold out of Gears of Golgotha, her debut novel) rocked the house made people laugh and sold copies of our books. Rebekah's book sparked a bidding war between three houses (I say somewhat egotistically here that I mentored her and am rejoicing in her success).

I sat on 7 panels. Had dinner with Jay Wilburn, sat on a panel with the infamous Armand Rosamillia and had quite the adventure when the fire alarm went off right at the beginning of the first panel.

And then the cherry on the top of a very big sundae was winning getting to hear Letters to Daniel called up as Runner Up for Best Documentary. My family was there to see it. The important ones anyway.

And to the announcement I am starting a new blog to cover my journey to the 2016 Walt Disney World Marathon. The letters appearing from henceforth will be about others and the journey to the impossible.

As it is, may we never meet, may you never know of me, I want the world to know your work inspired me like few others have. And as I bid this blog or at least my regular posting to it adieu I feel as if I might cry. Few things have meant as much to me as the joy of sitting with a book or in a darkened theater and watching a movie. And to think it all started with the viewing of Casino Royale. Thank you, Daniel Craig, may my work reach others as yours has touched and reached me.

Sincerely,
Amy McCorkle

Dear Daniel,

Okay, so I said I was going to hand this blog over, but it turns out I've only had one taker and I've lost the gentleman's very sweet account of how his wife inspired him to become a writer upon his return from war.

That being said, OMG! Letters to Daniel the documentary has achieved something I *never* dreamed possible. I entered it into the FREE FILM FESTIVAL and it has not only been accepted it has secured digital and theatrical distribution.

HOLY CRAPTASTIC!

If you could see me now!

It's one of those full circle moments where everything. And I mean everything comes together. This film, the memoir, and really, this blog has been there for me in way that I used poo poo others about.

Yeah I'm journaling to some degree, but it's not just a journal on display here, it's my life. And how rapidly it's changed over the last few years.

First came the books, then with the screenplays, now with the film. It's hard to believe May 7, 2013 marked the beginning of this blog. And how now, even though I know you don't see me, don't know me, have never heard of me you and you work have inspired me to be my best self at such a point in my life when I thought perhaps it wouldn't have happened at all!

Everything's been moving fast this year. Not that it wasn't moving fast before, but this year it seems to moving *really* fast.

And as time goes by it seems to go at breakneck speed. I find it difficult to just sit and relax and soak up and enjoy the moment. Some of that I'm sure is the anxiety from the bipolar disorder and the relentless need to always be moving forward to always be telling a story.

Even though I lost last night at the Louisville International Festival of Film I had the best time relaxing drinking ginger ale and chatting with Mysti Parker, my date for the evening. Missy couldn't make it and Pam was wiped from physical therapy, Sisters In Crime and had projects to work on.

So it was me and Mysti, ON A YACHT! Talking, laughing, drinking. Watching awards going to people who weren't even present to receive them. LOL. The awards were burnished mahogany glossed Louisville Slugger Baseball Bats with the category they had won and their project would be engraved and shipped to them.

I have never had such a good time losing before. Maybe because I didn't think I could win, or I felt out of place with the people around me. People who were phony and fake and well very different from the crowd at Imaginarium.

Otherwise I had Mysti there and after the awards were over we retreated to restaurant and had dinner. The clam chowder was delicious and brownie sundae was just too big to eat between the two of us.

I soaked up the moment. Most people were disappointed they didn't win. And there was a piece of me that was too. But I was able to soak up the fact there was NO PRESSURE on me or my film to do anything beyond screen at 11AM on a Friday morning in the basement of the library.

It was a lovely festival run by lovely people. And I take away the compliment one volunteer gave my film, that it was amazing. That really touched me. Because she meant it. Now my film has distribution on VOD, ISS, DvD, and theatrically. I am above all truly blessed. And I found out tonight three of my screenplays have been accepted into the festival.

If only you could see me now.

Sincerely,
Amy McCorkle

Dear Daniel,

I had a reading done by a tarot reader and she has been more accurate than anyone else. We're not a speaking terms anymore. And really I think it's for the best. If only because she's a good person and so am I and arguing brings out the ugly in us. So I wish her nothing but the best. I hope her life is blessed and filled with the kind of joy I'm getting to experience.

She said Letters to Daniel would be a breakthrough for me. And it has been. She said the film would be what took me to the next level and it looks like that's where things are headed. She said my screenplays would win awards and they have. She also said things would start to move very, very fast.

She was right on every account.

My cousin Rebekah was a rock star at Imaginarium. The kind of plucked from obscurity thing one always dreams about. But I wasn't. But I had helping hands all along the way. And the ride felt fast already, but to be honest it's felt like being a roller coaster the that crept slowly to the top and is dipping and rising twisting and turning and it just refuses to let up.

There's often a, send me more information quality. And I've always wanted to break into television. Not with a reality show. But with a dramatic series. And I've just gotten my first bite on Bella Morte the television pilot. I won't say from where but like I said this is a rollercoaster ride that just keeps going and going.

I've had a good amount of luck in my career. But I've been writing since I was 5 seriously since I was 13 and looking for publication since I was 18. There was no one beyond my Uncle Ron and Writer's Digest to guide me in early career. Then there were Michael Hauge and Dov S Simmens. Maurice Benard the actor sharing his personal story of triumph over bipolar disorder in order to help others. I wrote every day.

Through the confusion.

Through the pain.

Through the madness.

Through every obstacle that would come my way. With the help of key friends and family who continue to be there for me.

The success is crazy for me. I'm white knuckling it at the moment.

I've written 3 books, 4 scripts, and created 2 going on 3 documentaries. I'm pretty sure the bottom is about to drop out on me. I have that feeling peaking. I hope to have the third documentary done by the end of November beginning of December.

With Thanksgiving coming up on us I want to say I'm grateful for everything this blog, and you Daniel (symbolically, you nor anyone else affiliated with you have ever done anything for me, except kindly pass along my documentary and memoir to whoever it is that looks at that stuff for you), have shot my blossoming career into overdrive. Who knows what I'll to say the next time I sign here.

Pray for me and my mental health. I feel a crash and burn coming on. This time of year I'm notorious for them. With my mother in the hospital, which I'm happy to say she farted five days after surgery and got to eat Jello, saltines, and drink water after five days of ice chips. She might be home for Thanksgiving! Something else to be grateful for.

Sincerely,
Amy McCorkle

Dear Daniel,

I'm here, because things just, well they just keep getting better. I want to take a moment here to thank the people who saved my life. First, there's Missy, if you follow this blog at all you've heard me mention her name a million times in a dozen different contexts. If I blabbed on about her I might bore you. But here's the truth.

When we were in Texas and I was at my sickest, she was there. An overburdened psychiatric system that made the treatment I received at 7 Counties seem like the gold standard. And believe as good as it was, the system is made to keep people out. And there were times I cursed the day I ever walked through those doors. But Missy was always there. Always encouraging. Never judging. Sure she got mad. She we exchanged hurtful words. But the thing was she seemed to be helped by attendance to psychiatiric and therapeutic sessions. She learned what I did. S

Life with me was hard. No cake walk. I took my meds without question but there were days that I wondered if a magic switch would flip and life would get better. Would *feel* better. Not grandiose but happy, joy, the ability to concentrate. And yes even pain and sorrow. As a writer I felt my story. I didn't think it. So right before treatment bipolar disorder robbed me of my creative voice and all I did was write letter after letter, which I later learned was a form of hypographia that those with bipolar disorder are often afflicted with.

And then the treatment seemed to rob me of any hope getting my voice back. And then there was GLADIATOR. I saw the previews and a story came to me. It was hideous. It was burn it away, use it as a table evener bad. I threw it away. But I was happy to be writing again.

Missy lived the hardest part of the journey with me. The wild mood swings, the eight hour crying jags, going to bed hungry, waking up hungry. Not even having pen or paper to write with at times. And we CHOSE to do this.

I can honestly say Maurice Benard and his wife Paula's courage in sharing their story saved my emotional and physical life. He plays Sonny Corinthos on General Hospital. In October of 1999 nobody, and I mean *nobody* was talking about mental illness. But they were. And because of their fearlessness in sharing what their lives had been like I was able to see the symptoms in myself. Without their activism I may have lost my battle altogether.

And then there is someone who I usually say unkind things about. My sister Sara. I'm not really all that close to any of my siblings. Not my brother, and not my three sisters. If untangled that family tree that would be a blogpost all unto itself.

Sara was the one to tell me to ask to be evaluated for depression and manic depression.

That's right folks, I was diagnosed at a time when manic depression was the term for bipolar disorder. Honestly I think manic depression has a romanticism to it. Not I like the disorder, but it's been with me all of my adult life. And while acknowledge the very desperate need for medication and treatment I don't where I'd be without it. Without Sara telling what to do I may have languished to the point where the very tenuous grasp I had on reality at the time may have slipped away altogether and I would have done something stupid to myself that I couldn't recover from.

Missy, Maurice (in sharing his story, I don't know him), Sara thank for saving my life. Because when everyone else was looking away you were there at the most traumatic of moments doing triage in your own unique ways.

Russell Crowe. He breathed new life into my writer brain and set the wheels a churning. Scripts. Books. None particularly good. But A Beautiful Mind set me free in ways this wonderfully gifted actor and director will never know. That movie and GLADIATOR and CINDERELLA MAN helped heal creative wounds. For that I will always be grateful.

Pamela Turner, yet another name you hear rung loud and clear and often. None of this happens without her. She suggested digicon. She told me about Fandom Fest. Where I met two of my publishers. Hydra and Blackwyrm. Where I met my publicist. Where I met my agent. She's bought my medicine when I couldn't afford it. She's taken me to the hospital. She's taken me to 7 Counties. She's an awesome friend and has been there for through many of my crap sandwich moments.

And then there's mom and dad. They give me shelter and food. And of course as dysfunctional as it may be, they give me love.

And finally, the man of the hour, Daniel Craig. I recently signed with a literary agent. There's a television executive who wants to option some of my book titles. And I'm a finalist for a very prestigious ebook award for Letters to Daniel the memoir.

I just wanted to thank you for everything your work has done to inspire me in my own work.

Sincerely,
Amy McCorkle

Dear Daniel,

As the second year of this blog nears its end I find healthwise I'm glad the year is nearly over. Mom's health scare is behind us and Dad's knee replacement surgery is done and now we are a week from Christmas. With everyone's health accounted for all in all this has been an incredible year for this little blog and every form it has taken.

Two volumes of letters. The first volume collected as I have expressed has been named one of only four finalists in the non-fiction category for an EPIC eBOOK AWARD. It is the highest honor an ebook can receive.

This year professionally has truly been beyond any expectation I might have dreamt up for myself. First the fantastic sales at the conventions I attended this year. I thought FILM-COM would change things. Maybe it just changed my perspective on things. I attended nine events. On average I attend 1-3 and they're all local.

I was financially strapped all year. But in the end it has paid off. 7 awards. 2 nominations. 3 finals. My screenplays, books, and documentary based on this blog all soared against the competition. And my first #1 Amazon Bestseller in Bella Morte: Beginnings.

November was relatively quiet only in contest news. I made 3 documentaries and one music video before Thanksgiving.

Then December. Holy. Fucking. Shit.

A television producer told me he was interested in optioning some of my titles. Told me to come back in 90 days with a literary agent.

That was on a Saturday. The following Wednesday I found out I was an EPIC Finalist. And signed with a literary agent.

Now news that I may get a response from a huge hero of mine. I started crying this morning when I got the news. It's hard to process so much in so little time.

So many people helped me get where I am. And I've told them on several occasions through this blog and in person. By word and by action. They have my undying gratitude.

But this blog is called Letters to *Daniel.*

And when I talk about my career and crawling out of darkest of holes the turnaround started in May of 2010 when I wrote *Another Way to Die.* Honestly your work inspires me. Your activism where women's rights are concerned touches me. I know our paths may never cross, but your films have been everything from security blankets (Cowboys & Aliens) to storyline inspiration, I can't really narrow list down as one of my favorites is Mother and another is Casino Royale and those are very different kinds of films.

I know from interviews (which you seem uncomfortable with at best) that you eschew fame and live for the work. You love and protect to family and loved ones. You always fight for the integrity of the film you're a part of and you always bring you're A game to your performance.

I hope to be just as grounded as my career does what it does and takes whatever turns it will take. Daniel, I know you're not reading this. But I can say this enough. Thank you for the work and being the kind of performer that you are. I admire you greatly. In as much I hope my work shines as authentically as yours has.

Sincerely,
Amy McCorkle

Dear Daniel,

This is my year in review. I've made this blog about what is going on at this very moment and to show what it is that I'm grateful for. And this year I've had A LOT to be grateful for. From the personal to the professional.

Dreams coming true. Breakthrough moments.

Family members surviving health scares.

Unrequited crush.

My life was full this year.

Starting in January when the call for entries for the Imaginarium Convention's Film Festival went out. A simple conversation with Stephen Zimmer led to the creation of the Letters to Daniel documentary.

I finished the writing of Bella Morte: Devil's Backbone. I finished BLACKOUT:An Aurora Black Novel. And BLACK ICE:An Aurora Black Novel. I wrote co-wrote 4 screenplays. Rain Down On Me, Darius & Anastasia a web pilot, Episode 2 in that series, and The Gladiator Chronicles. I wrote 2 television series treatment. One for City of the Damned and another for the

Royals adapted from the book Falling Slowly that I started in Dec and will finish this month sometime.

I directed 3 documentaries and one music video. Carla's Halloween, Strong Southern Mamas, and Enter the Imaginarium. And I Love You a Christian music video.

Three books were released this year, BLACKOUT: An Aurora Black Novel, Letters to Daniel Volume 2, and Bella Morte:Beginnings. BLACKOUT and Bella Morte were bestsellers and Bella Morte was my first #1 hit on Amazon.

In December I started working on Falling Slowly. I'm a little less than halfway through that book now. Creatively, my cup runneth over this year.

And awards I've always wanted a trophy. I think it goes back to when I was five years old and I was standing on stage after a dance recital and everyone it seemed but me was getting a trophy. It was for perfect attendance. I didn't understand that you had to accomplish something to get a trophy. I'll admit over the years it became something of an obsession to win one.

And I've won just about everything you can win. Plaques, certificates, online announcements, medals. But the big wins always eluded me. I mean I couldn't even final. Talk about a watershed year. I double finaled in the Fright Night Film Festival with two screenplays to kick off the awards season for me. Then there was Indie Gathering. Two second place TROPHIES and three honorable mention medals. Then there was Imaginarium. I sold 30 books. Had premiere event with my first documentary Letters to Daniel, it was a smash. I had more people attend that screening than any of the other films. And was Runner-Up for Best Documentary. Then there was the Terror Film Festival. All three of my scripts entered finals. Then were nominees. And finally Bella Morte, the script got Honorable Mention in the short screenplay competition.

I attended the Louisville International Festival of Film and had more fun losing at the awards ceremony than anyone had a right to with a fellow author friend of mine, Mysti Parker. I lost but I screened at three film festivals and I won at two of them. I thought Letters to Daniel had sung its swan song at LIFF. As several festivals chose not to screen it. But then the FREEdom Festival changed all of that. I secured a distribution deal. VOD, ISS, DVD and Theatrical in NY and LA and FL.

To say I was flabbergasted and over the moon that more people were going to have a chance to see this film about dealing with bipolar disorder and sexual abuse and overcoming those obstacles would truly be a an understatement. I made this blog to show gratitude and give hope to those who might find themselves in similar situations and to help me cope with my current one.

I thought the memoir, the first slender volume of letters had run its course as well. Hitting number 2 on the Amazon Bestsellers list and spawning a second volume and a documentary. Helping people and helping me to heal at the same time. But then it happened. I opened email and there in the inbox it was staring back at me. Letters to Daniel was named an EPIC eBook Award Finalist in the Non-Fiction Category. In the small press and independent publishers world EPIC is the top tier awards competition. I entered Letters to Daniel because I felt it was strong enough to compete. But I knew it was a long shot. But there it was, my web badge and certificate.

And finally this. The one thing I had been hoping for. A breakthrough in television and film writing. There's the potential for my bestsellers, some of them anyway, to be optioned by a television producer. But he said I needed a literary agent.

This was the catch 22 all writers fear. He admired my CV. 9 bestsellers. Multiple award both as a screenwriter and a novelist. A paid gig (won on my authoring of Letters to Daniel). Again it all comes back to this.

But the miracle happened. I landed that agent. Or she landed me. Thank you Daniel. Thank you for inspiring me with your work and your professionalism. My dreams are coming true and if I ever get the chance, I will thank you.

Sincerely,
Amy McCorkle

Tim's Intro

Dear Amy,

I guess it won't be long until people are writing letters to you the way you have to Daniel Craig. And your friends couldn't be prouder. In today's culture we throw words around like they don't mean anything - words like Inspiration. Warrior. Hero. But as sure as I write these words today, there is someone in this world reading your work, learning about your struggle, and seeing herself in your words. And because of your work, she has hope. She knows there is help, that she's not crazy and this is not how she has to live. Because of you. You're someone's hero.I've watched you grow in the last few years, and it's been my pleasure. I've seen days when you couldn't leave your house, and nights when you couldn't sleep. We've had a triumphant screening and interview, and we've been shut down by the Galt House. I've seen those sleepless nights of anxiety turn into bursts of creativity where the hours passed awake due to excitement instead of anxiety. I've seen you make friends with my wife and my daughter, and I have this amazing mental picture of the brightest smile I've ever seen on your face, the night you guys just let an afternoon turn into a Girls' Night at our house. It's been like watching someone spiritually reborn. And it's inspiring to everyone who's ever fought for their own mental health and happiness, every time we see you smile.You've shared your laurels with me - movies and screenplays and bestsellers and now we're working on projects together. And now you're experiencing the best part of success, helping the people you love experience the same - in this time, you've gone from fighting for every little win to reaching out to take the hands of people like you and helping them to experience that same success. Your success has nothing to do with luck or privilege - you've been a warrior for everything you've earned.So enjoy this time of rising tides in your life. You deserve it. Celebrate it with the greatest creative burst ever to come from your keyboard. Let the last few years be a launching pad - a beginning, not an end. Your work is not done, your rise is not complete - you're only a fraction of what you're going to be. I - we - believe in you. And I feel like, for the first time in a very long time, you believe in yourself. And know how we, your friends, see you. Inspiration. Warrior. Hero.

Love always,

Tim

Missy's Intro

Dear Amy,

I am writing this letter for three reasons. The first, because you are my best friend of almost twenty years. Second, it has been an honor to watch you work your way up from a store clerk with a dream to being an award winning author, screenwriter, filmmaker and blogger. The third reason is that you are the most persistent person I have ever known and have been bugging me to complete this letter for some time now.

When you told me about Letters to Daniel I knew that at the very least it would be a positive way for you to journal your feelings. I believe that Daniel Craig and the parts he portrays touches a basic need in you to feel loved, heard and protected. I believe it is those things that draw people to you work in general and Letters to Daniel in particular. People want, no need, to be loved, heard and protected. Your honest nature inspires others. The fact that Letters blew up the way it did, with a multi award winning documentary, was beyond belief but knowing you, it should not have been.

They say that James Brown was the hardest working man in show business. Amy, he has nothing on you. You work continuously. You are that weird writer chick that eats and sleeps her career. I've seen you hustle a no into a yes. I've seen you bust open doors that were bolted shut. Any creative person knows that the ability to hustle is part of the game. That is not to say that you have not had your problems. But it has been a privilege to watch you turn those problems into success. You are a great writer and an even better friend.

Made in the USA
San Bernardino, CA
19 June 2016